THE CONTRA CONNECTION

by

G. Lee Tippin
Colonel U.S. Army (Retired)

Daring Books
Canton • Ohio

Published by Daring Books
Box 526, Canton, Ohio 44701

Library of Congress Cataloging-in-Publication Data

Tippin, G. Lee, 1935-
   The Contra connection / by G. Lee Tippin.
     p.   cm.
   ISBN 0-938936-66-2
   1. United States--Foreign relations--Nicaragua. 2. Nicaragua-
-Foreign relations--United States.   3. Counterrevolutionists-
-Nicaragua.   4. Nicaragua--Politics and government--1979-
I. Title.
E183.8.N5T57 1988
327.7307285--dc19   87-36532
                                           CIP

Printed in the United States of America.

THIS BOOK IS DEDICATED TO...

The memory of Dana H. Parker Jr., James P. Powell III, Civilian Materiel Assistance, and Mario Pozo, Nicaraguan Democratic Forces, who were killed by the Sandinistas in Nicaragua on September 1, 1984. "REST IN PEACE FREEDOM-FIGHTERS."

AND

To the men and women of the Nicaraguan Democratic Forces (FDN) who are fighting to free their country from communist domination.

AND

To the men and women of the Civilian Materiel Assistance (CMA) who have dedicated their lives to stop communism and who have donated time and money to provide assistance and supplies to the Anti-Communist Freedom-Fighters in Central America.

* * *

The situation in Central America is important to United States national security and has major implications for our capacity to act in the world. The proximity of the Isthmus of Central America to vital waterways and the U.S. border makes it impossible for us to escape the consequences if Soviet power should become firmly established on the continent. The Pacific Ocean insulated the United States from the consequences of withdrawal from Vietnam. No ocean protects us from the consequences of ignoring the growing threat in our neighborhood.

Nicaragua is now governed by an internally repressive, internationally aggressive, Marxist-Leninist regime. Nicaragua is a base for the projection of Soviet power in our continent and in our hemisphere. The liberation of Grenada demonstrated that communist expansion is reversible after all. In Nicaragua, democratic forces seek to reverse the establishment of a Soviet-Cuban military base in Central America. The "Contras" still seek democratic government. The people and the government of the United States have a vital stake in the outcome of the struggle for Nicaragua.

HONORABLE JEANE J. KIRKPATRICK

FORMER UNITED STATES AMBASSADOR
TO THE UNITED NATIONS

Foreword

I. A NATION BETRAYED

With the advent of the Jimmy Carter Administration, a new phrase appeared on the international political scene. That phrase was "Human Rights." Carter said that the United States would concern itself with the rights of people all over the world—and who could condemn such a lofty goal? However, as it turned out, with the exception of boycotting the Olympics in Russia, which was stupid, his human rights program only applied to certain countries and seemed to pertain primarily to the small and militarily weak nations, all of which just happened to be anti-communist: Nicaragua, Chile, Paraguay, Guatemala and Iran, although Iran was certainly not a weak nation—it was still fervently anti-communist and America's best friend and ally in the Middle East.

The human rights campaign that Carter unleashed upon the world resulted in thousands of deaths in Iran, Nicaragua, El Salvador and Guatemala; the turning over of Iran to a radical government violently opposed to the U.S.; the turning over of the Panama Canal to a Socialist government friendly to Cuba; a communist government in Nicaragua; and almost a Marxist takeover in El Salvador. The Iranian hostage crisis and the bombing of the Embassy and marine barracks in Beirut can be directly attributed to Carter's "Human Rights" policies.

Carter's stated policy in Latin America was clear: "To see that all of the right wing governments in Latin America were to be replaced and that Nicaragua would go first." Using Human Rights as an excuse, and with his willing leftist accomplices, President Perez of Venezuela and Panama's strongman, Omar Torrijjos, who was an open admirer of Fidel Castro, President Carter delivered Nicaragua into communist hands. This strategic mistake by the United States has already cost the country dearly and most likely will cost American blood in the future. The sad part of the whole affair is Carter could have had Nicaragua without the Somozas and without communism. But he chose to let the Marxists take over the nation. History may someday ask "Why?"

Carter used the issue of Human Rights to turn much of U.S. public opinion against the government of Nicaragua; and this same issue

v

of human rights, as it turned out, served the communist purpose also.

One week after taking office, Carter cut off all military assistance to Nicaragua, even though he knew at that time that Cuba was providing men and arms to the Sandinista rebels. The Carter-appointed U.S. Ambassador to Nicaragua was advised by the U.S. President not to get too close to Somoza, and the Ambassador promptly began an intimate association with the Sandinistas. Through his dominant influence in the Organization of American States, Carter put pressure on member states to condemn the government of Nicaragua. Carter's representative on the International Monetary Fund twice blocked badly needed standby credit for Nicaragua; and Carter suddenly pressured all shipping companies to boycott Nicaragua so that the coffee crop could not be exported. Carter successfully closed all markets where Nicaragua could purchase arms and ammunition. And when the government of Nicaragua fell and the Marxist Sandinistas took control, there were celebrations in Moscow, Havana and Washington, D.C. Strange bed-fellows!

Nicaragua was invaded by international leftist forces with brigades from many countries. It was never a secret that the revolution in Nicaragua was communist-inspired and supported by Cuba and Moscow. In 1971, Carlos Fonesca Amador, one of the Sandinista leaders, sent a message to the Communist Party Congress in Moscow. He wanted to be certain that the Communist Party knew of his loyalty and devotion. In that message, he described the Sandinistas as the "successor to the Bolshevik Revolution" and said further that the "ideals of Lenin are a guiding star in the struggle which the revolutionaries are waging."

The Sandinista leaders were trained and indoctrinated in Cuba and the Soviet Union. Castro provided men, weapons, logistic support, money, and open sanctuary. During the Marxist attack on Nicaragua, Panama openly became a haven for the terrorists and a base for the recruiting, equipping and training of communist forces. War goods traveled from Russia to Cuba, to Panama, from Panama to Costa Rica, and from there overland to the Sandinistas in Nicaragua.

The following news article appeared in the *Chicago Tribune*, on June 27, 1979:

"Castro has been active in mobilizing support for the Nicaraguan guerrillas in other countries. In February, 1979, he promoted a meeting of the Communist Party representatives from all the Central American countries plus Mexico and Panama. At this meeting, the Communist leaders discussed not only support for the Marxists fighting in Nicaragua, but also plans for future meetings to discuss revolutionary activity in other Central American countries.

"In March, 1979, Fidel Castro met personally with the leaders of the three factions of the Nicaraguan guerrillas. At this meeting in Cuba, Castro persuaded them to establish a unified leadership. He promised to give them arms, money, and weapons if they did this.

"Castro advised them to downplay their dedication to Marxism at this time. This, he counseled, was necessary to lure non-Marxist support for their efforts.

"Castro even advised the Nicaraguan rebels on battlefield tactics, counseling them to concentrate on hit-and-run tactics and avoid frontal attacks on the Nicaraguan National Guard."

The above story came from a CIA report which, of course, was given to President Carter. Yet a few weeks later, Carter said "that to his knowledge, Cuba was not directly involved in the overthrow of the Nicaraguan government." One wonders why the President lied!

II. A REVOLUTION BETRAYED

Seven years after the Sandinista regime took power in Nicaragua, it has failed to fulfill any of the promises that it made. Instead of establishing the Democratic Society for which the Nicaraguan people fought, there has been a gradual taking over of power by a small group of dedicated, hard-core Marxist-Leninists, whose goal is to communize not only Nicaragua but all of Central America.

While publicly promising elections and genuine democracy, the Sandinistas lost no time in transforming the nation into a Marxist-Leninist totalitarian police state. In the first two years of Sandinista rule, close to a quarter of a million Nicaraguans fled the country as refugees, including some 20,000 Miskito Indians. In March of 1982, *Time* magazine revealed that 42 Miskito villages along the Rio Coco had been firebombed, 49 churches were destroyed, 35 villagers from Leymus were buried alive by Sandinista soldiers, and thousands of Indians were imprisoned or had disappeared at the hands of security forces—all for resisting the restructuring of their society on Sandinista-Marxist lines.

Nicaragua has become the most militarized society in the history of Central America. Under Somoza, there were 11 military bases; now there are 65. Somoza's National Guard had only 11,000 men in it; and now there are 90,000 soldiers in the Sandinista Army, 80,000 more in the reserves, and they have plans to build up to a quarter of a million. There are now 170,000 troops in Nicaragua. In comparision, it would mean 16 million men under arms in the United States.

Military advisors from the Soviet Union, Bulgaria, East Germany, North Korea, Libya, and over 7,000 from Cuba guide the operations of the Sandinista armed forces, with the Cubans right in the field against the Contra. The East Germans have instructed the Sandinistas in organizing a massive and ruthlessly efficient internal security apparatus. The PLO and Libyans are conducting special training in terrorism for selected Sandinista soldiers.

The Sandinista Defense Committee operates over 10,000 "Block Committees" which monitor, Big Brother-style, citizens' activities, encourage neighbor to spy on neighbor, unleash mobs to intimidate opponents, and are in charge of distributing many services, including food rationing cards. If you don't exhibit sufficient "revolutionary fervor" to satisfy your local Bloc Committee, you may not have very much to eat.

The revolution in Nicaragua has been repeatedly betrayed by the Sandinistas. Many of the people who fought alongside them during the revolution have been imprisoned and tortured, or forced into exile; many have been killed! Those former opponents of Somoza, who now oppose the Sandinistas, are called "Contra."

The Democratic Forces of Nicaragua (FDN), or Contra, are fighting for the freedom of their own country. They want to force the Sandinistas to live up to their original promise of creating a democratic society in which basic human rights are respected and real, where free elections are honestly held, and of bringing an end to the foreign domination of their country: no more Russians, Cubans, East Germans, North Koreans, etc.

The Sandinistas and their comrades in Cuba and the Soviet Union have no intention of confining their Marxist enslavement to the people in Nicaragua. They have already declared open war upon Nicaragua's next door neighbors, with 120 attacks upon Honduras in 1985-86 and continuing subversion within Columbia, El Salvador, Guatemala and Costa Rica. And they make no secret of their ultimate goal: the communization of Central America and an all-out attack on the U.S. border.

In a 1983 *Playboy* Interview, Tomas Borge, Nicaragua's Minister of Interior, boldy conceded their intent. When reminded of critics' charges that the Sandinistas planned to export Marxist revolution "to El Salvador, then Guatemala, then Honduras, then Mexico," Borge declared: "That is one historical prophecy of Ronald Reagan that is absolutely true!"

Two years earlier, he had made it even clearer. While interrogating a civilian prisoner, he proclaimed that even if it took five, ten, or fifteen years, Nicaragua would eventually communize Mexico, and then send 100,000 people across the U.S. border "armed with machetes" to fill their quota of dead...

On October 16, 1985, Nicaragua's ruling Sandinistas formally implemented sweeping restrictions on remaining civil liberties, including the right of assembly, the right to travel within Nicaragua, the right to habeas corpus, the right to trial, the right to judicial appeal, the right to strike, the right to mail privacy, and the right to form political groups. The last opposition newspaper, *La Presna*, which had been operating under strict government censorship since 1982, was finally closed down in September 1986.

One dictatorship has been replaced by a dictatorship of another kind, and the Revolution has been betrayed!

"FIRST, WE SHALL TAKE ALL OF EASTERN EUROPE. NEXT THE MASSES OF ASIA. THEN WE SHALL EN-CIRCLE THAT LAST BASTION OF CAPITALISM, THE UNITED STATES OF AMERICA. WE SHALL NOT HAVE TO ATTACK, BECAUSE IT WILL FALL LIKE OVERRIPE FRUIT INTO OUR HANDS."

LENIN

FREEDOM FIGHTERS

I regret that I cannot be with you, but we have almost run out of food and medical supplies.

In addition, I have no blankets for my men, and winter is only a few months away.

After four years of fighting one of the world's great superpowers, our only victory has been to escape total defeat.

Even if the rest of the world continues to ignore the cause, we will fight on. For we are fighting not only for ourselves, but for all mankind. We are fighting for freedom and human dignity and the right to worship the God of our choice.

I urge you to tell the world of our plight and send whatever help you can.

God Bless you for caring enough to read my letter.

GEORGE WASHINGTON
VALLEY FORGE
September 1780

Acknowledgments

I wish to thank Rene Charette for the use of his home on Grand Cayman Island while writing this book. I thoroughly enjoyed the lovely beaches, swaying palms, beautiful blue waters and my favorite hangout: The Wreck of the Ten Sails Bar.

And a very special thanks to Herbert Humphreys Jr., owner of the Holiday Inn, Grand Cayman Island and President of Marine Archeological Research Limited, for his advice, assistance and friendship. Herbo, I look forward to writing a book about your adventures in treasure finding and the search for the main treasure of the Spanish Galleon, La Senora Nuestra de Maravilla.

G. LEE TIPPIN
AUTHOR

*"Con Dios patriotismo,
derrotaremos al comunismo."*

(With God and Patriotism,
we shall defeat Communism.)

Motto of the FDN and CMA

1

On June 28, 1979, the new government of Nicaragua announced the basic guidelines of their political program: "The establishment of democracy, justice and social progress"; the organization of the state "in order to pave the way for true democratic development on the basis of broad popular participation," including the participation of all those who fought against the Somoza government; the guarantee of full respect for human rights"; and "special guarantees... for the ... fundamental freedoms, including freedom of information and thought, freedom of religious belief, and free unionist and popular organization." Other parts of the program were the abolition of "repressive laws and repressive institutions," "suspension of illegal trials and sentences," and an "independent foreign policy." This new revolutionary junta promised that "all laws repressing the free manifestation and communication of thought and the freedom of information shall be abolished."

MANAGUA, NICARAGUA AUGUST 15, 1980

The four-story white office building, home of Nicaragua's largest daily newspaper, looked alive. To those people that worked there, the building was alive. It had a heart and a soul and a pulse beat.

It had aspirations and hopes. It was a building that had been the conscience of a nation for over 35 years. It was a building that never slept. At night, when the rest of the city was quiet, the presses that were the bowels of the building were working, grinding out the printed word, the accumulations of endless hours of human endeavor—printing the next morning's newspaper.

At the entrance to the building, and just to the right of the door, was a brass plaque on which was inscribed:

LA VERDAD
"THE TRUTH WILL KEEP YOU FREE"
ESTABLISHED 1946
FOR THE PEOPLE OF NICARAGUA

La Verdad in Spanish means "The Truth."

Just inside the entrance was a large reception room, and beyond that stairs led down to the noisy rooms where the paper was printed. On the second floor was a large spacious room with rows of desks and telephones. There was a quiet constant fury of activity in the room as busy reporters pounded away on typewriters or talked on a phone making hurried notes on yellow legal pads. At the far end of the room was a single enclosed office with a sign on the door that said simply, "MANAGING EDITOR."

Inside the office were two people. A distinguished looking gentleman in his early sixties, dressed in a short-sleeved white shirt and dark tie, sat at his desk talking to a beautiful raven-haired young lady. "I tell you, Maria, the country is in the hands of a few criminals. Those Marxist bastards have betrayed our revolution, and we are going to end up with a communist dictatorship—and it will be far worse than under Somoza. And I'm partly to blame because I sat by and let it happen!"

The young woman looked sadly at her father. He had aged since she last saw him. He looked rung out—defeated. He had devoted his life to fighting for freedom and democracy. Enrique Salazaar, owner and publisher of one of Managua's three daily newspapers, *La Verdad*, was a descendant of the early Spanish aristocracy. His father built a coffee and banana empire in Nicaragua. Enrique attended the best schools and eventually graduated from Notre Dame in the U.S. with a degree in journalism. He worked for a while for a newspaper in Indianapolis and then World War II broke out. Enrique enlisted in the Marine Corps and was wounded on Iwo

14

Jima. After the war, he returned to Nicaragua and followed his dream. He established *La Verdad*.

* * *

As a young man, Enrique had been a friend of the Somozas. After the War, he returned after having experienced a taste of American democracy and became an outspoken critic of the Somozas. Then he became a political opponent and a militant enemy, finally joining with the Sandinistas to help liberate Nicaragua.

Enrique was never fooled by the leaders of the Sandinistas. He knew that Borge, Wheelock and the Ortegas were Marxists who were trained in Moscow and Cuba. He knew the revolution was being funded by Cuba and Russia—however he mistakenly believed that the Marxists could be controlled and that Nicaragua would establish a Democratic-Socialist type of government after the revolution.

After the revolution, Enrique was one of the original twelve members of the ruling junta. However, the Marxists had planned well, and one-by-one the moderates were edged out and replaced with Marxists. The ties to the Soviet Bloc became stronger. Planeloads of Russian and Cuban advisors arrived, along with tons of sophisticated military equipment. The moderate members of the junta were powerless to stop the communist takeover. Finally, disgusted with his figurehead position, Enrique resigned.

Using his newspaper, Enrique began speaking out against the new regime. He received several calls from old acquaintances asking him to cool down his rhetoric—but he disregarded them and continued. Then, just two weeks ago, the government had issued a new ultimatum, in a growing list of ultimatums designed to curb individual and group freedoms: "All newspaper articles have to be submitted to the Office of the Minister of Interior for approval prior to publication." In other words, the Sandinista regime imposed government censorship of the press!

Enrique went through the ceiling. Even during the worst days of the Somoza dictatorship, his newspaper was not censored. Somoza had not dared to do such a thing! The former dictator once had Enrique arrested and thrown in jail for two weeks for speaking out—but he never censored *La Verdad*.

Enrique disregarded the Sandinista ultimatum and wrote an editorial on the new government's attempts to stop freedom of the press. The next day a platoon of soldiers surrounded his building and his paper was closed for seven days. This was the first time *La Verdad* had failed to go to print since the day it had been established. Enrique received an ominous letter from the Minister of the Interior warning him "not to disregard the government ultimatum again ."

* * *

Maria gently patted her father's arm. She knew that he would never stand by and allow the government to censor his newspaper—it was against his very moral fibre; he would die first. "Father," she asked, "what can you do? How can you fight them?"

"I can fight them with the truth! I can tell the whole world how a popular revolution has been betrayed by a handful of Marxists backed by Cuba and Moscow. I can tell the truth about the leaders who are no better than common criminals. Did you know that Ortega's greatest claim to fame before the revolution was that he killed a milkman while robbing him of sixty dollars?"

"Papa. There is nothing you can do here—it is too late. You said yourself that they are firmly entrenched and have all the power. They can do whatever they want to do. Why don't you and Mama come home to America with me. There, you will be free to write and say whatever you want to about the Sandinistas. Americans need to know what is going on here and you can tell them."

"My dear girl. Americans will not listen to me! They don't want to know what is happening here. The Americans are still living with the Vietnam War syndrome, and they are afraid to get involved in Central America. If they only understood that Nicaragua is just the first step in the communist march toward the United States—then they might listen. Why, the communists would not even be in power if it wasn't for Carter and his policies. We could have had a free Nicaragua—without the communists." Enrique paused and took his daughter's hand in his. "Chiquita, I cannot leave now," he declared emphatically. "The paper survived the Somozas, and it will survive these communist thugs. They cannot win against the truth!"

Maria knew that it was no use arguing with her proud stubborn father. He was not about to leave Nicaragua. To him, that would be total capitulation.

Maria and her ten-year-old son had arrived in Managua the week

16

before for a lengthy visit with her parents. Maria was married to an American career soldier. She met her husband, Richard Wade, while she was attending the University of North Carolina—until she met Richard. She always told people that God had dropped her husband from the air—right into her arms. They met when he missed his drop zone and parachuted into a backyard swimming pool where Maria was attending a party.

Shortly after they were married, Richard went to Vietnam. Their son David was born while he was away. Now, Richard was a Lieutenant Colonel and assigned to the Delta Force, America's counterterrorist unit at Fort Bragg.

Maria loved her husband very much and enjoyed Army life. Richard's work was demanding and he was a dedicated soldier—but he was a good husband and father. He had already been promoted ahead of his contemporaries twice, and everyone said he was headed for stars. That he would not make general never occurred to Maria. She expected it! Her husband was the stuff generals are made of.

Enrique picked up his pen and started writing. "Father, what are you going to do?" asked Maria.

Her father looked at her and smiled, "I'm going to write a story that will really get their attention!"

* * *

MANAGUA AUGUST 21, 1980
AND HE DID!

The next morning twelve thousand copies of *La Verdad* hit the streets of Managua; the three-inch headlines blared:

MARXISTS BETRAY REVOLUTION

In the story that followed, Enrique Salazaar blasted the new regime! He told in his own words how the Marxists gained control of the revolution; how they had forced out the more moderate leaders; how Fidel Castro had instructed the Sandinistas to downplay their ties with Cuba, until the revolution succeeded; how the Sandinistas used the Catholic Church and other religious groups. He explained the Sandinista plans for building a comminist military enclave and exporting the revolution to other Central American nations. He told how stupid and naive he and the other moderate leaders had been and how they had been used and fooled by the

17

Marxists; and he blamed himself and the other moderate leaders for allowing gangsters and murderers to get control of the revolution.

* * *

At 8 p.m. that evening, twenty-five men dressed in civilian clothing and carrying sledgehammers, axes and ball bats walked through the front door of *La Verdad*. Most of the night crew fled; a few loyal employees tried to fight the mob, but they were quickly beaten down. The intruders spent a half hour in the building. When they left, everything inside was a shambles.

Enrique Salazaar and his family were oblivious to the carnage that was taking place at his paper. Janice, his wife, was serving the dinner. They could afford maids, and she did have a housekeeper during the day; but at night she preferred to take care of her husband herself. Janice was an American from Indianapolis. Enrique met her when he was working there before the war.

They were having their last dinner together for awhile. Janice was going to go to the States the next day with her daughter and grandson. There was an air of sadness about the table because Janice and Enrique had never been separated for more than a week since the war.

Maria laid down her fork and looked across the table at her father. "Papa, I wish you were coming with us. It will be dangerous for you here."

"No Chiquita, I will be safe here. They wouldn't dare do anything to me. I am too well known." He smiled sarcastically, "After all I am a hero of the revolution!"

Janice walked over and put her arm around her husband. "I do not want to go without you."

"It won't be for long, Querida Mia—but I will feel much better with you at Maria's." He looked solemn, "I think they will close my paper this time. Then I may have to leave the country."

Their conversation was interrupted by the ringing of the phone. Enrique got up from the table, walked across the room and picked up the phone: "Hello, Enrique Salazaar, here. What!" His face turned ashen, "They what? Good lord! Yes, I'll be right down!" He slammed down the phone and turned to his family, a look of disbelief on his face: "That was the police. They said a group calling themselves a 'turbos divinos' (divine mob) broke into the newspaper and wrecked it. Four of my employees are in the hospital!"

Janice came to her husband, crying. "Oh no, Enrique Mio." They put their arms about each other. "What will you do now?" she asked.

"Well, first I am going down to the paper and see how much damage they did."

A loud knock at the door startled them. Maria left her parents comforting each other and walked to the door. A confused David sat quietly at the table. He did not understand what was going on. Maria opened the door slightly; then her arm was jerked abruptly as two men burst in brandishing pistols. Three more followed.

Enrique stepped forward, putting his wife behind him. "What are you doing h----?" His words were cut off as one of the men slapped him on the side of the head with a pistol barrel. Enrique was stunned; he staggered backwards, blood pouring down over one ear.

David jumped from his chair and came running across the room towards his grandfather's assailants. He flung himself at the man that pistol-whipped Enrique, screaming: "Don't hit my grandpapa!"

One of the men caught the young boy's arms and held him; another stepped forward and swung his pistol in a vicious chop. There was a loud crack of metal against bone, and David crumpled to the floor and lay still, like a broken doll.

Maria screamed and ran to her son. She bent over him; two men grabbed her and stood her up. She kicked and struggled—but to no avail.

One of the men, apparently the leader, walked over to Enrique who was supporting himself by the table: "Enrique Salazaar, I arrest you on behalf of the people of Nicaragua—you are a traitor to the revolution."

"How dare you force yourself into my home!" yelled Enrique. "Don't you know who I am? I was one of the leaders of the revolution!"

"We know very well who you are," said the leader. "You are Enrique Salazaar, imperialist pig; tool of the United States; and a traitor to the revolution!"

"Did Borge send you here?" asked Enrique.

The leader stepped forward and struck Salazaar with his open hand. Then he turned to two of his men and nodded. They began to beat the editor with their gun barrels. Enrique tried vainly to protect himself. His blood began to run on the white tablecloth he was leaning over.

His wife ran to his side, trying to protect him. One of the men struck a vicious blow to her face and she fell to the floor. As she tried to struggle to her feet, the leader put his gun barrel to her head and pulled the trigger.

The sound of the single shot echoed through the house. Maria stared in disbelief at her mother's body on the floor; then she screamed: "Oh, my God! Mama!"

Enrique crumpled to the floor and lay in a widening pool of blood. He tried to touch his dead wife, but he lost consciousness.

A hysterical Maria, already approaching insanity, was dragged into the bedroom. There, they ripped her clothes off and forced her down on the bed. She screamed in agony as the first man raped her. By the time the fifth man took her, she was beyond pain. When the last man finished, he put the gun to her head and pulled the trigger.

Before the men left, they set fire to the house.

2

TWA Flight 847, with 177 passengers aboard, took off from Cairo at 0900 hours, climbed to 29,000 feet and headed towards its first destination, Athens. The plane was filled with European and American tourists, along with a few Egyptians and Arabs. At 0930, a dark man, obviously an Arab, left seat 16-C and went to the restroom. He returned three minutes later. At 0945, another man, whose passport stated he was Lebanese, left seat 26-E and went into the same restroom. He returned to his seat a few minutes later. No one took notice of these two insignificant activities. At 1000 hours, both men got out of their seats and walked slowly towards the front of the aircraft. They stopped to talk to two other male passengers and handed them each a brown paper bag—then they disappeared into the first class section, closing the curtain behind them. One man in first class stood up to meet them. "May Allah be praised!" he said in Arabic.

* * *

WASHINGTON, D.C. MARCH 1, 1981

A late winter storm blanketed the Nation's capital; early morning traffic on the beltway was bumper-to-bumper and not moving. The ponderous wheels of the bureaucracy had ground to a halt—buried under 4 inches of fresh snow. The nation was being run by a small group of hardy souls who lived close enough to their offices to walk

The President of the United States sat at his desk in the oval office going over a speech he was to give the next day in Cleveland. The President was depressed He hated Washington in the late winter He thought it about time that he visited his ranch in California

He looked up as Larry Vance, his Secretary of State, walked into the room. He could tell from Vance's face that he was the bearer of bad news: "Mr. President, a TWA airliner out of Rome has been hijacked!"

"Damn!" said the President. This was something he had been dreading ever since he took office. He had promised the American people that he would take strong measures against terrorists—now he was faced with the fact.

"Sir, the plane is on the ground in Rome now, and the hijackers have demanded to speak to a representative of the U.S. government. They have already killed one passenger, an American! They just opened the door, shot him in the head and tossed him out. That is all the information I have now."

The President thought for a minute, then looked at his friend, "Has Delta Force been notified yet?"

"Yes, Sir. The Delta Force Commander and a team are already in the air and enroute to Rome."

"Okay, Larry. Keep me informed. As soon as you get an evaluation from Delta Force, let me know. Have Andy call a press conference and you handle it. Just tell them what we have. But make it clear—the United States will not be blackmailed by terrorists! If we can use Delta Force on this one, I want to use it. And you can tell the Delta Force Commander that I want him to get these terrorists!"

* * *

LEONARDO DA VINCI AIRPORT, ROME

The hijacked airplane looked lonely sitting on the tarmac 200 yards from the international terminal. It was a good position for the terrorists, because nobody could approach the aircraft without being seen. Just below the nose of the plane, a lone body lay, face down in a crumpled heap—a warning that the terrorists meant business and would not hesitate to kill again. Aboard Flight 847, 171 terrified passengers each wondered if he would be the next victim. The pilot had given the tower one message from the terrorists: they would not talk to anyone except an official representative of the United States Government!

Libertad "Libby" McGinnis, a fledgling reporter with ABN News, stood anxiously looking out of the window of the terminal at Flight 847. Libby, the daughter of an Irish father and Italian mother, had only been with ABN six months. She had majored in radio and TV at Boston College. After graduation she went to work for a local TV affiliate in Boston. She worked her way up from assistant producer to roving reporter and finally to anchorwoman. In her early days, she even pulled a stint as the local TV weather girl. She spent seven years as the anchorwoman before moving up to ABN National Staff. Now, she was back at the bottom paying her dues again. She was confident in her abilities, and there was no doubt in her inquiring mind that she would go all the way to the top. She was good at her work, and she knew it! "Tom Brokaw, Jane Pauley, Connie Chung—watch out! Here comes Libby McGinnis!"

Libby was a self-proclaimed liberal. She was born a liberal and she planned on dying a liberal. She distrusted anyone or anything that had to do with the establishment, the military and conservatism in general. She believed that the conservatives were hell-bent on blowing up the world. She felt that it was the duty of the liberal press to expose the conservatives and be the conscience of a government that continually exploited its second-class citizens.

In college she was active in the Anti-War movement. Libby's two greatest heroes among living Americans were Jimmy Carter and Edward Kennedy.

Her good looks helped in her business and she knew it. By anyone's standards she was a beautiful woman—and she turned heads wherever she went. Her long red hair, big green eyes and almost mulatto dark skin were a rare combination that accentuated her perfect figure—a figure she kept in tune with hours of strenuous exercise.

As luck would have it, Libby was already in Rome when the hijacking occurred. She was doing a special on the Vatican, and she was not even guaranteed it would get on the air. Her office in New

York instructed her to drop everything and cover the hijacking, at least until one of the "headliner reporters" arrived.

Standing beside the newswoman was her cameraman, Robert Scott. "Scotty" was one of the best in the business, a seasoned hand, having received his baptism of fire as a Marine combat photographer during the Korean War. His later work in Vietnam, with Tom Brokaw and others, made him almost a legend among his peers. Scotty liked Libby McGinnis; she had talent—she had the dedication and zeal that great reporters are made of. She was the kind of daughter he would have liked to have had—if any of his three marriages had produced offspring. He knew that she would have to be looked after and guided for awhile; but he hoped she did not lose any of her determination and zeal. Most reporters lost their edge after awhile—the great ones did not. She could be one of the great—as long as she remained hungry. Scotty was a quiet conservative who had worked so long with liberals that he had learned to keep his mouth shut. Sometimes Libby's liberal views danced on his nerves—but he just smiled and shook his head, knowing that someday she would discover the realities of life.

The American negotiating team had arrived a few hours ago and went straight to the control tower. They were easy to spot in their ivy league uniforms, carrying their badges of importance—thin black leather briefcases.

So far, the media had been kept in the dark, but a press conference was scheduled. Libby looked around the room at her fellow reporters and the busy camera crews. Everyone was just like her—they were hoping to get the big story. The goal of every newspaper reporter was to hit the front page; every TV news reporter wanted to get that 5 minute spot on the evening news; and if you got a story that was important enough to break into the regular programming—so much the better.

There was a stir in the crowd as two men walked into the room and stood on either side of a hastily arranged podium. The one in the dark gray suit spoke first: "Good morning, ladies and gentlemen."

The media, not known for their polite demeanor, stirred around for a bit, then finally settled to listen. Flashbulbs clicked and there was the low sound of video cameras whirring. The astute Libby had spotted the two negotiators when they entered the room and had edged herself and Scotty to the front of the crowd.

The man at the podium waited until the room was quiet, then

resumed: "I am James Nash from the U.S. Embassy in Rome. The gentleman to my right is Mr. Barnard Wilkerson from the U.S. State Department. Mr. Wilkerson is the leader of the American negotiating team."

Wilkerson was cut out of the same mold as Nash. He was wearing a light gray pin-stripe suit. He wore heavy black horn-rimmed glasses and a brown beard covered his face. His suit was a bit baggy, as if it were one size too big and he had slept in it for two days. He was an unassuming and typically ivy league upper crust whiz kid. "No doubt a conservative," thought Libby.

Wilkerson moved over behind the podium and cleared his throat, "Ahem." Libby noted that he looked nervous and unsure of himself. He did not look the crowd straight in the eye; instead he looked on a 45 degree angle to the floor. Libby turned to Scott and whispered, "A wimp! A conservative wimp!"

Wilkerson gripped the podium as if he were going to fall down if he let go. He cleared his throat again, "Ahem. Good morning ladies and gentlemen. We have been in telephone contact with the hijackers. They have made several demands." Wilkerson removed a paper from his pocket and read it verbatim, as if he were afraid to misquote: "First, they demand the immediate release of 240 Palestinian prisoners being held by the Israeli government. Second, they insist that the U.S. government pay them $25 million in American greenbacks. Third, they want the aircraft refueled with a flight clearance to Tripoli, Libya. And fourth, they want an on-board interview with one of the major American TV networks. The hijackers have set a deadline of 4 p.m. this afternoon for our answer. After that time, they have threatened to execute one passenger every five minutes, starting with the Americans on board. And now I'll try to answer some of your questions."

Hands shot up all over the room, including Libby's. Wilkerson pointed to one of the men. "Mr. Wilkerson, which American TV news network is going to conduct the interview?"

"That hasn't been decided yet. If our State Department approves—we will let the hijackers decide." He pointed to another male reporter.

"How many passengers are on board and how many of them are Americans; and do you have the name of the man that was killed?"

"There are 171 passengers on board; of that, we think 32 are Americans. We have asked the hijackers to allow us to recover the body—but they have refused."

Hands went up again, and the negotiator pointed to another male. "Sir! Have you been in contact with the President and will he pay the ransom?"

"We are in constant contact with the State Department, who is in contact with the President. The President has not made any statement yet."

A voice yelled out: "Does that mean you may pay the ransom money?"

"That means," answered Wilkerson, "that there has not been a decision yet." He pointed to another man.

"The President once said that he will never negotiate with terrorists. Does your being here mean he is reneging on that promise? And has the Delta Force been alerted—will they be used?"

"You will have to ask the President about his statement. As far as the Delta Force is concerned, I suppose they have been alerted—it is customary. As to their being used, that decision will be made much later." He stopped, looked around the room and finally pointed to Libby: "Yes, Miss?"

"Well thank you sir! I was beginning to think you were afraid of women," Libby chided sarcastically.

There was a moment of laughter in the room.

Libby noticed the negotiator did not look amused. She continued: "Has the United States asked the Israelis to release the prisoners?"

"We have been in contact with the government of Israel. Any announcement pertaining to the prisoners will have to come from the government of Israel."

Libby did not like the smooth talking Wilkerson—he had all the right answers. She said what she knew others wanted to: "Mr. Wilkerson, you have not told us a thing. What we want to know is what you are doing to free the hostages."

"I can only reiterate that we are doing everything humanly possible. Our primary concern is the safety of the passengers—and we will exercise every option to get them released safely."

Hands were still waving in the air, but Wilkerson disregarded them. "That is all I can say at this time. We will keep you informed," he turned and walked out of the room with the man called Nash following.

Libby turned to her cameraman, "Did you get some good shots?"

He looked back and smiled. "Libby girl, I always get good shots. By the way, you sure handled him."

"Don't be a smart ass—I still say he is a wimp. Sometimes I

wonder where Washington finds them."

The third member of her crew, a young Italian on loan from the Rome office, took the videotape from Scotty and hurried out. Within 15 minutes, the interview would be seen in the U.S. via satellite, providing her boss decided to put it on the air.

Libby and Scotty walked out of the room and down the corridor to the coffee shop. They had no more than sat down, when a man in civilian clothes walked up. "Miss McGinnis, Mr. Wilkerson would like to see you up in the control tower."

"What does he want?" she asked, thinking that the negotiator was going to chew her out for baiting him.

"He'll tell you, miss. Mr. Scott is to come along also."

They rose and followed the man out; Libby leaned over to Scotty and mumbled, "Well, well—it seems we are being summoned by the wimp."

A few minutes later they were ushered into the control tower, where they found a hum of urgent activity. Several men sat around a conference table on the other side of the room. Their escort turned to them: "Please be seated. Mr. Wilkerson will be with you in a minute."

The mini-conference finally concluded and the four men talking to Wilkerson left the room. The negotiator walked over to the news team and announced matter-of-factly: "The hijackers want to be interviewed by ABN News!"

Libby was stunned by the news! She could not speak as the excitement welled up inside of her. An exclusive interview with the hijackers! What a scoop—unless the big boys arrived! She gathered her wits and asked: "When?"

"At 2 p.m."

She looked at her watch; it was 12:30. Maybe she would get her chance at the big time.

Scotty broke into her thoughts: "No, Libby! I don't think you are ready."

"Oh, don't be so damn protective, Scotty; you know I can handle it."

The truth was he knew she could. And the other truth was he wanted to do it too.

"Now, I must warn you; there will be some danger," said the negotiator, his steel gray eyes never leaving hers, "but we will do everything we can to keep you safe."

It was the first time she had really looked into his eyes. They looked cold, almost cruel. It seemed like he was looking straight through her. He continued: "I will accompany you as far as the aircraft. The steps will be positioned just prior to our arrival. You and Mr. Scott will go aboard alone. You will have 15 minutes for the interview. I will wait for you outside and escort you back."

"I understand," she said.

"I hope you do, Miss McGinnis! Once we leave the terminal there will be no turning back—you must do everything I say—no matter what!" His gray eyes blazed a warning that made her shiver.

He was not the same man that had spoken to her at the press conference. Even his voice had changed, and he no longer seemed unsure of himself.

"You will remain here until it is time to go to the plane. Please sit down over there." He pointed to two chairs at the other end of the room. He turned and walked over and picked up the phone.

During the next hour the room was a bustle of activity, and Wilkerson was right in the middle of it. Men came in and talked quietly to the negotiator. Twice he talked on the phone to someone Libby figured was the hijackers. Once during a lull, his eyes fell on her, and suddenly Libby saw in them a loneliness to match her own. Libby McGinnis did not seem like a lonely woman—but she was. Six months ago, she broke up with her fiance of five years. Since then she had lost all faith in relationships. She had found solace in her work.

Libby and Scotty worked out a series of questions to ask the hijackers. Finally, the tense period was over, and Wilkerson walked over to them: "We'll go now. Remember, I'll lead you up to the passenger ramp. Then on my word you will walk slowly up the ramp. Don't make any sudden moves. These people are easily spooked and may even be taking drugs to keep themselves alert. One false move and they will kill—not only you but perhaps some of the passengers. I'll call out when your time is up—you must come out at that time. The gas truck is scheduled to begin refueling the aircraft at 2:20. After that, we don't know what is going to happen."

"Does that mean you have given in to their demands?" asked Libby.

"No. Only the interview and refueling. We'll give them answers to their other demands at three." He turned to Scotty: "Don't turn on your video camera until you get on the aircraft!"

Wilkerson turned and walked over to a small radio; then he spoke some strange words—for a negotiator: "All stations check in affir-

28

mative go. Roger Alpha. Roger Bravo. Roger Charlie. Roger Delta. It is a go! Execute final option."

Scotty whispered in her ear, "Libby, something's going on; I don't like it."

Libby didn't understand what was going on, but she sensed that something was wrong. Before she could ask any questions, the negotiator grabbed her arm and guided her out of the room. She tried to talk to him during their walk to the terminal door, but he did not pay any attention to her. When they walked out of the terminal and into the parking apron, the area was clear, except for the Italian military vehicles several hundred yards away. Two attendants wearing blue coveralls pushed the passenger ramp up to the aircraft and ran off. A refueling truck moved slowly onto the parking ramp and stopped 100 yards from the airliner.

Libby was shaking with fear and excitement; she had a sudden urge to run away—but she could not. This was her chance at the proverbial brass ring and she was going after it! Move over Connie Chung! Move over Tom Brokaw! Libby McGinnis is coming. She felt Scotty's hand on her shoulder in a reassuring gesture. She turned to him and managed a brave smile: "We are going to do it, Scotty!"

Up ahead, the body of the murdered passenger lay beneath the airliner—a grim reminder of the dangerous men waiting for them inside the plane.

When they were about 75 feet from the airliner, Wilkerson unexpectedly stopped and turned toward them: "Stay here!" he ordered. "If anything happens, run like hell back into the terminal!" He spun around and walked off before they could say anything.

"I don't like this at all," mumbled Scotty. "He has changed the scenario—something is going down!"

Wilkerson walked up to the passenger ramp and stopped. A terrified woman was shoved to the door of the plane; a hijacker stood behind her with one arm around her and the other holding a gun to her head.

Wilkerson spoke first, "We have a slight problem."

"What kind of problem?" yelled down the gunman.

Wilkerson took one step up the stairs and said in a low voice, "ABN will not allow their reporters to come aboard without a government representative along."

Libby turned to Scotty, "Why, he's lying!"

Under his breath Scotty said, "SHHH."

There was no answer from the hijacker. Wilkerson took one more step up the stairs and repeated, "I said, ABN will not allow their female reporter to come aboard for the interview without a U.S. government representative along."

The hijacker began to suspect something was wrong. He yelled a warning; his voice sounded almost hysterical. "Stop! The interview is off. Don't come any closer or I'll kill this lady. Go back to the terminal or I'll blow this lady's head off!"

The terrified hostage began to moan and cry. Wilkerson took one more step up the stairs while he was speaking in a low voice: "Don't be hasty. I'm sure we can work this out. I know you want to be interviewed. Listen, I am going to remove my shirt so you can see I'm not armed."

The negotiator slowly took off his tie and dropped it to the ground; then his suit jacket followed; and finally his shirt. Libby thought the scene on the passenger ramp almost sensual—like a male strip show without music. Then, as his shirt came off, Libby saw it—a gun! A dark automatic pistol was taped to his bare back. Now she knew what was happening. This was it—the final option. She mumbled to Scotty, "Turn your camera on."

"It's already on; start talking."

Libby put her mike up to her mouth: "This is Libby McGinnis, ABN News. Our camera is located near the TWA hijacked airliner flight number 847 at Leonardo da Vinci Airport in Rome. This reporter was scheduled to interview the hijackers holding 171 passengers aboard flight 847. However, there has been a sudden and dramatic change. Mr. Wilkerson, the State Department's chief negotiator, is on the passenger ramp leading up to the airplane, talking to one of the hijackers. The hijacker is holding a gun to one of the female passengers at the aircraft door. I do not know what is happening, but it appears as if there is going to be an assault on the airliner. Mr. Wilkerson has removed his shirt, supposedly to show the gunman at the door that he is unarmed; but as you can see, there is a gun taped to the negotiator's back. At this time, I cannot see anyone else around."

The refueling truck began to move slowly towards the airplane. Libby anxiously watched the drama unfold from her ringside seat. She narrated what she saw as best she could, as the old pro Scotty seemed to know exactly where to focus his video camera. She sensed that she was about to get a once-in-a-lifetime story. Cameras from the terminal were also focused on the hijacked plane—but Libby and Scotty were there in the arena; they were part of the drama.

The refueling truck was halfway to the plane before the hijacker at the door spotted it. "Stop that truck!" he screamed. "Get it out of here!"

"They must have their time wrong," yelled Wilkerson to the hijacker. He took another step up the stairs and turned slightly to the right, still keeping his back hidden from the hijacker. He commenced waving at the truck, yelling at the top of his voice. "Stop! Stop the truck!"

A hidden marksman, high atop the terminal, focused the crosshairs of his scope on his target. Wilkerson's arm suddenly dropped to his side. A single shot cracked across the runway; and an instant later a 280 grain, hollow point slug hit the hijacker and his head exploded in a cloud of red and gray. The hijacker was thrown back against the fuselage; then he pitched forward and lay still at the top of the steps. The hysterical female hostage stood and screamed. A second hijacker appeared at the door, pointing a submachine gun at Wilkerson; but the terrorist was too slow. The negotiator had jerked his revolver free and was firing as he moved up the steps. Two slugs smashed into the hijacker's face, driving him back inside the aircraft. Wilkerson brushed the female hostage aside and disappeared into the airplane. A second man, dressed in black with a mask over his face, appeared from nowhere and followed the negotiator up the steps. The man had evidently been hiding in a secret compartment in the passenger ramp. The refueling truck jumped forward as the driver floor-boarded the accelerator! In a few seconds, it screeched to a halt under the wing; and four men dressed in black leaped out of the tanker, carrying aluminum ladders. Two of them scrambled on top the wing while the other two went for the aft emergency exit. There was gunfire coming from inside the airliner now. Two helicopters appeared from behind the terminal; each had a man dressed in black hanging below on cables. The emergency doors popped out at the same time the men hanging below the helicopters arrived. They both swung into the airplane through the open exits.

Libby was shaking with fear and excitement, but she did not run. She crouched on the concrete—Scotty by her side—and continued her narration. The firing aboard the hijacked airliner suddenly stopped.

"It is quiet aboard the airliner now," said the newswoman. "All the firing has stopped. Italian military vehicles and ambulances have surrounded the aircraft. Wait! Someone is coming out of the plane!"

A young dark-haired man wearing a white shirt and dark trousers came running down the stairs of the ramp. He started waving his arms wildly and screaming in English: "DON'T SHOOT! DON'T SHOOT! I GIVE UP! PLEASE DON'T SHOOT ME!"

He ran directly toward Libby and Scotty. He was unarmed! Wilkerson appeared at the door of the plane and stepped out on the ramp He raised his gun and aimed. The young man was still screaming: "DON'T SHOOT! I'M UNARMED! DON'T SHOOT!"

Libby joinned him and yelled at Wilkerson: "DON'T SHOOT! HE WANTS---!"

She never finished her sentence. Wilkerson's arm bucked up and a single shot echoed across the tarmac. The young man did a complete flip in the air and landed on his stomach; a bloody hole covered the middle of his back, and his arms and legs were flopping against the concrete. Another shot followed and his head exploded in blood and bone. His body twitched twice and he lay still.

Libby was screaming into her microphone—horrified by what she saw: "OH MY GOD! HE JUST SHOT HIM DOWN IN COLD BLOOD! THE MAN WAS UNARMED AND TRYING TO GIVE UP AND HE JUST SHOT HIM DOWN IN COLD BLOOD. OH MY GOD! HOW HORRIBLE! HE JUST SHOT HIM DOWN IN COLD BLOOD!"

3

That night, millions of people watched Libby's tape, and her words "HE JUST SHOT THE MAN DOWN IN COLD BLOOD!" echoed throughout the world.

The next day's headlines could have read, "DELTA FORCE RESCUES HOSTAGES," or "U.S. COMMANDOS CONDUCT DARING RAID TO FREE HOSTAGES," or even "U.S. DELTA FORCE KILLS FIVE TERRORISTS." Instead the headlines were "U.S. DELTA FORCE COMMANDER SHOOTS DOWN TERRORIST TRYING TO SURRENDER!" and "COLD-BLOODED KILLING SHOCKS THE WORLD!"

The liberal American and World Press jumped on the bandwagon and condemned the "gestapo-like tactics" of the Delta Force Commander.

The next morning, Libby McGinnis was interviewed on *Good Morning America*. She talked about her "horrible experience," and by the end of the day America had forgotten the fact that 165 hostages were rescued. Within a week, liberal U.S. Congressmen, eager to find fault with the military and the Administration for their own political purposes, were demanding a full investigation of the Delta Force.

Using the Freedom of Information Act, Libby was able to get a copy of most of Wade's military records; but there were some she could not get because they were classified. Libby had been totally shocked by the unnecessary killing of the one terrorist, and she was curious to see what kind of man the Colonel was.

Scotty tried to talk her out of it: "Leave him alone, Libby; we have already done enough damage to him. The press is already comparing him to Attila the Hun. We got our story—now let's leave him be."

Libby could not put it down. She had to find out more about Colonel Richard Wade. However, the Colonel turned out to be a much different man than she expected.

Richard Wade's father was a career Infantry officer who was killed in Korea in 1953. His mother was killed in a car accident six months later. Wade was raised by a Japanese doctor and his wife who had been close friends of his father. Wade's foster father was also a Kung Fu Master who owned his own martial arts studio in San Francisco. Wade had a black belt in karate by the age of 17. In high school he was an "A" student and a star athlete. He received an appointment to the U.S. Military Academy at West Point. He graduated number two academically and made second-team All American as a running back. He turned down a professional football contract to go into the Army. He was All-Army Karate Champion for three consecutive years. In 1964, he married Maria Salazaar, the daughter of a wealthy Nicaraguan. Altogether, he spent four years fighting in Vietnam—mostly as a Green Beret. He was wounded three times and returned home as one of America's most decorated combat soldiers. Much of his duty in Vietnam was with Special Operations and many of his efficiency reports were classified, so Libby was unable to find out exactly what he did. According to reports written by his senior officers, Richard Wade was "a brilliant leader who would someday be a General."The words "Outstanding," "Future General," "Promote ahead," "Promote immediately," and "The best!" kept appearing in his efficiency reports. Wade was promoted ahead of his contemporaries twice, making Colonel before he had 15 years commissioned service. From a military point of view, Richard Wade seemed to be the quintessential officer—destined to make general.

His wife and young son were murdered by bandits in Nicaragua in 1980, along with his wife's parents. It was while reading about the death of his wife and son that Libby began having misgivings about what she was doing. Suddenly, she realized she was prying into someone's personal life. However, the more she dug into the life of the Colonel, the more obsessed she became about finding out more. On paper, he was the perfect soldier; a war hero; All-American football player; the ideal husband, etc., etc.—the all-American boy who made good. But she knew there had to be a flaw somewhere. Why else would he shoot a man down in cold blood?

She traveled and interviewed officers he had worked for and men whom he had served with; and all she heard was praise from what appeared to be a Richard Wade fan club. Many of his friends refused to talk to her when they found out who she was. She could not talk to any of the men in the Delta Force—because it seemed that no one knew who was in the unit. Everything about the Counter-Terrorist unit was classified. She found out that the only reason Wade's name was released to the public was because she had pictures of him on tape.

One of his former commanders, now a four-star General, told her: "Miss McGinnis, Colonel Wade is exactly as he seems. He is an outstanding, dedicated officer. Your Rome story not only ruined the career of a great soldier, but will probably deny the Army the services of a brilliant officer. And now that you have exposed him, he will be on every terrorist hit list in the world!"

Libby was shocked by the General's statement and he explained: "The reason we keep the names of the members of Delta Force classified is to protect them and their families from possible terrorist reprisal. For your information, our intelligence sources told us that three days after the Rome operation was aired on TV, Colonel Wade was placed on Khadafy's top ten hit list."

On an impulse, Libby called Fort Bragg and requested an interview with Colonel Wade. Their curt reply: "Colonel Wade will not give an interview!"

The TV reporter was surprised when Wade's Japanese foster parents agreed to talk to her. She hurriedly packed her bags and headed for San Francisco. The Hurachis lived south of San Francisco near San Jose. Libby was greeted at the door of the Hurachi home by an attractive middle-aged oriental lady. "Good morning, Miss McGinnis. I am Yoshiko Hurachi; please come in."

Libby followed the lady who called herself Yoshiko into a pleasant living room. The first thing she noticed was a picture of Wade as a cadet on the mantle. On it was enscribed,"To Mom and Pop—

With All My Love, Richard."

They were met by a white-haired man wearing a dark suit and tie. He offered his hand to the reporter: "Welcome to our home, Miss McGinnis; I am James Hurachi. Please sit down. Tea?"

Libby sat down in the chair he pointed to. "Yes, thank you."

Yoshiko poured the tea then took a seat by her husband who spoke first: "We have seen you on TV many times. You are even more beautiful in person."

Disarmed by his compliment, Libby could only say, "Thank you."

James Hurachi continued, "We understand you want to ask us some questions about our son, Richard."

Libby suddenly felt uncomfortable—out of place. She wished fervently that she had not come. She took an immediate liking to the charming couple. She decided to take the bull by the horns and get it over with. She swallowed and asked, "Mr. and Mrs. Hurachi, when you watched the Delta Force assault the hijacked airliner in Rome, what were your feelings?"

The lady answered: "We were very proud of our son; and we were happy that he was able to rescue the remaining passengers."

Libby went for the jugular: "What about when he shot the man running from the airplane? What did you feel then?"

Again, Wade's foster mother answered: "We felt sad; sadness for the man that was killed, and sadness for Richard because he had to kill him!"

"What do you think Colonel Wade felt when he shot the man?" asked the reporter.

The man finally spoke. "Miss McGinnis, I don't know what you are trying to learn from us. We saw exactly what you saw in Rome—what the camera saw. However, you must remember that the camera cannot see into a man's heart. Richard saw something different. He saw a crazed fanatical Muslim; a man who had already killed in cold blood; a man who had threatened to kill more—running towards you. There was no way he could know if the man had a gun or grenade or knife hidden in his shirt. He is trained to assume the worst. So he had to kill the man. This much our son told us—and he would never lie to his mother and father."

"Why hasn't he told this to the press?" asked Libby.

"Richard is a proud man," returned his mother. "He will not talk to the press; he doesn't trust the media."

The Hurachis took Libby into Wade's room and showed her his trophies and pictures. Hell, he was even an Eagle Scout. Libby apologized and left with a hollow feeling at the pit of her stomach. She knew there was not going to be a follow-up special on the Delta Force Commander.

* * *

When she returned to New York, she explained to her boss that she could not do a special on Wade. "I want to call the whole thing off!" she said.

"No, I want you to keep on trying," her boss said. "You are a good reporter and I know you can dig up some good dirt for a follow-up. You and Scotty cover the Senate Hearings. Should be a lot of publicity there."

"Yeah. Like the Nuremburg War Crimes Trials," chipped in Scotty, sarcastically.

Libby turned to her cameraman: "You like Wade, don't you?"

Scotty, who had also read the Colonel's records, answered: "Yes I do. Don't forget Libby, I'm a former Marine and I have seen combat. I think the guy is great. If I had to go back into combat, he's the kind of officer I would want to follow." He looked at her with a puzzled look on his face. "Why can't you leave him alone? I think you are obsessed with him. Hasn't what you have found out about him sunk in? The guy is a genuine 100 percent American hero. But we—yes, you and I—have made him into a Nazi—a cold-blooded killer. My God! He killed a terrorist. What's so bad about that? He was only doing what he has been trained to do. He was only doing his job!"

Libby looked at him, somewhat startled by his outburst: "Would you have shot an unarmed man trying to surrender?"

"How do you know he was trying to surrender? Maybe he was just trying to get another infidel. How did Wade know the man was unarmed? He could have had a grenade or knife in his pocket. How do you know the terrorist wasn't coming after you? Hell yes, I would have shot him!"

"But the man was unarmed," she protested.

"The Colonel didn't know that. He's been taught to assume the worst when dealing with terrorists—and act. Wade probably thought he was saving your life!"

"But the man was screaming that he wanted to give up!"

"Wake up girl! Wade could not take the chance; he had to kill the man. Don't you see that now?"

37

Libby was quiet for a moment. She took herself back to Rome and tried to imagine it from the Colonel's view. What she saw did not give her any comfort. "Why haven't you said something before now? I did not know you felt so strongly about him."

"There was no way to stop what happened. It was just one of those things. Besides, I wanted the story too. You reported what you saw in your own words—and you were great. Your emotional outburst helped to sell the story. It made the difference between something good and something great. I took the pictures; and they were great. We cannot feel guilty about doing our jobs. The colonel is just an unfortunate victim of circumstances. But I do think you should lay off him now. Forget about him. If you don't, you could get hurt."

Libby tried to follow Scotty's advice. But she could not get Richard Wade out of her mind. She had been shocked by what happened in Rome and had felt only revulsion and hate for the Colonel. She had wanted to see him punished. But now she was confused and feeling guilty over what was happening to him. Richard Wade stayed in her thoughts day and night. She had become a woman obsessed.

4

The President of the United States was in a quandary! What he knew to be a brilliant counterterrorist operation; what he thought would be a major blow and deterrent against terrorism and a coup for the Administration; and what he believed would be a major publicity victory had been turned into a debacle; a circus spectacle by the press and the liberals in Congress. The outstanding young Colonel who led the raid, who did exactly as his Commander-in-Chief requested—and that was to kill the terrorists—was being made the scapegoat. And he, the President of the most powerful nation in the world, was powerless to do a thing to help. He had initially praised the actions of the Delta Force; but everyone expected that. Now his closest advisors were telling him not to discuss the issue, particularly since the Senate was conducting an investigation.

* * *

Democratic Senator Thomas D. Fallon of Iowa used some of his blue chips to get himself appointed Chairman of the Senate Sub-Committee which was to investigate the U.S. Counterterrorist Unit's actions at the Rome airport. Thomas D. Fallon was no dummy; he realized that this was a chance to embarrass the conservative Administration and strike a blow for liberalism against the Military-Industrial Complex that was running the nation. It was his chance for a victory against an Administration that he perceived was leading the nation into another Vietnam-type war in Central America. He also knew that the publicity from the hearings would help him to get re-elected and perhaps propel him into a position of greater influence in his party. Fallon had been an activist and a leader of the Anti-War Movement in the late sixties. He was elected on an anti-war and anti-nuclear platform. A secret admirer of Marx and Lenin, he hoped someday to see a Socialist Government in the U.S.

Senator Fallon looked out across the hearing room at the throng of reporters and smiled. He had a feeling this was going to be his day. He picked up the gavel and rapped the table twice, bringing the hearing to order, and spoke in his best oratory voice: "Good morning ladies and gentlemen and distinguished colleagues. The purpose of this hearing is to investigate the methods used by the U.S. Counterterrorist Unit known as Delta Force, and especially their motives and actions in their attack on the TWA Airliner in Rome. As you all know, five hijackers and one innocent passenger were killed during this assault; and one of the unarmed hijackers was shot down while attempting to surrender. This last act, which has received so much world attention and condemnation, was committed by the Commander of the Delta Force. I want to emphasize that no one is on trial here. The Committee wants to hear the testimony of certain key witnesses and key people, gather the facts, and to the best of our abilities, make recommendations on how these types of operations can be improved in the future."

The first witness before the Committee was not a person; it was the now famous "videotape"—the tape that had already been seen by most of the world and that had skyrocketed Libby McGinnis to the top of her profession. The last scene showed Colonel Wade taking deliberate aim at the hijacker running toward the camera. You could clearly hear the hijacker pleading for his life. Then Libby McGinnis could be heard asking the Delta Force Commander not to shoot. There were two shots and the tape stopped as the hijacker kicked himself to death on the concrete parking ramp. The last words on the tape were Libby's: "He shot him down in cold blood!"

The next witness was Libby McGinnis, ABN News.

Senator Fallon smiled his best smile: "Miss McGinnis, please tell us, in your own words, everything that happened that day."

Libby calmly told her story—only this time she went out of her way not to condemn the man she now knew so well.

When she finished, Fallon asked, "Did Colonel Wade tell you that you were going on board the aircraft to interview the hijackers?"

"Yes Sir."

'He hid from you the fact that the Delta Force was going to assault the aircraft and that you and Mr. Scott would be in extreme danger—is that correct?"

"He did not tell us about the assault, but he did say we would be in danger. We knew the risk we were taking. It is part of our job."

"Colonel Wade passed himself off as a negotiator representing the President of the United States—is that correct?"

"The Colonel said he was with the State Department; he did not say he was representing the President."

Fallon had listened to Libby on the *Donahue Show* and he expected her to be a stronger witness against Wade. He sensed that somehow she had changed and excused her from the stand.

The next witness was Robert Scott; however, when Scotty began speaking out, defending Wade's actions, Fallon cut him short and excused him. Scotty returned to his seat beside Libby, mumbling something about the son-of-a-bitch being a communist!

Scotty was followed by several other members of the media who witnessed the incident in Rome from inside the terminal. They were all hand-picked by Senator Fallon, and they generally agreed that the assault was unnecessary and should have been handled by negotiation and that Wade's shooting of the unarmed hijacker was a wanton act of murder. They were followed by an "expert in counterterrorism," a professor from Connecticut who said that violence and counterstrikes against terrorism were not the answer and could only do harm in the long run. He said what we needed to do was to get to the root of the causes of terrorism and correct them. He finished by saying, "The leaders of the world powers must work together and correct the social evils that cause people to turn to terrorist acts."

Libby sat listening to the testimony, not believing what was happening. She certainly did not like Wade or what he stood for, but this was entirely uncalled for.

Finally, Colonel Richard Wade was called to the stand. He was wearing his Army Greens and six rows of decorations covered his left breast. This was the first time Libby had seen him since Rome, and he looked tired and haggard. Gone were his mustache and glasses. He looked out of place, being the only one in the room in uniform. Libby wondered where the rest of the Army Brass was. She thought they would be at the hearing en masse to protect their fair-haired hero. She turned to Scotty: "I wonder where the rest of the big brass are?"

"They won't be here," he returned. "Don't you see what is happening here? Wade's being sacrificed at the altar."

"What do you mean?"

"You'll see. You'll see."

When the Colonel took his chair, his eyes fell on Libby. She could only see hatred in his cold gray eyes. She shivered and turned her eyes away from his.

Senator Fallon spoke first: "Colonel Wade, you are Commanding Officer of the American Counterterrorist Unit called Delta Force—is that correct?"

"No Sir! I am not! I have been relieved of duties pending the outcome of this hearing."

His words shocked the room. Relieved of command was tantamount to the Army admitting that Wade had acted incorrectly.

"But you were in command of the Delta Force when the rescue attempt was made on TWA Flight 847 in Rome?"

"Yes Sir. I was."

"Colonel Wade, I sent you a subpoena directing you to list the names, ranks and experience of the members of your team in Rome. Have you complied with that request?"

"No Sir! I have not complied with that directive."

"May I ask why?"

"The names of the members of Delta Force are classified. To release their names would put the men and their families in danger."

"Come now, Colonel," shot back Fallon sarcastically. "You don't really believe that, do you?"

"I know that—Sir."

"Well then; will you give me those names in a closed hearing?"

"No Sir, I will not."

"You realize that you are in contempt of a government hearing, don't you?"

"If you say so, Senator!"

Colonel Richard Wade was the sacrificial lamb and he knew it. Just a few days before, he had been called in by General H. C.

Smith, Commanding General of Army Special Operations. "Colonel Wade, we all know your operation in Rome was brilliant and you personally acted in the proper manner. Hell, I think you should be given a medal. However, this whole media thing has gotten out of hand. The press is murdering us, and the liberal assholes in Congress are after the Delta Force. If it continues, the Chief of Staff believes that funding for Delta Force will be cut off. Then all the work we—all the work you have done—will be for nothing. We must have Delta Force. The nation needs Delta Force. These Senate Hearings will be the key. Delta Force will live or die based upon the results of the Hearings."

"What are you trying to say General?" asked Wade. "Are you trying to tell me that you are not going to testify before the hearings?"

"That is correct. I am not going to testify—Chief's orders. You are going to be the only Army type there."

"You mean I am going to be the only man there in uniform?"

"That's correct!"

"What if I refuse to testify?"

"That's your decision. I'm sorry to do this, but I am officially relieving you of your command until the hearings are over."

"That will look as if the Army believes I did something wrong."

"Yes I know, and I'm sorry; but you and I are expendable."

"But in this case, I'm the expendable one—right?"

"I'm afraid so, Richard. If only you hadn't blown away that bastard right in front of a camera."

"I told you; the camera was not supposed to be on."

"Yeah, but unfortunately it was. Too bad you didn't miss the terrorist and hit that girl reporter."

A terrible feeling of loneliness came over Wade. The General was right. Ever since his wife and son's death, Delta Force had been his life; he had helped build it. The last thing he wanted to do was to see the Force go down the drain. Wade was still a good soldier, and he would do as he was told. But he could not help feeling bitter over the unfairness of it all. He knew there was no use continuing the conversation. Wade knew he had just lost a friend. He looked at the general, smiled and shook his head: "H. C., the next time the Chief takes a shit—don't forget to move your face." He turned without saluting and walked out of the General's office.

Fallon interrupted his unpleasant thoughts and brought him back to the unpleasant present: "Let me ask you this Colonel. Who made the decision to assault the TWA airliner? Did the President give the final approval?"

"No Sir. He did not. I made the final decision to go."

Scotty whispered in Libby's ear: "He's lying! He's lying to protect the President!"

Fallon paused and tapped the table in front of him with a pencil; then he continued: "You are saying that you took it upon yourself to make the assault—without the approval of the President?"

"That is correct, Sir! It was my decision!"

"Is that by any chance why you have been relieved of your command?"

"Yes Sir. That is why I have been relieved of my command."

"During the final assault on the hijacked airliner, your men killed five gunmen and one innocent passenger—is that a correct statement?"

"My men saved 165 passengers and killed five terrorists who had already murdered one passenger and were threatening to murder more. Unfortunately, one passenger was killed during the final assault."

"You killed one of the gunmen yourself, didn't you, Colonel?"

"I killed three of the terrorists, Sir!"

"Well, well," the Senator said sarcastically, "That was good shooting Colonel. You must be proud of yourself. I understand that one of the gunmen was running away from you, trying to surrender. Yet you shot him in the back. Why Colonel? Why did you do that?"

"One of the terrorists was running toward two innocent bystanders; and yes, I shot him in the back."

"And put a second bullet in his head as he lay on the ground! You are a good shot, Colonel! Did you know he was unarmed?"

"No Sir. I assumed he was armed."

"But he was not armed. Is that correct, Colonel?"

"That is correct, Senator."

"And you took it upon yourself to shoot down an unarmed man who was trying to give himself up? Is that what you teach your men in the Delta Force, Colonel?"

"I teach my men to kill terrorists, Senator."

* * *

Libby could not help it; she was beginning to feel sorry for Wade. She was actually getting sick to her stomach. The hearings had turned into a Fallon witch-hunt. He was making it a one-man show. And to make it worse, Wade was purposely taking all the blame—everyone in the room could see that. She wondered why any man would intentionally crucify himself. Then again, she knew about as much about Wade as anyone, and way down deep she knew he would sacrifice himself.

* * *

Senator Fallon continued the inquisition: "Colonel, let us get back to your decision to conduct the assault, as you call it: 'The Final Option.' What if your assault had failed and the hijackers had opened fire on the passengers, killing most or all of them? What then, Colonel Wade?"
"The attack did not fail, Senator!"
"Colonel, what factors made you think it would succeed?"
"In my judgment, it would succeed—so I took a chance."
"Oh, so you took a chance with the lives of 165 people?"
"Yes Sir, I did—plus the lives of my men."
Senator Fallon looked at his watch: "Well, I think it is time for a short break; then we can continue with the questions."
"NO SIR! We can't!" bellowed Wade who stood up and started walking toward the Senator. "This farce has gone far enough." He reached in the pocket of his tunic and removed a piece of paper, which he handed to Fallon. "Here Senator, this is a copy of my Letter of Resignation! You can frame it and put it on the wall of your trophy room." Next he removed his blouse and ripped off one of his eagles. He dropped the bemedaled blouse to the floor and handed the Senator the eagle. "And pin that to your ass, Senator!"
The startled Fallon looked ridiculous as he began pounding on the table with his gavel. Wade turned and started to walk out of the room. He stopped in front of newswoman Libby McGinnis and whispered, "Congratulations!" Then he walked out of the room.
Libby was stunned! She felt Scotty's hand on her shoulder, as he mumbled to himself: "He's got more balls than any man I ever met."

* * *

45

Two weeks later, on the front page of the *New York Times*, there was a photograph of Libby McGinnis receiving an award as "The Outstanding TV Newsreporter of the Quarter." On the fourth page there was a short story about the findings of the Senate Committee that investigated the Delta Force. Essentially, the Committee cleared the Army of any wrongdoing and recommended that the Delta Force continue. There was one sentence in the last paragraph which said, "Colonel Richard Wade, former Delta Force Commander, has resigned from the Army"

* * *

Libby McGinnis filed her papers and photos of the former Colonel away in a drawer. On an impulse, she kept one photograph. She could not understand why Wade still stayed in her thoughts. He represented everything that she was against, yet he held a certain fascination for her—a fascination she could not figure out. She was at the top of her profession now, thanks to her coverage of the Rome incident. She had everything she wanted—except peace of mind.

She kept having the same nightmare: She was standing on the runway in Rome. It was snowing and she was shivering. Dark figures with scarves wound around their faces were running toward her. They were Arabs! Another figure, with his face covered by a black mask, moved to her side and began shooting the Arabs. There were bodies falling all around her. Then finally the Arabs stopped coming, and the masked man turned to her and ripped her dress off; however, as he reached up to removed his mask, she always woke up. It didn't matter; Libby knew the masked man's identity!

* * *

Libby tried to find out what happened to Wade, but he had simply disappeared from the face of the earth. Not even his foster parents could tell her where he had gone.

MIAMI, FLORIDA   JANUARY 1986

Five men sat huddled in animated conversation around a kitchen table, in a small house in the suburbs of Miami. The table was cluttered with empty coffee cups, newspapers, maps and assorted documents. The eldest, a gray-haired, distinguished looking man in his mid-fifties, picked up one of the documents and passed it across the table. "According to this intelligence report we just received from Managua, Enrique Salazaar, the former editor of *LA VERDAD*, which was once Nicaragua's largest newspaper, is still alive and being held in Salon Prison near Managua."

The man speaking was Alfonso Caldera, leader of the Nicaraguan Democratic Front or FDN. The FDN—or Contra as the Sandinista government of Nicaragua calls them—were the guerrillas fighting the Marxist-Leninist regime in Nicaragua. "Contra" is Spanish for counterrevolutionaries.

The FDN was originally organized in 1981, and was backed and supplied by the U.S. Central Intelligence Agency. However, in 1984, the U.S. withdrew support because of the pressures of a liberal Congress. Since then the FDN has struggled to build its growing guerrilla Army with little outside help. Poorly equipped and armed,

Opposition Front, being imprisoned by the former dictator in 1978. He never supported the Sandinistas because he recognized, from the very beginning, the "Marxist-Leninist" course the Sandinistas were taking. After the revolution, Caldera made a concerted effort to work with the Sandinistas in rebuilding Nicaragua; but by the end of 1982, having become totally disillusioned with the steady drift toward communism, he went into exile.

Just to Caldera's right sat wealthy Memphis businessman, Robert Hunter. Hunter, a fifth generation Memphian, was a staunch anti-communist. Only 38 years old, he had already fought communists in Africa, Southeast Asia and Central America. His expertise in guerrilla warfare had earned him the position of advisor and con-fidant to the FDN and the rank of Colonel. He was not only a com-bat participant in the war against the Marxist-Leninist regime in Nicaragua; he was also one of the principal financial backers of the FDN. In 1984, when the U.S. withdrew its official support from the Contra, Hunter and some of his friends stepped into the breach. It was largely through their efforts that the FDN was able to con-tinue their war. Hunter had contributed large quantities of his own money to fight the communists in Central America.

Robert Hunter was a man with a mission in life. He was well

aware of the communist threat to Central America and the ultimate consequences for the United States. He believed the key was Nicaragua. If the communists were able to consolidate their military enclave in that nation, then there would be hell to pay throughtout Central America. He was willing to risk everything, including his life, to stop the communist expansion.

Hunter owned and managed a vast business empire with hotels in the British West Indies and Bahamas. His real estate and investment companies had major interests in the U.S. and throughout Central America and the Caribbean. Active in politics and government, he was a member of the President's National Security Advisory Board and the National Defense Council. He also owned two Marine Archaeological Research ships; and when he was not fighting communists, he was running his business interests, or otherwise engaged in National Security matters—he relaxed by diving for treasure in the Caribbean.

Hunter began early, training himself for his adventurous life. He attended a myriad of special schools: SCUBA, Airborne, martial arts, Ranger, marksmanship and special weapons. He was also a Captain in the Merchant Marines and a qualified pilot.

There was one other thing that Robert Hunter was: he was the President's man. He had close personal ties with the White House, and his clandestine activities had prior approval of the President of the United States! He kept his association with the Commander-in-Chief a secret from everyone except his Chief of Security, Rene Marcel.

The man seated next to Hunter was Tom Patterson, Director of a group called Civilian Military Assistance.[1] Patterson, a former Marine and combat veteran of Vietnam, was also a dedicated anticommunist. In 1983, he decided he wanted to do something to stop the communist takeover of Central America, so he paid his own way to Honduras and contacted the Contra. He returned home and bought supplies out of his own pocket. He placed advertisements in local newspapers and national pubications asking for supplies and equipment for the Freedom-Fighters. His organization grew rapidly into a national body of over 3000 members. CMA was truly a grass-roots American organization. In 1985, CMA provided trainers, medics and over $4 million worth of non-lethal supplies and equipment to the FDN. Even more important, they provided moral support at a time it was badly needed. CMA showed the FDN that there were Americans who did care!

Liberal Congressmen, left-wing organizations and communist sympathzers had worked diligently trying to discredit the CMA. The group had been accused of being everything from Nazis, to mercenaries, to CIA agents. In reality, the organization was exactly what it claimed to be: "A group of individuals dedicated to stopping the spread of communism."

The leader of one leftist organization, the Mid-South Peace and Justice League, publicly called the CMA a "bunch of terrorists, not unlike Khadafy." In a secret meeting in Memphis, he told his people that the "idea of CMA" was dangerous to the cause. He said he was not worried about the small amount of supplies the CMA furnished the Contra rebels; but he was worried about the growth of a conservative "idea" in the Mid-South.

The fourth, and by far the largest, man at the table was Jim Turpin, a huge 290 pound giant of a man. Turpin, also a former Marine but medically retired because of wounds received at the Battle of Hue in Vietnam, was Deputy Director of CMA. He had several nicknames including "Big Jim," "Bubba" and "Sailor." Of course, there would be no reason to call him "Little Jim," and every man in Arkansas and Tennessee over 235 pounds is called "Bubba." Turpin was all hard muscle and was as dangerous in a fight as he looked. In his younger days he had been known to clean out many a bar in the Memphis area. Jim Turpin was a favorite of the Contra because of his down-home sense of humor and his "good old boy" approach to solving problems. He had a simple solution for handling communists: "NUKE THEM!"

Seated next to Turpin was Hunter's Chief of Security, Rene Marcel. The former French-Canadian ran away from home at age 15 and joined the Royal Canadian Navy. When he was 16, he was working convoys sailing the dangerous North Atlantic route to Murmansk, Russia. A year later he was transferred to anti-submarine duty in the Eastern Atlantic. His ship sank the last German U-Boat only two months before the War's end. In 1951, he joined the Canadian Army; and during the Korean War he fought with the Royal Canadian Special Force Brigade. He was wounded in 1953, and evacuated home. Not satisfied with the quiet life, Marcel found himself fighting in Rhodesia and the Congo. He joined Hunter's Corporation in 1980, and because of his considerable military experience soon found himself Chief of Security. In the last six years, Marcel had been by Hunter's side during a number of clandestine operations.

* * *

Hunter looked up from the document Caldera had handed him: "I thought Salazaar was killed by bandits."

"That was the official word put out by the government," answered Caldera, "but we found out several months ago that it was one of Borge's Divine Mobs that broke into the Salazaar house."

"Then Borge may have ordered the murder of Salazaar's family?"

"It looks that way. But that's the way things are in Nicaragua these days. We have documentation of over 700 liquidations by the government in the last two years."

"If we could rescue Salazaar and he could tell his story to the world, it would greatly help our cause," continued Caldera. "Right now, we are receiving so much bad publicity that our very existence is in jeopardy. It's amazing what inuendos and half-truths can do to you."

"It's that old writer's trick of 'omission and commission'," said Hunter. "You add a little bit here, and you take out a little there, and you can come up with whatever conclusions you want. There is no doubt in my mind that we are facing a world-wide communist disinformation program aimed at weakening the very fibre of the United States; and the tentacles of this monster reach right back into Moscow. The communists found out from the Vietnam experience that the best way to break the American resolve to win was to conduct an effective propaganda campaign right in the United States. Unfortunately, our media, our good old liberal press, is an integral part of this communist program. The disinformation program for Nicaragua was started in 1978, to pressure the U.S. to leave the Sandinistas alone, originally lobbying against U.S. aid to the Somoza government, then for aid to the Sandinista regime, and today against aid to the Sandinista's armed opposition. This well-planned and coordinated disinformation program has consistently held the same objective: to help the communist cadres gain and consolidate their control over Nicaragua.

Hunter stopped and took a sip of water, then he continued: "The vanguard for this program in the U.S. is the American Communist Party along with some other radical groups controlled by Russia and Cuba. Their accomplices, some knowing and other misled naive fools, are some of the so-called peace groups, liberal religious groups, liberal Congressmen, and finally our own liberal press."

51

"If we could free Salazaar, it would be a major defeat for this disinformation program. He is a credible, respected newsman— the world would have to listen to his story. Alfonso, if you can send a team in to rescue Salazaar, I will finance the operation."

"I don't know," returned Caldera. "I'd like to; but an operation of this type calls for special talent. I'm not sure I have people experienced enough to do it."

Hunter leaned across the table and placed his hand under his chin. "I know of such a man! A very unusual man that has that kind of talent—and ironically he's Salazaar's son-in-law. Have you ever heard of Colonel Richard Wade? He was married to Salazaar's daughter."

"Salazaar's son-in-law? Yes! I met him several years ago at a party at Salazaar's home. Wasn't he kicked out of the Army?"

"No. He resigned. He was railroaded by the press and some liberal Congressmen. He took the blame for a situation where there shouldn't have been any blame, so the Delta Force could survive. Anyway, that's beside the point. Wade may be the best special ops man in the U.S. I met him last year when he went into Iran and rescued two American businessmen. If he thought there was a chance that his father-in-law was still alive, nothing could keep him out of Nicaragua. Has the underground heard anything about Wade's son or wife being alive?"

"No. His wife's death was confirmed; and as far as we know, the boy is dead. However, we thought Enrique was dead too. So, I guess there is a chance," returned Caldera. "Where is Wade now? Do you know?"

"The last I heard," answered Hunter, "he was living on Grand Cayman Island in the British West Indies under an assumed name."

Tom Patterson spoke for the first time: "The CMA cannot officially get involved in this type of operation. We would be violating the National Security Act. However, we might be able to find some experienced volunteers that we could put you in touch with."

"Me for one!" piped up Turpin. "I'll just temporarily resign from the CMA and go as a private citizen. Where do I sign up?"

They all laughed at Turpin's typical exuberance. "Just like a Marine," said Hunter. "Hi-diddle-diddle, straight up the middle."

"I'm serious! I want to go!" exclaimed the giant. "I'm as good a man in a firefight as you'll find."

"Okay Jim," said Hunter, "you are the first volunteer!"

Caldera changed the subject. "Does Wade have any idea that the

52

Sandinistas were behind his wife and son's death?"

"No, I don't think so," returned Hunter. "I suppose he just accepted the government's version. I think he should know the truth, and I'm planning on telling him. He would be a good man to have with us, Alfonso. Let me go down to the Islands and talk to him"

6

GRAND CAYMAN ISLAND, BRITISH WEST INDIES

The underwater scenery and fish life was dazzling. The gray and white coral twisted and turned into caves and pillars. Yellow and purple and green fish of all sizes and shapes glided through the coral caverns. The human swam effortlessly along a coral ledge and past a fantastic growth of elkhorn. A moray eel poked his head out to watch the human. A giant ray flapped overhead and slowly passed from sight. The five-foot barracuda divers had affectionately nicknamed "Old Snaggle Tooth," because of a broken incisor, tagged curiously 10 feet behind the human. Old Snaggle Tooth had never been known to attack a human—but he often scared the hell out of newcomers to his territory. Once, he did bite a girl, but it was an accident and her fault; she forgot to let go of the fish she was offering him. Two fat groupers, each weighing over a hundred pounds, swam up to the diver and smiled. He reached out and rubbed their noses. Then he reached into a bag tied at his waist and removed two small fish. Each grouper swallowed one and waggled off. Old Snaggle Tooth resented this; so he slickered-up to within six inches of the diver's face and stared, as if to say, "Hey pardner, where is my lunch?" The diver recognized the look and

54

removed a fat fish from his pouch and offered it to the barracuda. Old Snaggle Tooth gulped it down; the diver swam off with the barracuda tagging dutifully behind.

The barracuda had been following these strange creatures for over 12 years. So far, they had not caused him any problem—and often he got a hand-out—but this was his domain; so he always kept a wary eye on the interlopers. He figured that because of their size they must be some kind of groupers. He loved to eat grouper! But he made a policy of never attacking anything larger than himself.

The diver was just off the southwest tip of Grand Cayman Island, between Smith's Cove and Pull-And-Be-Damned-Point. It was one of his favorite areas; a drop off to 130 feet started about 200 yards from shore. The sheer cliff was covered with various coral, sponges and gargonians. It was not normal procedure or recommended that divers dive alone—however this man seldom used normal procedure.

The diver finally surfaced and pulled himself aboard his anchored Zodiac boat. A well-tanned, long-legged, attractive blonde lay stretched out naked on the short deck. She raised up on one elbow and spoke in a low Texas drawl: "Y'all were sure down there a long time sugah—do you do this every day?"

The man wriggled free of his wet suit. He was tall, bronzed and well-muscled. A short beard covered his face. The blonde watched him hungrily. From the look in her eyes, it was obvious that the diver was safer in the water with the barracuda.

The man set about stowing his equipment, as he mumbled an answer: "Every day that I can."

"Maybe that's what makes you such a tigah!" she drawled.

He glanced over at her and growled.

She giggled. "Come on down heah, Tigah, and scratch mah itch. I've got this ferocious itch, heah."

He stripped off his bathing suit and knelt beside her. She raised up, put her arms around his neck and pulled him on top of her.

Dixie Lee was a wealthy divorcee from Houston. Her ex-husband had been in oil or something like that. Like many wealthy and unwealthy women, she was drawn to the Cayman Islands for sun, excitement and hopefully a little romance. The dusky-skinned island beach boys were kept busy servicing these hungry women from the north who wanted to add a little spice to their lives. The boys didn't mind at all—after all, you had to keep the tourists happy; that was the unwritten law of the Island of Love. And once in awhile

55

a grateful female tourist might present her young stud a gold necklace as a token of her esteem.

Dixie Lee had met the diver several nights earlier at the Wreck-of-the-Ten-Sails Bar in the Holiday Inn. She took one look at the bearded, sun-tanned man at the bar and decided, then and there, that he was going to be her romantic interlude for this trip. After one Reggae and a calypso by the Barefoot Man and his band, she had him hooked—and he had more than lived up to her fantasies. She still didn't know much about him and really was not concerned wtih his social status or politics. The important thing was that he was a good dancer and one hell of a lover.

Actually, the man Dixie Lee called "Tigah" and whom his few acquaintances knew as Frank Wilson, was much more complex and troubled than she or his friends realized. He was the outsider who lived by himself in the small cement-block house at the northwest corner of the island. He was friendly but quiet. He drank some, but not to excess. He dove, snorkled, fished and did a lot of jogging. Once in awhile, he left the island for several weeks, but he always returned.

Disillusioned with the world, Colonel Richard Wade, alias Frank Wilson, had picked Grand Cayman in order to hide from the world. His family had been brutally murdered, and his once bright career was ruined. He had dedicated his life to defending his country; and finally, even his country had turned against him. A week after the Senate Hearings, Wade had landed in Grand Cayman. Then two things happened to change his life again. First, he ran out of money. Then, since he was a man of action, he got bored very quickly. He flew back to the States and contacted an old friend in the CIA and offered his services—for money. "I will not become one of your regular agents," he told them, "but I will work on a contract basis. My fees will be high! I'm an expert in special operations and I have been trained to kill—so I might as well get paid for it."

So the former Colonel became a "contract agent" for the U.S. Central Intelligence Agency; and as in his Army career, he soon became one of their best. His code name was "Barracuda"; maybe that was why he was so fond of Old Snaggle Tooth. In many ways, he and the old warrior of the sea were a lot alike. The fish hunted alone too, and when he killed it was quick and quiet.

Only a handful of men in Washington knew the identity of the Barracuda. In the last five years Wade had worked at his deadly trade in the Middle East, North Africa, and Central America.

He purchased a home on Grand Cayman and settled in to be a part-time recluse. He did not own a radio or TV or read newspapers. When the Agency had a mission for him, he was contacted by message at the Holiday Inn and he would fly to Miami to meet his "contact" and receive instructions.

After a time, he also became bored with just fishing and diving—so he took up women as an added hobby. The average tourist stayed six days, so Wade entertained a smorgasbord of beautiful, available and willing women. And it was relatively safe because "she" always had a plane to catch in a few days.

Dixie Lee wrapped her luscious, long legs around him and whispered in a husky voice: "Make the boat rock, Tigah! I'm hungry all ovah—make me feel good!"

The boat began to rock—you have to keep the tourists happy—it's the law of the island!

* * *

Later that day, Wade stopped by the Holiday Inn and found a message in his mail box:

MR. WILSON: URGENT THAT I SEE YOU. I HAVE
NEWS OF NICARAGUA. ROOM 400. ROBERT
HUNTER

Wade remembered Hunter. The Memphis businessman was aboard the U.S. destroyer that picked him up in the Arabian Gulf, a year before, when the former Colonel had gone into Iran and rescued the two American businessmen that were being held by Khomeini's radical government.

A few minutes later, Wade was in room 400 sitting across from Hunter, sipping a rum punch. Even though Wade had only met Hunter once before, he knew something of the wealthy businessman-adventurer's reputation. Hunter was known as a man of action: a man who put his money and his life on the line for those things he believed in. Wade knew that Hunter had close ties with the Man in Washington—but he didn't think Hunter knew about the Barracuda.

Wade was wrong! Hunter was one of the "handful" of men that knew who the Barracuda was and what he did. The two men sat for a while making small talk about the island and sizing up one another. Hunter knew most of Wade's recent activities. There was, of course, his daring rescue of the two Vesco employees in Iran the year before. Two years ago, Wade had eliminated two Holy Jihad leaders in Beirut—a partial payment for the bombing of the American Embassy. There was the death of the Cuban General in Angola and, just a few months ago, the PLO Terrorist leader in Cypress.

Hunter finally decided that they had made enough small talk: "Colonel, I'm sure you are wondering why I wanted to talk to you. Well, I have some information that I think you will want to hear. I have recently recieved word from the FDN that your father-in-law, Enrique Salazaar, may still be alive and is being held in Managua.

His words jolted Wade to the quick! It was impossible! He had buried Enrique in the family plot in Managua; along with his wife and son and mother-in-law.

"It was not Contra or Somocistas that attacked your family—it was one of Borge's divine mobs; and we believe Tomas Borge ordered the attack." Hunter went on to explain to Wade the facts that he had at his disposal.

It could be true, thought Wade. The only body he had been able to identify was his wife's. The authorities told him the others were burned beyond recognition. The fire was extinguished before it reached Maria's bedroom. He thought back to his trip to Managua for the burial. He was met at the airport by an official of the Ministry of Interior and taken directly to the Minister's office. Tomas Borge greeted him warmly and told him how sorry he was about his wife and son. Borge explained what a tragic loss to the country the death of Enrique Salazaar was. "Enrique was like a brother to me," he said. He praised Enrique as a "Hero of the Revolution" and a "champion of liberty and justice"! Borge promised to do everything in his power to bring the "Somocista murderers" to justice. Wade was given the VIP treatment in Managua. There were parades in honor of Enrique; and the family was buried with full honors.

At the time, Wade did not have any reason to disbelieve the Nicaraguan government's official version of the deaths. At the time, it seemed logical that former Guardia soldiers would want to murder Enrique. And in 1980, Wade, like most Americans, was not aware that the revolution had been taken over by Marxist-Leninists. Like everyone, Wade at that time believed what he read in the American newspapers. Since then he had learned to doubt the printed word.

He returned from Nicaragua a changed man. He had buried his youth, his love, and his heart and soul in the ground with his family.

He lived only for his work, and he wished for the solace and peace that death would bring. And then, his work was taken from him, too. After the Rome incident, his resignation from the Army seemed like part of the logical progression to oblivion. Becoming a special "Black Agent" for the Agency also seemed logical.

Hunter interrupted his thoughts. "Colonel, we want to send in a team to rescue Salazaar, and we would like you to lead it."

"Who are 'we', Mr. Hunter?"

"I represent the FDN and some Americans from the private sector. Enrique Salazaar is a highly respected man—both in Nicaragua and the U.S. Even more important, he is a credible journalist. If we can free him and he can tell his story to the world, it would be a major blow to the communists. And if we can persuade him to accept a leadership position in the FDN, it could be the deciding factor in getting military aid for the Contra. Are you interested?"

"Yes! Of course I'm interested. If there is any chance that Enrique is still alive, I will get him out!"

"Money will be no problem," said Hunter. "Whatever you need will be available."

Wade was quiet for a minute, pondering the complexity of the operation. "The first thing I need to do," he announced, "is to go to Nicaragua and conduct a recon. I'll need contacts inside the country."

Hunter could see the wheels turning; he knew he had picked the right man for the job. He reached out and shook Wade's hand: "Colonel, I'm glad to have you aboard. Now, how about having dinner with me?"

7 _____

The man in seat 26-F looked out of the window of the jet-liner and caught a glimpse of the coast of Nicaragua below. He was glad to be sitting in the rear of the plane, away from the exuberant group leader, Brother Timothy. The Maryknoll Brothers' constant elaboration on the virtues of the Sandinista regime tended to get on one's nerves after a time. The good Brother was a so-called "expert on the Sandinista government and Liberation Theology in general." Anyway, he considered himself an expert—after only three trips to Nicaragua. He was also very good at elaborating on the atrocities committed by the Contra and the dire policies of the government in Washington.

The bearded man in seat 26-E was not listening to Brother Timothy. His mind was filled with thoughts of days gone by and of a woman and child whose bodies were lying in a cemetary near Managua. But even in the midst of his dark thoughts, he could manage a slight smile when he remembered the unusual circumstances of his first meeting with his now dead wife...

PINEHURST, NORTH CAROLINA 1964
Maria Salazaar, then a junior at the University of North Carolina,

was spending a few days at her roommate Sally Smith's home at the edge of the Uwharrie National Forest. The sprawling ranch-style home was located atop a low hill. To the west, the thick pines of the National Forest seemed to stretch indefinitely, while on the east was a wide grassy valley.

It was late summer, and the weather was hot and muggy. Sally's parents were hosting an evening pool party for the two girls. It was 11 p.m. and the pool area was alive with people having a good time. They were unaware that a camouflaged C-130 Hercules airplane was approaching from the east at an altitude of 24,000 feet. And there was really no reason for them to be concerned, because the airplane was supposed to drop its human cargo several miles from the party.

Inside the approaching aircraft, four men watched the rear end of the plane slowly yawn open. The men looked a bit like Darth Vaders with parachutes. They were dressed in black jump-suits, oxygen masks and safety helmets. One of the four men was a very scared, anxious lieutenant named Richard Wade. The tightness of his harness and equipment caused him to stand in that unnatural stoop known only to paratroopers. His mouth was dry and he had to urinate, but it was too late to think about taking care of any natural body functions. This was to be Lt. Wade's graduation jump. After tonight he would be HALO qualified. HALO (High Altitude Low Opening) techniques were one of the several ways Green Berets were taught to infiltrate deep behind enemy lines. This was the last of 16 free-fall jumps, ranging from 7,000 to 24,000 feet, he had made in the last six weeks.

The red light began to blink, indicating three minutes to jump time. The four jumpers shuffled awkwardly to the open back door and looked out at the black hole of the night. A thin layer of clouds drifted below them. The light turned green, and without hesitation, one by one they stepped off into the dark void.

Wade tumbled for a time, then he spread his arms and legs and arched his back, stabilizing his fall. He began to enjoy the exhilaration of free-fall. He could see the stars appear on the horizon and blanket the sky. Down below he could see farmhouses dotting the landscape. He could pick out the cars and trucks on Highway 81. When he passed through a cloud, he experienced an instant of vertigo and began tumbling again. He finally got himself straightened out and decided it was time to look for the Drop Zone lights. Off to his left, he spotted a circle of lights. He turned and began tracking in that direction.

The Lieutenant's parachute automatically opened at 1,000 feet. He reached up and grabbed his toggles and steared toward the circle of lights. Then it suddenly dawned on the young jumper that the Drop Zone was to be marked with a "T"! Too late, he realized he was going to land in someone's backyard; and the circle of lights were Tiki torches around a swimming pool! He quickly decided that the safest place to land, both for himself and any innocent bystanders, would be in the pool.

Maria was enjoying the party. It was nice to be away from the rigorous grind of college. Sally's parents were grand people, and they treated Maria as one of the family. It had been 9 months since Maria had seen her mother and father in Nicaragua—and she was more than a little homesick. Sally put on a slow record; and a very nice looking young man named George, a Pre-Med student at Baylor, asked Maria to dance. He put his arms around her just as they heard a pop in the sky. The guests looked up to see a dark figure swooping out of the heavens toward them. There was a splash, and Maria was covered with water as the black-clad monster hit mid-pool. The parachute collapsed, covering several of the guests. The figure rose to the surface of the pool and lay face down.

Lt. Wade was stunned by the landing and thought for a moment that he was going to drown. Luckily, several men acted quickly and dragged him from the pool. He found himself laying on his back, looking up at the most beautiful girl in the world. Her big dark eyes were wide with concern.

Maria looked down, thinking the man who had dropped out of the sky was dead. But he opened his eyes! Then he reached up and removed his mask and helmet. His first words were "You are one beautiful angel!"

Lieutenant Richard Wade and Miss Maria Salazaar were married six months later in the Chapel at Fort Bragg, NC.

* * *

Wade's thoughts of pleasant times and pleasant places—a world of memories—were interrupted by the announcement to fasten safety belts. He glanced forward to see Brother Tim still standing in the aisle preaching about the virtues of the Sandinistas. Wade had asked Hunter why he thought so many American peace and church groups that go to visit Nicaragua return with such glowing views of the

Marxist regime there.

"I don't know for sure," he answered, "but there is a good book on a similar topic written by Paul Hollander titled, *Political Pilgrims*. He tells about the Thirties when people went over and raved about Stalin's brave new world; then went to China and raved about the wonderful world of Communist China; and then to North Vietnam to rave about Ho Chi Minh. This same phenomenon is going on in Nicaragua today and is the latest in a series of Communist nirvanas that these type of people are always searching for."

* * *

Libertad "Libby" McGinnis, The American Broadcasting Network's popular and noted TV newscaster, watched the Boeing 727 taxi slowly up to the terminal. She glanced over her shoulder at Robert Scott; he was already filming the approach. The ABN News Team was in Nicaragua doing a special report on the visiting Peace Group phenomenon. The 727 was carrying a Peace Group from California who were here as guests of the Nicaraguan government. The purpose of the visits, according to Tomas Borge, Minister of Interior, was "to allow the American people see firsthand exactly what was going on in the country and to show them how the new government was working to improve the quality of life of the Nicaraguan people."

The news team had already been in Managua a week, doing the background work for the special. So far, Libby was impressed with what she saw happening in Nicaragua. It seemed as if the government was popular with the people and making great strides toward economic and political progress.

Scott, the skeptic, told her it was all "hogwash!" "Just remember," he warned, "you can't judge what's inside a book by looking at its cover."

"You are wrong," she retorted. "Everything I have seen points to progress and better education. I just don't see why our government can't leave these people alone and let them develop on their own."

"Libby, you are only seeing what they want you to see," returned the cameraman. "This is simply a well-staged show for your benefit—and you are eating it up. Underneath it all is a Marxist government, a proxy of Moscow—plain and simple."

The newswoman disagreed with Scotty—but they often had their friendly disagreements—especially about politics. They were still the best news team on TV.

The group arriving today was sponsored by the West Coast Peace and Justice League. On the list were people from all walks of life: doctors, lawyers, teachers, ministers, businessmen and home-makers. And they were coming to see for themselves the new Socialist Utopia that was Nicaragua under the Sandinistas.

As the visitors filed through the door into the terminal, Libby stepped forward and stopped the leader, a skinny little man wearing the brown robes of a Catholic Monk: "Pardon me, Sir, I am Libby McGinnis, ABN news. Are you Brother Timothy?"

Brother Timothy stopped and smiled into the camera. "Yes, Miss. I am."

What is the purpose of your bringing this group of Americans to Nicaragua?"

Brother Timothy smiled again for the camera: "This is my third visit to Nicaragua, and I know from seeing firsthand the great strides the Nicaraguan government is making in the areas of land reform and curing illiteracy and poverty. I want to show these good people traveling with me the things I have seen. I want them to know that President Reagan and his Administration are conducting a monstrous hate campaign against the good people of Nicaragua. And this campaign is based on lies! They will see that the United States should be helping the legal government of Nicaragua, instead of using the CIA to train the Contra rebels. They will see that this is not a communist nation: that it is a Christian Social Democracy and that its leaders are dedicated to improving the quality of life for the people."

"Will they also see," asked Libby, "the largest army in Central America? One that is armed with Soviet weapons and equipment?"

"Unfortunately, a strong army is needed now to protect the people from Reagan's trained mercenaries," answered the Brother.

"What order do you belong to, Brother Timothy?"

"I am in the Maryknoll Order, and my diocese is in Detroit. However, on your previous question, President Ortega has stated publicly that the Nicaraguan Army only has defensive weapons; and if the U.S. would stop supporting the Contras, he would cut the size of the Nicaraguan Army." Brother Timothy was turned on now—a walking advertisement for liberalism and the Sandinistas. He also became a bore—fast! Libby stood there, shifting from one foot to another, listening politely as the Brother went on and on.

She was going to have to do a lot of editing of this tape. The newswoman glanced back along the beaming, anxious faces of the Peace Group who seemed to be absorbing every word that Brother Timothy said. Then she saw him—the bearded man slouching nonchalantly at the rear of the group. The eyes! She knew those eyes. He was thinner and he was darker, but she knew the man behind the eyes—he still plagued her dreams and thoughts. Cold chills ran down her spine, and she almost dropped the mike.

Wade had recognized the reporter the instant he walked into the terminal, but it was too late to turn back. His only hope was that she would not recognize him. When he saw her reaction when she spotted him, he knew there was no way of avoiding the confrontation. He decided to act boldly; he headed straight toward her. He strode up and put his hand on Brother Timothy's shoulder and spoke in a soft voice: "I say Brother Tim, who is this charming lady?"

The Monk was caught in mid-dissertation; he stopped and cleared his throat. "Oh, why, yes. Miss McGinnis, this is Robert Alford; he teaches Political Science at Berkeley."

Libby tried to speak, but could not find her voice.

Wade further surprised her by extending his hand. "I'm pleased to meet you, Miss McGinnis."

She automatically put her hand out and he took it. His grip was firm and his gray eyes burned into her. His message was clear.

Robert Scott watched the scene unfold. He did not recognize the former Colonel until he took Libby's hand. The cameraman thought quickly. Something was wrong here or Wade would not be using an alias. He knew one thing for sure—it was no time for Libby to go spouting off the Colonel's real name. He stepped up to rescue someone—but he was not sure whether it was Libby or the Colonel: "Libby, we'll have to get the rest of the interviews later; I'm out of film. Sorry!"

Libby knew the cameraman was lying. Scotty was a pro; he would never run out of film during an interview. But she was grateful for the interruption.

Wade looked at Scotty and winked a thanks. He let go of Libby's hand and smiled: "Well, I'm sure we will see more of you, Miss McGinnis." He picked up his travel bag and walked off.

Scotty grabbed Libby by the arm and ushered her out of the terminal. She was still shaken by her encounter with the ghost of her past when they reached the parking lot. She finally stopped and turned toward her friend: "Scotty, what do you suppose he's doing here using a different name?

"I don't have the slightest idea! Maybe he's changed his name and has a new life."

"You don't really believe that, do you?"

"No, but I don't think it is any of our business. We best just forget we saw him."

That evening, Libby and Scotty sat in the Caravel Hotel Restaurant having dinner. Seeing Wade had been a shock for the redheaded reporter. She had not seen or heard of him since he walked out of the Senate Hearing. Scotty suddenly touched her arm: "There he is!"

Wade had entered the restaurant with two other members of the peace group. When he spotted the news team he excused himself and walked over to their table: "Good evening Miss McGinnis, Mr. Scott. It is good to see you again."

Scotty stood up and shook hands with the former Colonel, and asked: "Won't you join us?"

"No thank you. I'm going to eat with some of my friends." Then in a low voice he said, "Thanks for not giving me away."

Before either one of the newspeople could say anything else, Wade turned and walked away.

Libby could not understand her emotions. At first she was shocked when she saw him at the airport—then unexplainably a feeling of anticipation came over her. Now there was fear. Maybe he was here to get even with her, to embarrass her, or even worse. She decided that she was not going to give him that satisfaction; in fact, she was just going to ignore him.

Later that night, Richard Wade, alias Robert Alford, sat alone in his hotel room, sipping on a glass of iced Russian Stolichnaya Vodka. The Russians did make good vodka; and for some strange reason, it was plentiful in Managua these days. He, too, was filled with a storm of unusual emotions. Libby McGinnis, here in Managua—of all the damned coincidences. What if she told the authorities who he was? He had an option; he could bug-out and contact the local underground, but he needed the relative freedom of his cover for a few days. The beautiful redhead brought back memories—painful memories of a life he had almost forgotten— back when he was part of the human race. She also brought back something else: he still remembered how much he was attracted to this beautiful woman who had innocently been caught up in his life and who had played such a big part in changing it. And maybe, just maybe, one of the reasons he wanted to stay with the Peace Group was to see Libby McGinnis again.

8

At 10:00 p.m. the next morning, the "American Peace Group," 22 in all, was ushered into the office of Tomas Borge, Nicaragua's Minister of Interior. Borge, one of the leaders of the revolution, was a hard-core Marxist-Leninist who received his training in Cuba in 1968-70. He stood out above the other leaders, being the oldest and most experienced. He also was the most powerful man in Nicaragua and might someday emerge as number one. As The Minister of the Interior, he is Director of the Penal System, General Director of State Security, Director of the Sandinista Police, and Director of the Special Forces of the Pablo Ubeda Brigade (engaged in fighting the Contra). As Director of State Security, he manipulates the so-called "turbas divinos" (divine mobs) which stage threats, demonstrations, harassments and witch hunts directed at opposition elements, particularly the Catholic Church. Such a "turbo" heckled the Pope during his 1983 visit.

Tomas Borge had named them Divine Mobs, because he said they were the people in charge of saving the other people's souls from the enemy, that is the devil or the counterrevolutionaries or the Yankee Devil. The mobs are formed by the block committees, which are modeled after the Cuban block committees. All of their members are part of the informer network. State Security controls them. State Security sets them up. Tomas Borge was an expert in combining mystical and religious ideas with politics.

Borge was responsible for some of the least humanitarian of the Sandinista's words and activities. He was personally in charge of the operation at Zona Franca Prison in 1981, when 16 prisoners were killed and 27 wounded while trying to stage a protest of the mistreatment they were receiving. As head of the Ministry of Interior, he was also in command of the forces that planned and executed the murder of an influential opposition leader, Jorge Salazaar; and he also played a key role in the repression of the Miskito Indians.[1] On Monday, August 9, 1982, he also led the Sandinista Defense Committee's mobs in taking over protestant churches and other buildings, on the pretext that protestants and other religious sects were engaged in "open and shameless counterrevolutionary activity." The newspaper headline read, "20 SITES CONFISCATED: POPULAR PROTEST AGAINST THE SECTS."*

This "Servant of the People of Nicaragua" and Hero of the Popular Revolution owns several estates (confiscated from their former owners); has seven cars including two Jaguars and a Porsche; gets a cut out of all TV products imported into the country; and owns two airplanes, which are kept busy flying drugs from Columbia and Panama[2] to islands in the Caribbean and then smuggling them into the U.S. His mistress, a former wife of a well-known rock star, occupies one of his villas and drives one of his Jaguars when she's in Managua. She is also a close friend of many liberal congressmen in Washington, where she wines and dines them on behalf of the Sandinistas.

The room was filled with folding chairs and the Peace Group filed in and sat down. Tomas Borge was standing behind his desk. Wade looked across the room at the man who, according to Robert Hunter, may have been responsible for the death of his wife and son. A feeling of hatred and rage boiled up inside of the former Colonel. He had an almost uncontrollable urge to leap across the room and strangle the Minister of Defense. He took a deep breath and regained his self control.

On the wall of Borge's office was a picture of Jesus Christ, wearing green combat fatigues and holding an AK-47 Russian-made assault rifle above his head. The caption on the poster read, "JESUS

---

* See Appendix B, Religious Persecution in Nicaragua.

FUE UN REVOLUCIANARIO!" (JESUS WAS A REVOLU-
TIONARY!). On Borge's desk, where everyone could see it, was
an open Bible.

The Minister of the Interior came around from behind his desk
and embraced Brother Timothy; then he turned and sat back on
his desk, facing the group: "Welcome to Nicaragua, my fellow
Christians. On behalf of the people of Nicaragua, I welcome you
to our country; and God Bless You for coming."

Two orderlies came into the room carrying trays of coffee, tea
and iced sodas and began passing out the libations. Borge walked
back behind his desk and sat down. He looked out at the group
and smiled. He was confident in his ability to manipulate and exploit the "deluded" religious group. It was part of the Sandinista
international political strategy to use foreign visitors and religious
groups as instruments of support for its public posture. Borge's office carefully orchestrated such visits in order to obtain the greatest
propaganda value. The visiting delegations are organized by left-
wing Nicaraguan solidarity groups in the United States and Europe.
The group tours are carefully planned and orchestrated; and the
tourees see only what the government wants them to see. In most
cases the members of these groups are told by the organizers that
they have an obligation to speak out when they return to their countries on the "Nicaraguan Reality" that they have experienced. Actually, what they have seen and experienced is only a carefully
prepared facade which masks the real situation in Nicaragua.

"The purpose of your visit to Nicaragua is to see the reality of
Nicaragua," said the smiling Borge. "You will see that the Church
here is part of the people's revolution against tyranny and exploita-
tion. You will see the Church and the revolutionary process working together to stamp out poverty and illiteracy and to improve the
quality of life of the people. I think you will be amazed at the progress we are making in education and land reform. This is a nation
that is truly run by the people, for the people—without the wealthy
aristocrats and the influence of your American Wall Street keeping the people in continual servitude. We are working towards a
deeply religious, classless society. This is truly an experiment in
Social Democracy.

"Unfortunately, you will see many soldiers and people's militia
being trained. But this is a matter of survival; and the blame falls
directly upon your own government. Now, I ask you, what does
a powerful nation like yours have to fear from our little country?

Absolutely nothing! We mean no harm to America; and we have always considered Americans our special friends. Your government and the CIA are backing and training former Somoza soldiers in Honduras and Costa Rica; and your president has stated publicly that he wants to see our government overthrown. These Contra, that are trained by the CIA, attack innocent villages along the border and murder church leaders and school teachers. We are obligated to protect these people from the rebels. You will see proof for yourself of some of the atrocities that have been committed and hear testimonies of some of the victims."

Borge paused and took a sip of the thick, sweet paste the Nicaraguans call coffee; then he continued: "The Bible says, 'The meek shall inherit the earth.' This has truly happened here in Nicaragua. We have given millions of acres to the poor farmers who used to work as slaves for the rich landowners. I notice that some of you have been looking at my poster. I designed that myself. You see, Jesus Christ is my savior and inspiration. Jesus was also a revolutionary! He rebelled against tyranny and Roman imperialism. He wanted a better life for the poor and the exploited. That was the purpose of our revolution. If He were to return today, I believe that Jesus would want to live here in Nicaragua, helping our religious oriented revolution build a better society."

Libby had interviewed Borge several days earlier, and she had already heard his basic speech. She glanced over at Wade; his face was impassive and he seemed to be listening intently. She wished she knew what the former Delta Force Commander was thinking. She had seen the wolf in sheep's clothing act like a sheep before; and she had a feeling way down deep that he was up to no good.

Borge talked for thirty minutes. He quoted the Bible often, giving the impression that he was a Bible expert. Wade was impressed—it was quite a performance. It was finally over, and the group was escorted out of the building to the waiting bus. Wade could tell from the attitude of his fellow "travelers" that they were sold.

After they departed his office, Tomas Borge sat back in his chair, pleased with himself. His Administrative Assistant walked into the room and asked, "How did it go, Sir?"

Borge could not keep a straight face any longer; he burst out laughing. Finally he stopped and wiped the tears from his eyes. "What a bunch of idealistic fools! It always amazes me how easy these deluded idiots are to handle. I just give them a few quotes

71

from the Bible and tell them what they want to hear, and they eat it up. However, they are important temporary allies and tontos utiles (useful fools)!"[3]

Borge picked up the Bible and handed it to his assistant: "Jose, there is no more effective way to combat the enemy than with his own weapons. And these do-gooder idiots who were just here are very important to our cause. Take this trash and get it out of my sight!"

* * *

The next stop for the Peace Group was at a Children's Revolutionary School. The students, who were between 9 and 13, recited poetry and sang songs about religion and the revolution. They presented a petition to Brother Timothy and asked him to give it to President Reagan. The petition asked the American President not to invade Nicaragua or drop bombs on their school. It also pleaded with him not to train and support the bloodthirsty Somocista Contras who were murdering children and raping women. One child then stood up and told how her village was attacked by the Contra, and her mother and father were shot down in cold blood. A contradiction in her story occurred when she talked about the American mercenaries that accompanied the rebels. Wade found that part a little hard to digest.

There was one song that the children did not sing for the American Peace Group; a song they sang every day; a song that all Nicaraguan children were required to memorize; a song composed by no other than Tomas Borge, himself. One of the verses reads...

> LOS HIJOS DE SANDINO
> NI SE VENDEN NE SI RINDEN
> LUCHAMOS CONTRA EL YANKEE,
> ENEMIGO DE LA HUMANIDAD.
>
> (THE CHILDREN OF SANDINO
> WILL NOT SELL OUT, WILL NOT GIVE UP,
> LET US STRUGGLE AGAINST THE YANKEE,
> ENEMY OF ALL MANKIND.)

Nor did they get to see the math textbooks that depicted AK-47's and hand grenades rather than apples and oranges. Nor did they get to see the young children training with AK-47's four hours each week. The visitors saw and heard exactly what they were supposed to see and hear—according to the gospel by Borge.

* * *

The group's next stop was at a rehabilitation home for former prostitutes, a "Punta Rehabilitad." Here, the former working girls told how they were forced into prostitution during the Somoza regime, by poor parents who were nothing more than slaves working for the rich landowners or by the wealthy landowners themselves to help pay their parents' debts. But everything had changed now, since the revolution. The new government was taking care of them and teaching them new and useful skills such as nursing and sewing.

After each girl gave a speech on how wonderful their life was in the new Nicaragua, the members of the Peace Group were allowed to mingle around and ask the girls any questions they wanted to. Libby watched Wade approach one of the girls and talk to her in Spanish. The girl giggled and whispered back to him. Wade edged over to the newswoman and said in a low voice, "I asked her how much for all night, and she said 20 dollars American. At least the price has gone down under the new regime!"

Note 1. There is little justification for the inhuman treatment of the Miskito Indians of Nicaragua by the Sandinistas. At one time there were roughly 70,000 Miskito Indians inhabiting the largely desolate Atlantic Coast, making their livelihood mainly as hunters and fishermen. Under the Sandinistas' rule, one-third of the Miskitos have been relocated to camps where they remain under military guard. Another third have fled to Honduras, where they live as refugees. The remaining third still live on the Atlantic Coast subject to harsh martial law. In the process of this uprooting, thousands of Indians were killed and hundreds have disappeared.

When the Sandinistas took power, they did not acknowledge the traditional network of Indian leadership and authority and attempted to destroy the Miskitos' local system of government and replace the Indian leaders with Sandinista Defense Committees. These policies alienated the Indian population and caused widespread unrest.

The Sandinista Army moved against the Miskitos in force in 1982: bombing and burning villages and destroying crops and livestock. Thousands of Indians were killed in the process. The Sandinistas forced 10,000 to march through the jungles for 15 days to be confined in relocation camps.

On 18 February 1981, Tomas Borge visited Stedman Fagoth, Miskito Indian Elder, in his jail cell and told the Indian leader that he was most willing to eliminate even the last of the Miskito Indians, if that was necessary, to be able to take Sandinismo to the Atlantic Coast of Nicaragua.

During 1982, the attacks continued; and by the end of year, 170 villages had been wiped off the map and their inhabitants either were placed in relocation camps or were killed or had escaped into Honduras. A history of these attacks is provided by the leaders of the Miskito Elders Council who managed to escape the holocaust. They reported the military occupation of several towns in which the population was confined to their village; even causing some children to starve.

(Testimony of Othniel Seiden, M.D., before the hearing before the Task Force on Central America, June 1984)

"This was my first exposure to what can only be called atrocities. I saw numerous refugees from Nicaragua who were now absorbed into these Miskito villages in Honduras. There was little I could do for their wounds for they were old wounds and scars: severely scarred backs obviously from whippings, scarred feet from whippings along the soles of their feet, scarring the sclera of the eyes—I was told that a method of interrogation by the Sandinistas is to throw sand and pepper into the eyes to get people to talk. The worst atrocity that I think I saw was cut tendons. The Sandinistas apparently liked to cut the tendons between the thumb and forefinger. Whether this is done so they can't pull triggers or if it's done so that they can't be gainfully employed for the rest of their lives—I don't know the motives but the scars were there.

I saw severed Achilles tendons, and I saw severed tendons behind the knees. It did not take long for me to realize that the Miskito Indians are picked out for genocide—genocide as individuals and genocide as a culture."

The mass relocation of entire populations and the destruction of indigenous cultures has been a constant in Marxist practice around the world: Stalin "resettled" the Kulaks; the Cambodian reds "resettled" their entire urban population and killed over 2 million people. From a Marxist standpoint, the destruction of those who obstruct the way to utopia means very little. The tragedy of the Miskito is but the most recent in a long series of communist suppressions of ethnic minorities.

Note 2. "Captain Charlotte Baltodano, Tomas Borge's chief of his office staff told me that Borge had made contact with the Columbian cocaine dealers through Captain Paul Atha, the director of 'H and M Investments', a MINT (Ministry of Interior) dependency controlled by Borge which handles business activities in Nicaragua and abroad in order to obtain U.S. dollars. Baltodano said that the Government of Nicaragua supplies the traffickers with Aero Commander and Navajo planes and access to the Montelimar Airport as a refueling stop between Columbia and the United States. She said that the Ministry had become involved in drug trafficking in order to obtain money for mounting clandestine operations by the Intelligence

74

and State Security Department outside of Nicaragua."

Alvaro Jose Baldizon Aviles
Former Chief Investigator of
the Special Investigations
Commission of the Nicaraguan
Ministry of Interior.

Note 3.

"Tomas Borge, Nicaraguan Minister of Interior, prepares himself for visits from foreign Christian religious organizations or speeches to these groups by studying the Bible and extracting appropriate passages for use in his conversations or address. When the foreign visitors have departed, he scoffs at them in front of his subordinates, bragging about his ability to manipulate and exploit the 'deluded' religious group.

"In January 1985, Borge ordered my office to seek out and provide him with persons in dire economic straits or with serious health problems who would then be used in staged 'shows' before visiting foreign political or religious groups. A quota of six such persons was to be furnished every 15 days. In May 1985, such a show was staged for the benefit of a visiting delegation of the West German Democratic Union/Christian Union (CDU/CSU). In this show, a blind man who had earlier requested an accordian so he could earn his living was presented with an instrument. The instrument was to be repossessed from the blind man after the show."

Alvaro Baldizon
A recent high-level defector
from the Nicaraguan Interior Ministry.

9

That evening, Brother Timothy hosted a cocktail party for the American Peace Group, at the lounge in the Caravel. Libby, wearing a white cocktail dress, was standing off from the crowd watching the activity. Several officials from the Nicaraguan government were in attendance. There was even a rumor circulating amongst the Americans that their new hero, Tomas Borge, might make an appearance.

Suddenly, the TV newswoman was startled by a voice behind her: "You sure do have beautiful legs, Miss McGinnis."

The redhead turned abruptly to find a smiling Richard Wade standing there with a drink in his hand. She ignored his compliment and asked, "What are you doing here? Why are you in Nicaragua?"

"Why, haven't you heard? I'm here to learn the truth."

"Then why aren't you using your own name?"

He did not answer her question; instead, he said, "I think you are the most beautiful woman in the world!"

Libby was stunned for an instant by his words. Then she lashed out in a low voice: "And I think you are the most contemptible man in the world. You—you are nothing more than a vicious animal."

Again, he disregarded her comment. Instead, he asked, "Did you know that humans are the only animals that make love face-to-face?"

Libby could not answer him. She just stood there, glaring at him. Her Irish temper was rising fast. She wanted to slap his arrogant face.

Wade could see that he had gone too far. Where he was concerned, Libby McGinnis did not have any sense of humor. The woman really hated his guts. He decided he had better tone down his conversation before she lost her temper and made a scene. "I do want to thank you for not giving me away."

"Why are you here?"

The former Colonel shrugged his shoulders and stepped back. His eyes scanned her from head to toe, and he said in Spanish: "Usted tiene una cuerpa magnifica!" Then he turned and walked off. Over his shoulder, he whispered, "And great legs!"

Libby understood fair Spanish. "Cuerpa magnifica" meant beautiful body. Scott sidled up to her. "I saw you talking to the Colonel. What did he say to you?"

"I loathe that arrogant bastard!" she mumbled.

* * *

Later that evening, Libby and Scotty were in her room editing the day's tapes. Libby could not concentrate on her work; she was still seething over her encounter with Wade. She had purposely avoided him all day, and he had only acknowledged her presence once. She wondered why he had approached her tonight. Why didn't he let well-enough alone? She had to admit, he was a good actor. He played the part of a college professor very well. She wished to hell she could get him out of her mind. Finally, she could not stand it any longer, and she blurted out: "The Colonel is a good actor. He plays the part of a college professor very well. But he's still an arrogant bastard."

Scotty looked up quickly and put his finger to his lips. "SHHHH!"

Libby looked back startled. She knew what he meant—a wiretap. "Oh come now Scotty. They wouldn't bug us."

Her cameraman shook his head from side to side. "Don't be so naive girl. Yes they would!"

* * *

Maria was calling for him! He could see her, up ahead, through the dense fog. Shrouded figures were striking her with canes. He began running as fast as he could, but his feet were mired in thick mud. A shrouded figure rose up in front of him. He struck the figure down, and it disappeared into the mud. He ran and ran and ran and finally he was getting close to his struggling wife. But now it was not Maria—it was Libby McGinnis and the reporter was laughing at him. More shrouded figures rose up out of the mud and began clawing at him. One of them started shaking his arm.

"Wake up Senor Alford—Wake up!"

Wade bolted upright in his bed and found himself staring into the barrel of an automatic pistol. The man behind the gun spoke again: "You must get dressed and come with us. We just want to ask you a few questions."

Wade's head cleared fast. "What are you doing here? What is the meaning of this?"

"We are the police, and we want you to come with us."

Three other men stood at the rear of the room; all were carrying small submachine guns.

Wade climbed out of bed and dressed slowly, while he watched for an opening where he could make his move. It did not come; these men knew their business. When he was dressed, two of the men stepped forward; and Wade felt a sense of frustration as the handcuffs clicked tightly around his wrists. He knew that somehow they had found out he was an imposter, so he had to make his move and escape as soon as possible.

They took him down the back stairs and shoved him into the back of an antiquated Army ambulance. The U.S. markings, although tarnished by rust and time, were still visible. Wade's hopes for escape faded as they manacled his legs to the floor of the ambulance. His lethal feet were now out of action. He sat back and relaxed; he knew his time would come.

They off-loaded him in the alley behind the Central Police Station and took him down some back stairs into the basement. He ended up strapped to a wooden chair in a small room lighted by a single light bulb in the center of a low ceiling. Two men came in and took his fingerprints; a few minutes later another entered and snapped several photos of the prisoner. Then they left him alone. He figured it must be close to daylight. He sat alone with his fears for what seemed like a long time. He could only imagine, in the darkest recesses of his mind, what was in store for him. Did they know who he was? How had they found out he was an imposter? There was only one logical conclusion: Libby McGinnis had betrayed him!

Finally, the door opened and two men walked in. One was wearing the uniform of a Sandinista Army Colonel; the other, in civilian clothes, was unmistakably an Arab. The Colonel spoke first: "Mr. Alford, I am Commandante Raul Castro Padilla, Deputy Chief of Security; and this gentleman," he waved in the Arab's direction, "is Major Achmed ben Abdullah."

The Arab smiled, but it was not a friendly smile—more like a Cheshire cat. The Arab removed a clasp knife from his pocket and opened it. He walked over to Wade and placed the blade against his throat. Then, with a laugh, he sliced the buttons off Wade's white shirt. Wade did not even flinch.

The Sandinista Colonel continued: "Mr. Alford, we know that you are a CIA Agent—so there is no sense wasting time, ours or yours. What is your real name and what is your mission in Nicaragua?"

Wade put on his best confused look: "I don't know what you are talking about! I don't understand this! Why have you arrested me? I'm a friend of your government. This is all some kind of horrible mistake!"

Commandante Padilla smiled. "Come now, Mr. Alford. Let us not play games. As you say in America—the jig is up!"

The Arab laughed, "I never understand what jig is up means."

"No! I'm not a spy. This is a mistake. Talk to Brother Timothy from our Peace Group; he will vouch for me. Please call the American Embassy. This is a horrible mistake!"

Padilla paid no attention to the prisoner's pleading. "You claim to be a professor at Berkeley, Mr. Alford. Well, we have checked with our friends there, and there is a Robert Alford with the Political Science Department; but you are not him! It seems Professor Alford is only five-foot-six and weighs 145 pounds. So you see—we know that you are lying!"

Wade was surprised that they had blown his cover so fast. He knew the Sandinistas had a solidarity network in the States; but he had underestimated their efficiency. Bob Alford was a friend of Hunter's; and it was easy to talk him into vacationing in the Los Padres National Forest in California for a few weeks while Wade took his place.

"This is a terrible mistake!" said Wade, trying to show fear and panic. "I demand to see someone from the American Embassy!" His protest was cut short as the Arab struck him with a powerful smash to his face with his doubled fist.

Wade's head exploded with pain, and the chair tipped over sideways from the force of the blow. Padilla and Achmed lifted the chair and the dazed prisoner from the floor and set them upright.

The Arab leaned over and whispered in Wade's face: "We Libyans[1] hate all Americans. I enjoy drinking American blood after I cut their throats. However, if you tell us the truth, you will live. If you don't, I will make you suffer great pain; yes—great pain!"

"My name is Robert Alford," gasped Wade. "Please get in touch with the American Embassy. They will get this thing straightened out."

"Achmed is an expert at inflicting pain," announced Padilla. "I will give you one minute to tell us the truth—then if you don't, I will turn you over to my Libyan friend."

Wade knew that further acting was useless. He remained silent, trying to steel himself to the pain he knew was coming. Padilla watched his wrist watch tick away the minute, then he smiled. "Too bad, Mr. Alford. I'm afraid you are going to have to be persuaded. Achmed—go ahead!" Commandante Padilla walked out, closing the door behind him.

Achmed smiled and stepped toward the prisoner. Wade's head exploded again as the Arab's roundhouse right caught him square on the cheekbone. The chair flipped over backwards. Achmed went to work on the American's ribs with a series of kicks.

Bolts of pain shot through Wade's body as Achmed's kicks crashed into bone and muscle. The Arab finally stopped and lifted the chair back to its upright position. Then he stepped back and lighted a cigarette. "What are you doing in Nicaragua? Who are your contacts here?"

Through clenched lips, Wade mumbled, "My name is Robert Alford—and I am not a CIA Agent."

The Arab stepped forward, taking a deep drag on his cigarette. "The pain is just beginning, you American dog!" he growled. He placed the fiery tip of his cigarette against the prisoner's chest and slowly ground it out.

White, hot pain shot through the America's chest. His neck muscles drew taut and he arched involuntarily up from the chair!

* * *

The American Peace Group were all "bright-eyed and bushy-tailed," as they eagerly loaded onto the waiting bus. They were dressed in slacks and jeans, tennis shoes and old shirts. Today, they were going to join a farm cooperative and work side-by-side with the farmers in the fields. Brother Tim had promised them a most memorable day.

Libby was wearing jeans and a bright print shirt; Scotty was in his usual rumpled safari jacket. Libby scanned the crowd for a glimpse of the man she loathed—but she did not see him. Her anticipation was a dead giveaway to Scotty who said, "Don't worry Libby, he'll be here."

"I'm not watching for him," she shot back, wondering to herself why she was lying to her friend.

However, the former American Colonel did not show up! The bus pulled out without him. Libby's questions were soon answered when Brother Timothy stood up at the front of the bus and announced, "Mr. Alford will not be joining us today. He became ill during the night and had to be taken to Central Hospital. I'm happy to report that it is nothing serious and he should be with us tomorrow. He just needs to rest today. Probably just a case of Montezuma's Revenge."

The members of the party politely laughed at the Monk's little touch of joviality. Libby felt relieved—and she was mad at herself for feeling anything. She could not understand why she was worried about the man; after all, she hated him and he hated her. She turned to find a frown on Scotty's face and asked, "What's the matter?"

"Oh, nothing I guess. I just have a bad feeling."

Note 1.

The Sandinistas have built close ties with Khadafy of Libya. During the 1970s, and prior to taking power, Sandinista militants trained in Libya, and Libyan funds were used to purchase arms from Vietnam and North Korea. Tomas Borge, Nicaragua's Minister of Interior, went to Libya in 1980, to obtain financial assistance and discuss joint agricultural ventures. In April 1983, Brazilian authorities seized four planeloads of arms from Libya en route to Nicaragua labeled "medical supplies for Columbia." In addition, Libya's "People's Bureau" in Managua has provided assistance to Central and Latin American terrorist groups.

The Sandinista government has issued Nicaraguan passports to radicals and terrorists of other nationalities, including radicals from the Middle East, Latin America, and Europe, thus enabling them to travel in Western countries without their true identities being known. PLO agents working in Central America and Panama use Nicaragua as their base of operations. The Sandinistas' willingness to provide new documentation and a base from which to travel is undoubtedly one reason why Nicaragua has become a haven for terrorists and radicals from Europe as well as Latin America.

10

Doctor Fernando Amador arrived at his office in the Central Police Station around noon. This was his usual routine because his main office and clinic was in the suburbs of Managua, and he always spent his mornings there. The Cuban doctor had only recently been posted to Nicaragua after serving two years with the Cuban Expeditionary Forces in Angola. Managua was a welcome relief after the spartan existence in Africa. Here, the accomodations were decent and good Caribbean Rum was plentiful.

He walked into his office to find the Deputy Chief of Security, Commandante Padilla, sitting behind his desk, reading a book. Colonel Padilla looked up, "Good morning Doctor, I expected you sooner. You were notified about the American spy we picked up, were you not?"

"Yes, but I had some work to do at the clinic. I got here as soon as I could. Where is this spy?"

Padilla yawned, "Down in interrogation room three with Achmed."

"Don't tell me you turned that Libyan animal loose on him?"

The Colonel shrugged his shoulders. "What else could I do?

Achmed was on duty when they brought him in. Besides, Achmed usually gets good results."

"Achmed's a brute! He gets carried away with his work. I just hope he hasn't already killed the American. These Arabs are bloody barbarians."

When the Cuban Doctor entered the interrogation room a few minutes later, he saw a chilling sight: The prisoner was strapped, naked, to the wooden chair. His shoulders and chest were covered with red, blistery welts which, on close inspection, turned out to be cigarette burns. A pile of cigarette butts lay strewn on the floor beside him. The prisoner's head lolled forward. "Por Dios!" exclaimed Amador. He lifted the man's head up. One eye was almost swelled shut and a deep gash on the right cheek oozed blood. He released the prisoner's head and turned on the Libyan: "What have you done, you animal? I can see I should have gotten here sooner."

"There is no need to be concerned, Doctor. The American dog isn't dead; I have just been softening him up. These cases usually take a little time before they are ready to answer questions. I'll leave him in your good hands—besides I am out of cigarettes." Achmed winked and smiled at the Doctor.

"And I take it that he did not give you the information you wanted?" asked the Doctor, sarcastically.

"No. He did not talk yet. This one is very stubborn. All I need is just a little more time."

Amador fixed his glare on the Arab: "You are a stupid oaf—a clumsy animal. If you are the best that Khadafy has then it is no wonder your country still lives in the dark ages. Now get out of my sight, while I repair your damages!"

The chastised Arab looked hurt for a moment; then he shrugged his shoulders, smiled and walked out of the room. He was used to these tirades by the eccentric doctor.

The doctor stood looking at the prisoner for a few seconds, shaking his head and clicking his tongue. Then he opened his medical bag and began to administer aid to his patient.

* * *

The stinging odor of ammoniam nitrate jolted Wade to consciousness. His throbbing head cleared slowly. His body felt like it had been attacked by a thousand angry hornets, then run over by a Mack truck. As his senses returned, he found an elderly gentleman dressed in white dabbing gel on his burns. The soothing ointment felt good.

"Ah ha, you are awake. I'm sorry about your beastly treatment, young man. What animals these Arabs are! However, I do not think Achmed did you any permanent harm. He gets carried away once in awhile. I think you will be as good as new in a couple of days; but I am afraid you will be a little sore."

The doctor poured a glass of water and raised it to the prisoner's parched lips. Wade gulped it down. His dehydrated body needed the water. The doctor then continued to dab gel on the burns. "I am doctor Fernando Amador. I am from Cuba; and I am on temporary duty here in Nicaragua. And what is your name, young man, and how did you get into this mess?"

Wade went back into his act: "Doctor, why am I here? I'm no criminal. This is all a horrible mistake! I'm a friend of the Nicaraguan government. Please call the American Embassy. I know we can clear this whole thing up. Please help me."

"I think we can arrange that as soon as we get a few formalities straightened out. I'll go make a couple of phone calls."

Wade's hopes soared.

The doctor left the room and returned a few minutes later with two uniformed guards. They released his straps and handed him his shirt and trousers. When he stood up, a wave of dizziness swept through him as he dressed. When he was finished, they strapped him back into the chair.

"I called your embassy," the doctor informed him, "but they claim they have no record of a Robert Alford being in Nicaragua. The gentleman I talked to said that your name was not on the list of the visiting Peace Group. So, I'm sorry, but I'm afraid we cannot release you yet." The doctor sat down in one of the chairs a guard carried in. "There now, isn't this more civilized?" Amador opened his little black bag and began removing small glass vials and lining them up on the field table.

"Are you the prison doctor?" asked Wade.

"Well, yes—in a way I am. I'm a doctor and I work with the prisoners. I graduated from the University of Madrid. However, I'm not practicing the kind of medicine you think. Normally, I specialize in research; but here in Nicaragua I am the Chief Interrogator for the Office of State Security. Here I work mostly as a teacher, but sometimes I handle the tougher cases myself. I think you fall in that category—don't you? You have evidently been well-trained to handle physical punishment. I congratulate you for your resilience."

Wade's hopes fell and he suddenly felt very alone. A cold chill ran through his body and he shivered. Evidently, he had the doctor pegged all wrong.

"I see by your eyes that you are disappointed, my boy. Well I will try and make our association as painless and as short as possible. But you must realize that it depends upon you. If you would just agree to answer all my questions, we could end this interrogation right now. I really recommend that you do so. You know what the questions are—so what is your decision?"

"I don't have the answers to your questions," returned Wade. "I'm no CIA agent; I came to Nicaragua as a guest of your government."

The doctor shook his head and clicked his tongue: "Tsk, Tsk! Well young man, I'm afraid you have made the wrong decision. See these vials?" He held up one of the small glass bottles. "Let me give you some background on my field of research: We have know for years that bee and some snake venoms relieve—and in some cases cure—certain bodily ailments. People in Southern France have used bee venom to relieve muscular ailments for over 1000 years. The Ancient Egyptians believed that a small drop of asp venom in a gallon of water increases longevity. I have spent over twenty years studying the effects of the venom of various poisonous snakes; and I have made some amazing discoveries. Someday, the medical world will honor my research. While I was in Africa, I was fortunate to have thousands of patients to study."

The prisoner was baffled for a moment by the doctor's conversation; then he began to see what the doctor was leading up to. He shivered at the prospect. At this moment, his future looked very bleak.

The Cuban doctor picked up one of the glass vials and studied the clear liquid inside. He held it out for the prisoner to see: "Agkistrodon b. billineatus, commonly known as Mexican Cantil, a deadly snake found of course in Southern Mexico." He put the vial down and picked up another: "Bothrops astox. This is one I know you have heard of; the Fer-de-Lance; one of the world's most poisonous snakes—a real charming fellow that strikes without warning or provocation." Doctor Amador began pointing, in order, to the other vials on the table: "The Coral Snake, or Micrurus lemniscatus; a beautiful creature; only six inches long, found in your country and Mexico—but very deadly. Here is the King Cobra, or

Naja hanah; and my favorite, the Bushmaster, or Lachesis muta; and last, but certainly not least, the rare Maja nigrocollis, or Red Spitting Cobra from Southeast Asia."

Wade sat quietly, studying the doctor and trying to imagine what the medico had in store for him. He had a feeling of dread; this harmless looking old gentlemen scared the hell out of the tough, iron-willed soldier.

"I see by the look on your face that I have peaked your curiosity, Mr. Alford or whatever your name is. The human body is a beautiful machine, and it is a sin to scar or blemish it. I have spent my entire life searching for cures to certain illnesses and to ease human suffering. However, I found during my experiments that injecting diluted snake venom in people causes extreme pain. As a matter-of-fact I can use various solutions of venom and actually control the degree of pain in a patient. The process is usually not fatal; although I will admit that some of my research volunteers did die. However, I like to feel that those who perished died for science and for the benefit of mankind." The doctor stopped and took a drink of water, then he continued his lecture. "Different venoms attack different systems in the human body: the nervous system, muscular system, digestive system, respiratory system, and so forth. I'm afraid, my boy, that you are going to experience horrible pain."

This guy is crazy as a loon, thought Wade. He was ready for the Arab to return. Physical punishment, although painful, was something the soldier understood. "You're crazy!" he blurted out.

"Oh no, my American friend. I'm far from crazy. As a matter-of-fact, I have an IQ of 160. I am a medical genius, and my research is for the future benefit of mankind. I do not like this interrogator work; but it does allow me to experiment on humans. I don't want to cause you pain—but that is your choice. However, I will give you one last chance. Who are you? What is your mission in Nicaragua? And, who are your contacts in Nicaragua? Three simple questions. Three simple answers. No one will ever know, and you will avoid extreme pain. You will tell me what I want to know sooner or later, anyway. And by telling me now, you can avoid excruciating pain. You will beg me to kill you! And in the end, you will tell me what I want to know. Now are you ready to cooperate?"

"I'm telling you the truth! I'm no CIA agent! My name is Robert Alford, and I am in Nicaragua because I am a Marxist; I sympathize with the revolution. I have worked very hard for the cause in America."

"You are still lying to me. You see we know that you are an American and imposter—Miss McGinnis told us!"

Wade felt a new despair. Libby McGinnis had told them! He had misjudged her, and twice the woman had ruined him—but this time she had pronounced his death sentence. But there was something wrong or else why hadn't she told them his real name?

The doctor removed a hypodermic needle from his black bag and peeled off the plastic tip. He stuck the needle into one of the vials and pulled the plunger up, filling the syringe. He pushed the plunger slightly and a drop of clear liquid dropped from the needle tip. He held the hypo in front of the prisoner's face and smiled: "This contains a solution mixture of two percent Mexican Cantil and twelve percent Fer-de-Lance venom. The remainder is a harmless water-base liquid. There is not enough venom to kill you; but I guarantee you will be very, very sick. These venoms will attack your nervous and muscular systems. Do you want to talk?"

Wade realized further protestations were useless. He clenched his teeth and shook his head.

The doctor shrugged his shoulders. "Okay, my friend; but I am going to say that I told you so." He dabbed Wade's arm with an alcohol pad and smiled. "We can't let you get an infection—can we?" He poised the needle above the fleshy part of Wade's forearm.

Wade struggled instinctively, but it was useless; he was securely strapped in the chair. Amador stuck the needle into flesh and muscle and pushed the plunger home.

* * *

Libby sat hunched over her small portable, copying her notes from the day's visit to the government cooperative farm. The land had once belonged to a wealthy Nicaraguan who, according to the government spokesman, "was converted by the idea and goals of the people's revolution and had donated the land to the new government for redistribution to the poor campesinos he had once exploited.

"Now, the campesinos grew their own crops and donated a share to the government to be distributed among the poor people in the cities who had once been exploited by the American imperialists and Jews who once controlled the economy." Brother Timothy introduced workers who told stories of atrocities they had witnessed committed by the CIA-backed Contras. Before the day was over, even the liberal TV newswoman could see that the whole day had been contrived and planned.

There was a quiet rapping on her door, and she opened it to find Scotty. The cameraman walked past her and turned on the radio. Then he stepped close to her and whispered, "I called all of the major hospitals in Managua, and none of them have ever heard of a Robert Alford."

"Maybe he's back in his room," she said.

"No, I checked. He's not there. I think something has happened to him."

Libby felt an emptiness in the pit of her stomach—a feeling she could not understand or control. "Maybe we should call the embassy."

"And tell them what? That Robert Alford, whose name is not Robert Alford, is missing? I guess we had best just leave it alone."

"What got you so interested in Wade's welfare all of a sudden?" asked Libby.

"I don't know. I just have a feeling that something's happened to him; and the government is covering it up. Maybe he took off on his own; but I don't think so, based upon Brother Timothy's statement this morning."

After the cameraman left, Libby went to bed and tried to sleep, but she could not get the handsome Colonel off her mind. Damn him, she thought, why couldn't he just stay out of her life!

11 _____

At first, there was only a slight ringing in Wade's ears; then the muscles across his chest began to tighten, and he experienced difficulty in taking a deep breath. He did not know whether this discomfort was caused by the effects of the snake venom or by his own anxiety. Fear and nervousness can often cause a person to feel imaginary pains; and he was afraid. This old man scared the hell out of the strong-willed soldier. Physical torture was something a man like Wade could understand and, to a certain extent, prepare himself for. What the doctor was doing to him was unthinkable, like being involved in an old black and white horror movie—like something straight out of Frankenstein. It was fear of the unknown.

The tightness in his chest slowly increased. It felt as if an iron band was being cinched steadily about him. Panic gripped the former American Colonel as his entire body began tingling as if currents of electricity were being applied to his nerve endings. Then the muscle cramping started, first in his feet then moving up to the calves of his legs. Wade wanted to reach down and rub them away or to walk them off, but he could not move.

When the cramps hit his stomach, it was hard and fast, like getting hit with a ball bat. The electricity coursing through his body turned to fire as the snake venom relentlessly attacked his nerve endings. His body began to tremble uncontrollably. Doctor Amador issued an order in Spanish, and the guards unstrapped the American. Wade tried to stand up to fight the awful hands of pain that were tearing at him. He wanted to stand to get a deep breath. He wanted to walk off the cramps that were knotting the muscles of his body. He wanted to stand up to put his hands around the doctor's throat and crush it like copper tubing! He took one awkward step and crumbled to the floor. He doubled up in excruciating pain, his legs drawn tightly up against his chest. Sledgehammers of pain and agony slammed into every muscle and fibre of his body. He felt as if the muscles across his chest were going to crush his rib cage. Then an iron band of pressure and pain began squeezing his head; it felt like two hot pokers being forced into his ears. Every nerve in his body cried out in agony as if they were to the point of exploding. Finally, he started to scream from the horrible pain that galloped unrestrained through his once strong body.

Slowly his muscles began to relax as the knots came untied; and the pulsating torrents of pain subsided. Every muscle in his body quivered. He managed to get two deep breaths before the ordeal began anew; and the agony rolled back over him like a gigantic wave— pounding, pounding, pounding! Wade had known pain before—but nothing like this. It felt as if every nerve, every cell, every molecule of his body were being stung by angry hornets. Through the currents of pain, he heard the doctor talking: "Why are you in Nicaragua? Three very simple questions. Tell me and I'll make the pain go away."

The attacks began to rise and fall like ocean waves. They would slow and stop; then gradually build, higher and stronger; crashing with a horrible force against the ravished edges of his mind. He began to lose consciousness at the end of each attack—but the welcome blackness was short-lived as the pungent smell of smelling salts brought him back to pain.

The doctor had been correct about one thing; Wade was ready to die. He preferred death to the agony he was feeling. At this moment he craved the permanent relief that death could bring. Finally, after what seemed like hours of torturous pain; somewhere beyond agony and despair; somewhere beyond the fiery pits of hell; a wonderful, soothing black veil closed down over his eyes, and he slipped into the unfeeling world of darkness. This time, not even the little vial of ammonia could revive him. Amador checked the unconscious prisoner with his stethoscope and found the heartbeat. The doctor shook his head in admiration. The prisoner was a physical wonder; he had never seen anyone withstand as much pain. He would have to let the American rest for awhile or else he would surely kill him. He turned to the guards. "Take him to a cell." Then the Cuban doctor sat down and began writing in his journal.

* * *

MEMPHIS, TN

Robert Hunter sat at his desk studying the message from the leader of the FDN, Alfonso Caldera:

> INTEL RESOURCES INDICATE A 14-YEAR-OLD BOY BELIEVED TO BE COL. WADE'S SON IS BE-ING HELD IN A YOUTH REHAB CAMP (FRAN-CISCO MORENO SPECIAL SCHOOL) NEAR MANAGUA. SHOULD WE HAVE UNDER-GROUND INFORM WADE WHEN HE MAKES CONTACT?
>
> ALFONSO

The businessman-adventurer had just returned that morning from Washington where he had a clandestine meeting with the Vice President of the United States. Among other things, they had discussed Wade's mission to Nicaragua. Hunter was still unaware that the former Delta Force Commander was in the hands of the Sandinista State Security Forces.

Hunter thought for a few minutes; then he pushed the button on his intercom, summoning his secretary. She instantly popped her head in the door. "Yes, Sir?"

"Michelle, please get me Alfonso in Miami."

A few minutes later, the Contra leader was on the line.

"Yes Alfonso," said Hunter, "I think our man down south should get the good news as soon as he makes contact. Meantime, your people down there need to double their efforts to find Salazaar."

"We have," returned the FDN leader, "but we haven't found out a thing. When is your man due to make contact with our people?"

"Should be within the next couple of days. Will your people assist him in getting the boy?"

"Of course. We'll do everything we can. Maybe the boy knows something about his grandfather. By the way, what's new in Washington?"

"I don't have to tell you the Aid Bill is in trouble. The liberals are doing everything they can to defeat the bill. The President is worried. We have heard that Nicaragua has given over twenty-five million dollars to a Washington Publicity Firm to make the Contra look bad."

"I don't know how much good it will do now, but I'm going to Washington tomorrow," said Alfonso. "I have to do something to diffuse the lies about the atrocities supposedly committed by the Contra. I just don't know why the media doesn't print the truth."

"The liberal media are experts at omission and commission, Alfonso. You should know that by now."

After hanging up, Hunter sat there shaking his head. He felt sorry for his friend Alfonso. The bad publicity conjured up by the opposition just before the Senate was to vote on the Contra Aid Package had been devastating and generally a pack of lies. The Contra were a group of Sunday school girls in comparison to the Sandinistas. Hunter had seen first-hand what the Sandinistas were doing to the Miskito Indians. He had talked to hundreds of Nicaraguan refugees who had been tortured by the Piracuacos (rabid dogs), as the Contra called the Sandinistas. And yet our U.S. press hardly mentioned the treatment of the Miskito Indians or published the statements of the Nicaraguan refugees. And this business of always bringing up the Vietnam War was ridiculous. There was no way Central America could be compared to Vietnam. There was one thing that the American people should understand and did not; and that was that if the Contra did not succeed in Nicaragua, then sooner or later American troops would have to shed their blood.

12 _____

MANAGUA, NICARAGUA

The insistent knocking on her door woke Libby McGinnis from a troubled sleep. She turned on her bed lamp and glanced at her wrist watch. It was 3 a.m.! She stood up, slipped on her robe and slippers, and shuffled tiredly to the door. "Who is it? What do you want?" she asked in English.

A voice spoke back in English, "I am sorry to bother you at such an hour Miss McGinnis. I am from the police. I just want to ask you some questions."

"Can you come back in the morning?"

"No. I'm afraid I must talk to you now." Without unlatching the door chain, Libby warily cracked open the door and peeked out. Two uniformed policemen stood outside. "What's this all about?" she asked.

One of the policemen leaned forward and smiled politely, "It is just routine Miss McGinnis. We want to ask you a few questions about your friend Mr. Alford."

A cold fear shot through the newswoman. "If you are talking about the Alford with the American Peace Group—I hardly know him."

"It won't take long Miss McGinnis. Please get dressed and come with us."

"Can't I answer the questions right here?"

"No, I'm afraid you must come down to the station with us. It should not take long. Please hurry and get dressed; we will wait here."

Libby's hands trembled as she dressed in a pair of chino slacks and khaki blouse. When she was on assignment, she usualy wore her hair up; but tonight she let it flow over her shoulders. She stuffed her mini-tape recorder and notebook into her over-the-shoulder bag and cautiously opened the door.

The two policemen ushered her down the back stairs and out into the alley behind the hotel. One of them opened the back door of an old Army ambulance and waved her inside. At first she was puzzled by the clandestine exit, but then decided it must be to protect her privacy—after all, she was a well-known news personality. And she was used to VIP treatment.

Inside the ambulance, she found a scowling Scotty, waiting for her. She looked over at him. "Scotty, what on earth is going on?"

He looked back, smiled, and shrugged his shoulders. "I haven't the foggiest idea; but apparently it has something to do with your Colonel."

"My Colonel—my ASS!" she mumbled.

The ride to the Police Station was surprisingly short, only a few blocks from the hotel. They parked in a dark alley and were escorted into a back door. Scotty was led away by two uniformed soldiers, and Libby soon found herself in a comfortable room with a leather couch and chairs and even a rug on the floor. It reminded her of a doctor's waiting room less the usual outdated magazines. She even caught the faint odor of antiseptic. They left her alone and she sat back on the couch with her thoughts. She really was not afraid, because she had not done anything wrong. Running into Wade was strictly coincidental. Besides, she was too well known, and she worked for the most powerful news agency in the world—so they would not dare give her a hard time.

She sat there for two hours before anyone came into the room—and by that time she was fighting mad. She was not used to this type of treatment; and she was ready to give someone a piece of her mind. Her first visitor was wearing the uniform of a Sandinista Army Colonel. An elderly white-haired man dressed in a medical smock and with a stethoscope draped from his neck followed the

Colonel.

"Good morning, Miss McGinnis," the officer said politely, "I am truly sorry for this inconvenience."

Libby attacked: "I demand to know the meaning of this! Why am I being treated like a common criminal? Do you realize just who I am? I want to see someone from the Ministry of Interior, immediately!"

The Colonel smiled, "I am from the Office of Security in the Office of the Minister of Interior. My name is Commandante Raul Castro Padilla. And this gentleman is Doctor Fernando Amador."

The doctor displayed a kindly smile and nodded his head.

"I am extremely sorry for this inconvenience," continued the Colonel, "and I am sure that we can clear this up quickly and you can be on your way."

Libby interrupted him. "Why have I been dragged out of my bed in the middle of the night and treated like a common criminal? And why have I had to sit here two hours before someone had the courtesy to talk to me? I assure you that my government and my news agency are going to get a full report on my treatment!" Her green eyes blazed at the two men. "And what have you done with my friend, Mr. Scott? I demand that you bring him here immediately!"

The Commandante turned serious. "Miss McGinnis, I don't believe you understand the grave trouble you are in."

"What do you mean, trouble that I am in?" she shouted. "I haven't done anything wrong!"

"Spying is a serious charge, Miss McGinnis!"

Libby stopped short and looked at the Colonel, dumbfounded.

Padilla opened a brown envelope and removed a photograph, which he held out for the newswoman to look at. It was a picture of Richard Wade, former Colonel US Army, the man that Libby McGinnis loved to hate. "Do you recognize this man?" Colonel Padilla asked.

"Yes." she answered, "He is with the American Peace Group; but I don't understand. What has he done?"

"Did you ever meet him before he arrived in Nicaragua?"

"No, of course not!"

"Who else do you have working with you here in Nicaragua?"

"I don't know what you are talking about! What is the purpose of these questions?"

"Mr. Alford is an imposter and is a CIA agent. But of course,

96

you already knew this. We want to know his real name and what your mission is here in Nicaragua!"

For the first time, Libby began to feel fear. It suddenly dawned on her that the Colonel was accusing her of being a spy—an American CIA agent! My God! Her a CIA agent? It was unbelievable!

"I don't know a thing about Mr. Alford or what he does. The very idea of myself or Mr. Scott being spies is preposterous! I don't see how you can be serious."

"Believe me, Miss McGinnis; I am dead serious!"

"I demand to see someone from the American Embassy," yelled Libby.

"You are in no position to demand anything," snapped Padilla. "You are lying. You know who Alford is and why he is here." He pulled a small tape recorder from his pocket and snapped it on. Libby's voice came out loud and clear! "The Colonel is a good actor. He plays the part of a college professor very well!" Scotty had been right. They had bugged her room. There was no way she could deny knowing that Robert Alford was an imposter.

Padilla clicked the recorder off. "You do recognize your own voice, don't you Miss McGinnis?"

Libby felt herself beginning to panic. "That was a mistake!" she stammered. "I just thought that Alford looked like someone I used to know; a long time ago—but I was wrong!"

"Come now, Miss McGinnis; you really do not expect me to believe that, do you? Especially after Mr. Scott checked all the hospitals looking for him."

"Scotty was simply concerned for a fellow American who we thought was ill."

"If you were concerned, why did you not call the American Embassy?"

"We were going to this morning."

"I'll tell you what I think, Miss McGinnis: Alford is a CIA Agent, and he came to Nicaragua on a mission for the US government; and I think that you and Mr. Scott are his contacts, even perhaps part of his operational team."

"That's absurd!" protested Libby. "Your government knows me and my reputation. How dare you suspect me. Does Minister Borge know that I am here?"

"In my business, we suspect everyone—and I especially suspect you. Your actions have been very suspicious. With your press credentials and reputation you can come and go freely: an ideal cover for a CIA Agent."

"This whole thing is ridiculous! I'm no spy and you know it," the redhead snapped back. "You're paranoid and my story is going to say so. If you don't let us go, I guarantee you are going to regret it."

"I don't think you are in any position to make threats, Miss McGinnis. Let me tell you a little more of what I know: Several months ago, a very high-ranking officer in the Palestine Liberation Organization was murdered in Cypress. The assassin was clumsy and left behind fingerprints. The fingerprints match Mr. Alford's. So you see we are positive that he is a CIA assassin. If you are his accomplice, that makes you a murderer and subject to the death penalty. We are not a stupid little backward nation. We have telecomputers connected with a worldwide network. Don't you realize that we are part of a world revolution, and we have allies everywhere?"

The newswoman was no longer listening to what the Sandinista Colonel was saying. Now she knew what Wade had been doing since she saw him last and it sickened her. And somehow he had pulled her into his world of violence. And she was smack in the middle of the former Colonel's troubles. She wondered who he had come to Nicaragua to kill.

Doctor Amador interrupted Padilla's political tirade and said quietly, "Perhaps if Miss McGinnis saw Mr. Alford, it might refresh her memory."

Libby sat back on the couch and tried to understand what was happening to her. Surely the Nicaraguan Colonel was bluffing about suspecting that she and Scotty were CIA Agents. Perhaps it was simply a questioning technique, and he was just trying to scare her into admitting something. As long as she continued to deny working with Wade, she would be all right. She felt a stab of relief when the doctor recommended bringing Wade into the room. It meant the former Colonel was alive.

The door opened and two guards entered, supporting a shirtless, semi-unconscious man between them. Colonel Padilla grabbed the man by the hair and held his head upright. Libby almost choked at the chilling sight. Wade's face was covered with black bruises; blood ran down the right side of his face; his chest and shoulders were pockmarked with red puffy blisters. His whole body was quivering, and he acted as if he could not breathe. The guards unceremoniously dumped the former American Colonel on the floor, where his body drew up into a ball and he went into convulsions.

"My, he looks a bit discombobulated, doesn't he?" said the Doctor.

The room began to sway in front of Libby. Doctor Amador caught her as she fell and thrust a vial of smelling salts under her nose. She revived and stood there speechless, watching Wade's agony on the floor.

"Your Mr. Alford is a very stubborn man. I'm afraid if he doesn't tell us what we want to know, he may soon be dead. He won't be able to take many more of my special injections," announced the doctor.

Libby finally lost control and began to cry hysterically. "What have you done to him?" she sobbed.

The doctor answered her question: "Mr. Alford is feeling the effects of injections of poisonous snake venom—just small concentrations mind you, but enough to make him very uncomfortable. However, I do have the antidote to relieve his pain."

Libby found herself saying, "Please do something to help him! This is inhuman!"

"I can do that; but that is up to him—and you. So far he has not been very cooperative. Now if you tell us what his mission is here and who your local contacts are, I will take away his pain; and we will also avoid putting you through the same thing."

The ominous threat chilled Libby to the very marrow of her bones. Everything that was happening was unreal—like a horrible nightmare that she would awaken from any moment. Her life had abruptly changed, within a few hours; she had been thrust into a world of violence and torture; and she did not know whether or not she could handle it.

The door opened again and a soldier entered and handed Commandante Padilla a message. "Ah good," he said after reading the note, "Achmed has had some success with Mr. Scott. It seems our Mr. Alford is a former American Army Colonel named Richard Wade—but he denies that he and Miss McGinnis are working with Wade. He says the meeting in Managua was just a coincidence. Achmed thinks he is telling the truth."

"That's true," said Libby. "We just met him here by accident. We met him several years ago, when he was still in the Army."

"Then you should have told the authorities, Miss McGinnis. You have been lying to us!" said Padilla.

Libby shook her head in the affirmative, her wide eyes glued on the pathetic figure on the floor still writhing in agony. "Please do something to help him!" she pleaded.

"He will be all right in a little while. Now tell us everything you know about Colonel Wade."

Libby told them what she knew about the Rome incident and the Senate Hearings.

Wade's convulsions subsided, and he lay trying to catch his breath. At a nod from Padilla, the two guards dragged the former Colonel off the floor and deposited him in one of the leather chairs. As his senses returned, he looked across the room to see Libby sitting on the sofa.

"I see you are back with us, Colonel Wade," said Padilla.

So they now knew his name! Wade shot a hard look at the woman he believed betrayed him. His cold gray eyes stabbed into Libby's heart. She shook her head and said, "I didn't tell them who you were."

"She is telling the truth Colonel," announced the doctor. "Your friend Achmed persuaded Mr. Scott to tell us your name."

"You bastards!" muttered Wade through clenched teeth. Somehow, by sheer will power, Wade struggled to his feet. His next move was surprising for a man in his weakened condition. He lashed out with the palm of his hand and knocked one of the guards to the floor; he pivoted in a semi-circle and caught the other guard flush on the jaw with a high kick; then he headed for the Sandinista Colonel. But his strength waned and he crumpled to the floor; then the convulsions started again. The embarrassed guards both struggled to their feet and started to kick the prisoner. Padilla finally ordered them to stop.

Libby watched in horrified silence as Wade's spasms slowly subsided. She was at a loss as to what to do or say. She wanted to help the former Colonel, but she was paralyzed with fear. She thought that now that they knew she and Scotty were innocent they would surely let them go free.

When Wade returned from his short trip to hell, he found himself sitting in a leather chair with his hands bound behind his back. The Cuban doctor was leaning over him, examining him with his stethoscope. "You are quite a specimen, Colonel Wade. Still dangerous after all you have been through—I have never seen it before. Perhaps I will have to increase the dosage on your next injection."

"I came to Nicaragua alone," confessed Wade. "Miss McGinnis and Mr. Scott are not involved with me. If you let them go free, I will tell you what you want to know."

"That is very noble of you Colonel; and I wish we could," returned Padilla, "but I'm afraid it is a little too late for that. You see, they have seen too much."

"You can't hold us," spoke up Libby. "The Embassy will be looking for us. You can't cover our disappearance."

"Oh yes we can, Miss McGinnis. You see, it seems that early this morning you and your cameraman, Mr. Scott, and a driver furnished by the government drove out to the village of Malagua which was attacked by the rebels yesterday. A logical visit for any good reporter. But alas, when you did not return, we sent out a search party which found your vehicle overturned and riddled with bullets. There was a lot of blood but no bodies. Several witnesses will say that you were attacked by Contra."

"You can't get by with that!" exclaimed Libby, realizing that they probably could. She felt completely helpless. She looked across the room at her new ally; at the only one in the room she could trust; the only man that had the abilities to get her out of this mess; the man whose career she had ruined.

"Oh yes; we can get by with that," returned Padilla. "In fact the resultant publicity from your disappearance will help our cause. You will become our martyrs. Your press is so gullible and easy to manipulate that they will demand all US Aid to the Contra cease immediately. Especially if they believe two of their own were murdered by the Contra!"

13 ⎯⎯⎯⎯⎯⎯⎯

The two prisoners sat quietly looking at each other across the room as Colonel Padilla and the doctor held a short conference. Wade could see the fear in the girl's eyes, and he cursed himself for getting her involved. He was a professional, and capture, torture and sudden death were always just one mistake away; however, Libby McGinnis had no business being a part of his problems. He had to do something to free the girl.

Colonel Padilla turned away from the doctor and announced, "You will be moved to Doctor Amador's clinic in the country. Colonel, you still have many questions to answer, so I suggest you consider what might happen to Miss McGinnis if you do not tell us the truth."

Wade felt another attack coming on. The last three had been increasingly less severe. Evidently the effects of the last injection were beginning to wear off. What had the Doctor said? "The attacks will last several days but will decrease in intensity and gradually disappear." The cramping started again! The prisoner decided to play it to the hilt; he wanted his captors to think he was totally incapacitated. He grabbed his stomach and fell to the floor. The pain was severe enough so he did not have to do much acting.

Two guards picked up Wade and dragged him through the door; another grabbed Libby roughly by the arms and shoved her ahead of him. She stumbled and fell to her knees. Colonel Padilla jerked her to her feet by her long hair, and she felt physical pain for the first time since her arrest. Libby was propelled out the back door and shoved into the same ambulance she arrived in. Scotty was already inside. His face was a mass of bruises and cuts, showing the results of the Libyan's handiwork. The two news people embraced and held each other. "My God Scotty!" she exclaimed. "What did they do to you?"

"I'm OK!" he answered. "Have they hurt you?"

"No, but . . . ." Her words were cut short as the back door opened and an unconscious Richard Wade was tossed unceremoniously into the back of the ambulance like a sack of potatoes. Two guards carring AK-47 assault rifles climbed in, followed by Doctor Amador. The ambulance lurched forward.

But Richard Wade was not unconscious; more like semiconscious. He lay on the bouncing bed of the truck trying to regain some strength. The Sandinistas had made a mistake believing he was incapacitated, and Wade intended to make them pay for it. But he had to make his move before they reached their destination.

Amador commenced to explain his experiments to Libby and Scotty. It was almost as if he had to convince them that what he was doing was for the benefit of mankind. The thought kept coming to Libby that she was back in an old movie about Nazi Germany, and Amador was the evil German Doctor. She began to realize that Nicaragua was like Nazi Germany—complete with a Gestapo, torture, concentration camps and yes, even evil doctors. She wondered how she could have been so fooled, yet she realized that the American public was also being fooled; and she had almost become a part of the massive disinformation program. Right now, more than anything, she wanted to survive to tell the world the truth about what was really happening in Nicaragua. She wondered how she could had been so naive.

The angry hornets in Wade's head finally calmed to a dull hum as his latest spasm gradually subsided. He decided that he had to make his move now. He began moaning and jerking his body; he drew his legs tight up against his chest.

Libby pleaded with the doctor: "Can't you please do something to help him?"

"There is nothing I can do now. He will have these attacks for several days, but they will gradually disappear. When we get to my clinic I'll give him something to sleep. However, I must remind you that all this depends upon getting the truth from him and you. If he tells the truth, he will be spared further pain. If he does not, then both he and you will experience great discomfort."

"What is going to happen to us if he tells the truth?" asked Scotty.

"You will be treated well!"

Scotty knew better. He and Libby were as good as dead. The Sandinistas could not afford to let them live. A cold dread spread through him, and he tightened his hold on his terrified friend.

Libby shivered with fear. She was not fooled by the doctor's promise; she knew what was in store for them.

Scotty felt her shiver. He had to do something—but what? He had never felt so helpless in his entire life.

Suddenly, the writhing, moaning figure on the floor came to life and kicked upward. His feet caught one guard on the side of the head. There was a loud crack as the man's neck broke; he tumbled sideways to the bed of the truck to lay there with his head at a strange angle. Before the other guard could react, Wade sprang to his feet and smashed him on the jaw with both hands clenched together. The guard went down and the former Delta Force Commander followed up with a vicious kick to the back of the guard's neck.

Scotty reacted instinctively. He pushed Libby aside and wrestled the doctor to the floor. Wade picked up one of the assault rifles and stuck the barrel into the doctor's mouth. The surprised doctor tried to scream, but he found it impossible while biting on a gun barrel. Wade turned to Scotty: "Hold this—if he moves, shove it down his throat!"

The ambulance driver realized too late that something was amiss in the back. By the time he stopped the vehicle, Wade had opened the sliding panel separating the driver's compartment and rear and was holding the barrel of a rifle to his head. The former Colonel had a short talk with the driver in Spanish and the ambulance drove off.

The action had happened so fast that Libby was still speechless. She was awed by what Wade had done. In an instant he had become a fighting machine—just like those guys in the Kung Fu movies. It was unbelievable! Rambo could not have done any better. She had forgotten that he had a black belt and was once a National Karate Champion. She had an almost overpowering desire to hold him; and she wanted him to hold her and reassure her that everything was going to be all right. At least she knew that now they had a chance. All they had to do was to get to the US Embassy, and they would be safe. She reached out and touched his arm and asked, "How long will it take us to get to the Embassy?"

His answer jolted her: "We are not going to the Embassy!"

Libby stared at Wade in disbelief. "What do you mean we aren't going to the Embassy? That's the only place we'll be safe. We have to get there as fast as possible!"

"I don't think we would make it! The Embassy is on the other side of Managua. When the good doctor doesn't show at his clinic, the Sandinistas will know something is wrong; and we wouldn't get within two blocks of the Embassy. They will also block off other embassies. And another thing, a large number of the US Embassy employees either work for or have been bought off by Thomas Borge. So even if we made it, we would be in danger. And there is another reason."

"And I suppose that third reason is you still have to kill someone!" she snapped back angrily.

Wade was surprised by her statement. "What do you mean by that?" he asked.

"Colonel Padilla said that your fingerprints proved that you were a professional assassin!"

Wade knew that his last job in Cypress had been sloppy. They had almost nailed his ass; and in his hurry to get away, he knew he had left fingerprints. He did not realize that the Sandinistas were tied into the international terrorist network so efficiently. "You should not believe everything you hear, Miss McGinnis. I would have thought you learned that in the last few hours."

"If we are not going to the Embassy, where are we going?"

"I have friends here. They will help you and Scott get out of the country. You should end up with a great story, perhaps even better than your last big one."

Libby shut her mouth. The proud, strong-willed newswoman knew she deserved that last remark. But, oh how this man exasperated her. She had tried to reach out to him in a tender moment, because she needed his comfort and strength; and he had cut her down. She turned to Scotty and said loudly enough for Wade to hear, "He's an arrogant asshole!"

Scotty felt like smiling for the first time since his arrest. At least they were alive, thanks to Richard Wade; and he for one was quite willing to do whatever the former Colonel said. "Don't worry Libby, he will get us out of this. Let's just do exactly as he says. He's the only chance we have."

A few minutes later, the ambulance stopped by a phone booth. Wade got out, borrowed a coin from the obliging driver, who wanted to stay alive, and made a quick call. He hung up, had a short confab with the driver and hopped into the back of the ambulance.

The Cuban doctor had been sitting with his back tight up against the corner of the ambulance, with Scotty still holding the gun barrel jammed in his mouth. Wade opened the doctor's black bag and rummaged around inside. He finally found what he was searching for and withdrew a hypodermic needle and two glass vials. He stuck the needle into each vial and filled the syringe; then he turned to the cameraman and spoke evenly: "You can take the barrel out of his mouth now."

A terrified look came across the doctor's face as he watched the needle in Wade's hand. "What are you going to do with that?" he gasped.

Wade said quietly, "I don't have to tell you what is in this, do I, doctor? I think you know the whole speil. This is the pleasant stuff I have running through my veins right now, isn't it. Would you like to know how I feel Doctor?"

Libby was watching the drama unfold. She echoed the doctor's question: "What are you going to do?"

Wade turned to her. "Do you have any idea how many people this maniac has killed with his experiments, how many people he has tortured?"

"No, I don't. But you just can't kill him in cold blood!"

"Do you know of any other way to kill him?" asked Wade. "Some people need killing, and Doctor Death here is one of them!"

Amador was shaking all over. "No! Please don't hurt me!" he pleaded. "Think of how important my work is to mankind."

"Mankind is just going to have to get along without you, Doctor." Before anyone else could say anything, Wade jabbed the needle in the thick muscles of the doctor's thigh and pushed the plunger home. The doctor's eyes opened wide in disbelief, and he began to whimper and cry.

Libby caught her breath when she saw the hypo needle bury itself in the doctor's leg; then she covered her face with her hands.

"Believe me doctor, I know just how you feel," said Wade. "And I can guarantee you it is going to get worse. What did you say to me? You are going to beg for death. What's that old saying? He who lives by the sword dies by the sword! I guess the same could be said for the needle."

Amador's body began to convulse; and his screams echoed through the moving ambulance. Wade decided to end it. He hit the Cuban Doctor with a killing karate chop to the base of his neck and the sadistic old medico fell forward onto the bed of the truck and lay still.

Libby was horrified at what she had just witnessed; and yet, logically speaking, she had seen justice done. Was it this simple in Richard Wade's world? The man killed as if it were easy—an every day happening—without remorse. What kind of a man could do that? And yet, she felt no pity for the doctor; and she had not even given the dead guards a second thought. My God, she thought, what is happening to me?

A few minutes later, they were met by a car. Wade ordered the driver to pull over. He motioned Libby and Scotty out and into the back of an Isuzu. Two men who had climbed out of the Japanese car got in the ambulance and took off.

The driver of the Isuzu held out his hand to Wade. "My name is Jorge Dunn!"

14

Jorge Dunn's modest home was located in the countryside about 20 miles from the city limits of Managua. His cement-block single story house was typical of the area. Dunn was one of the leaders of the National Democratic Front Managua Underground. He would have to be considered middle-class in a nation that had never really known a large middle-class. Historically, Nicaragua was a nation of have-a-lots and have-nothings. Jorge was, by trade, a skilled printer and typesetter and had once worked for Enrique Salazaar at *La Verdad*. When Salazaar was killed and the newpaper shut down, Jorge went to work for the only other opposition newspaper remaining in Nicaragua: *La Prensa*. However, since March 1982, *La Prensa* had been required to submit all material prior to publication to the Office of Communication of the Ministry of Interior, where it was carefully censored. The newspaper had many times been unable to publish an edition because it was unable to replace on time the materials banned from publication.*

Jorge joined the underground movement fighting the Sandinistas when he found the new regime was not going to guarantee

---

* The Sandinista regime closed *La Prensa* for good in October 1986.

Jorge joined the underground movement fighting the Sandinistas when he found the new regime was not going to guarantee "unrestricted freedom of expression" as it had promised. Like most Nicaraguans, he found out that one dictatorship had been replaced by another—called communism. Jorge Dunn was quick to point out to his followers that Somoza was a tyrant, but he had never closed the newspapers.

* * *

Wade had been operating on sheer adrenalin. He was weak from the beating and the ravages of the injections; and he had not eaten any food for over 24 hours. Shortly after arriving at Dunn's home, he was struck by another attack. Jorge and Scotty carried him into a bedroom; and Jorge's wife, Luisa, and Libby tried to ease his pain by massaging him with rubbing alcohol. Finally, after thirty miserable minutes, the Colonel's trip back into hell stopped; and he slipped into the welcome blackness.

When Wade fell asleep, Libby returned to the small living room and sat back exhausted on the sofa. She rubbed the black and blue marks on her arm where Wade had grabbed her during his agony.

Scotty brought her over a heaping plate of frijoles negras y raz (black beans and rice). "Here eat this; it's good and you need your strength."

Libby tasted the unappetizing-looking concoction. Scotty was right; it was good. She wolfed it down; she hadn't realized how hungry she was.

Scotty sat down beside her and put his hand on her shoulder. "Don't worry Libby, we'll get out of this OK. If anyone can get us through this mess, Wade can. Your Colonel is quite a man!"

Libby looked up "There you go again. What do you mean, my Colonel?"

"Girl, if you don't see it by now then you aren't as intelligent as I think you are. I think you have been in love with Wade since Rome. I know you have been obsessed with him since then—but I believe it's more than that."

"Don't be ridiculous Scotty," she said defensively, "I could never love a man like him."

"Don't be so sure. He's the most man you will ever meet and you know that. You may not realize it yet, but you need a man like him."

109

"I don't understand what you are trying to say."

"Well, it's hard to explain; but you are quite a woman yourself. And I think Wade needs someone like you."

"Scotty, I love you—but sometimes you are full of shit!"

* * *

Wade awakened slowly. He had a feeling that he was coming up out of a deep black hole. He opened his eyes to see the beautiful green eyes of Libby McGinnis looking down at him. He smiled and asked, "How long have I been out?"

"About 12 hours; how do you feel?"

"I'm famished. When do we eat?"

Libby managed a smile and it felt good to her. Yesterday, she wondered if she would ever be able to smile again. It was really good to be alive. "The management has plenty of black beans and rice. Actually it's quite good," she answered.

"My favorite cuisine," Wade swung his feet over the side of the bed and sat up. The room swam in front of him for a moment, then settled into place. Every muscle in his body was stiff and hurt with each movement he made.

"You should stay in bed," declared Libby. "I can bring your food in here."

"No thanks. What I really need is to work this stiffness out." He stood up and walked awkwardly around the room. "I feel as if I've been through a meat grinder."

Libby looked at his battered face and red welts across his chest and shoulders and shook her head. "You look like you have been through one, too."

"How's Scotty?"

"He's sore, too, and looks a bit rough; but he's OK.

"Is there any way we can get in touch with the Embassy, at least to let them know we are still alive?" asked Libby.

"No, not yet, it's too risky. Jorge will contact his people outside of Nicaragua and our State Department in Washington will be told that you and Scotty are safe. Your news agency will be notified." He turned to her and said quietly, "I promise you, in a few days you will be safely in Honduras." His eyes held hers for an instant too long, and he took one step toward her. She stared back boldly, inviting him to take her into his arms. It was something they both wanted; but it was something they both feared. They stood there looking at each other. Then his eyes saddened as if to say "It could never be—our worlds are too far apart." He turned and walked out of the room.

Libby followed him, stunned and hurt by his walking away from her. She confronted him in the living room and asked, "If I write a story about what has happened, can your friends get it to ABN?"

"No! It would be too risky for you at this time."

"This story has to be told," she returned, her voice rising in anger. "Americans must be told the truth about what is happening in this country."

"Americans have been told what is going on here—but your liberal press doesn't see fit to print it," returned Wade.

"I'm a respected reporter; ABN will tell my story."

"Don't be too sure! They might and they might not. In any event, you will be able to tell your story to the world in a few days. I am sorry, but you and Scotty are just going to have to be our guests for a few days, until we can safely move you out of the country."

"What you are saying is that now we are your prisoners," she snapped back angrily.

"If you want to call it that—yes!" he returned.

"And just how are we going to get to Honduras?"

"Probably walk!"

"You are a bastard!" she yelled, showing her Irish-Italian temper. She turned and stomped out of the room. Wade watched her leave the room and just shook his head. He was not being smart-mouthed when he said they would walk to Honduras—he was dead serious!

* * *

That evening they feasted on chicken and, of course, black beans and rice. Libby choked down the thick black coffee the Nicaraguans loved so well. Luisa was as attentive to her charges as a mother hen to her chicks. Jorge's wife did not appear to be concerned about the possibility of the Sandinistas coming to her house. She was actually enjoying having guests in the house—regardless of the circumstances.

Jorge returned from work at 8 p.m. and joined them at the kitchen table. He had brought home a bottle of rum, and they were enjoying a welcome drink. He finally turned to Wade: "I have some very important news for you. I wanted to tell you last night, but you were in no condition. We have located a boy at the Francisco

Moreno Special School that we think is your son, David Wade!"

His son might be alive! The words hit Wade like a runaway locomotive. But it was impossible, because his son was dead. He had buried him and he had grieved for him. At first he could not speak—he was too filled with emotion. He took a deep breath and swallowed before he spoke. "That's not possible. My son is dead! I buried him!"

"But you never saw your son's body, did you? And you never saw Enrique's body. We have learned that the Sandinistas lied to you. Both your son and Enrique are still alive. Your son is being held in a Youth Rehabilitation Camp only 20 miles from here! However, we still have not been able to locate Enrique."

The room floated before Wade, and he thought for an instant that he was going to pass out. He remembered the last time he had held his son in his arms. It was the day before his wife and son had left for Nicaragua. He remembered the visit from the Post Chaplain informing him that Maria and David were dead. He remembered the agonizing flight to Managua and the funeral. He remembered identifying Maria's cold body, and the poor job the morticians had done in trying to repair her battered head. But he did not see David's body; the authorities told him the boy had been burned beyond recognition. He remembered watching the coffins being lowered into the ground, and he thought he was burying his soul. His heart grew cold, and he vowed never to get close to another person again. He returned home and buried himself—in his work.

Libby watched Wade change and soften with the news from Jorge. She saw tears in his eyes, and he grew silent for a time as if he was remembering other times and other places. The newswoman wanted to reach out and touch the former Colonel.

Jorge continued: "We found out about your son by accident. One of the members of the underground recently got a job as a maintenance man at the school, and he has talked to your son. He never reported it until he found out that the boy was Enrique's grandson."

"I would like to meet this maintenance man," said Wade.

"Si Senor, he is coming over tonight."

* * *

The maintenance man, Mario Caldazon, told Wade that he had been at the school for about three weeks when he was approached by a boy who said he was an American. The boy asked him to tell someone in the American Embassy that his name was David Wade, and he wanted to go home to America. Mario told the boy that he would try to pass on his message. However, he figured the best thing to do was have the underground pass the message to the FDN, because he was afraid to go near the US Embassy.

Wade stayed up most of the night, studying maps of the area and the sketch of the Youth Camp that Mario had prepared. Mario told him that there were 150 boys in the camp. They were not treated badly; but they were punished for infractions of the rules. Their schedule was rather stable: in the mornings they worked in the fields; in the afternoon they attended school; in the evenings they received political indoctrination. One day each week, usually Saturday, they took military training with the local People's Militia. The Youth Camp was run by a Cuban Director, and several of the teachers were Cuban; so the boys received a heavy dose of Comrade Fidel.

The boys lived in three two-story wooden barracks similar to American World War II Army barracks. The camp covered an area of 100 acres, surrounded by a 10 foot high wire mesh fence. The main compound, in which the barracks, mess hall, school and administration building were located, covered seven acres. This inner compound was surrounded by a 15 foot high chain-link fence. There was one guard post at the entrance to the main compound. The outer perimeter fence was patrolled irregularly by two soldiers in an old pick-up truck. Several walking guards patrolled the inner fence line. The guards did not live at the camp; they were furnished by a Sandinista Army unit whose camp was five miles away. The maintenance man believed they changed guard shifts every six hours.

Wade would have liked to make a personal reconnaissance of the youth camp before he made his attempt to free David; however, he did not have the time. He had to get Libby and Scotty out of Nicaragua as soon as possible. He had not told Libby, but she had probably become a high priority item to the Sandinistas. They could not afford to allow a media person of Libby's reputation to tell her story to the world. Wade decided to go for his son the following night.

Mario suggested that Wade meet his son at the tool shed in the main compound. The small building was isolated from the other buildings; and it would be easy to find because of a shallow ravine that ran by it. Mario agreed to tell David that his father would meet him at the tool shed at 0200 hours.

Everything had changed as far as Wade was concerned. He had hoped Robert Alford could move about Managua in relative freedom, searching for news of Enrique and re-familiarizing himself with the city. Now, he was responsible for the safety of Libby and Scotty—two innocent people who were caught up in his problems. And his son had suddenly returned from the dead! No one on this earth could keep him from his son!

The beautiful redhead was a special problem. She brought back feelings that he thought were long dead. This strong, self-willed woman with the big green eyes attracted him as no other woman since his wife. He realized that she loathed him and everything he stood for, but he still dreamed of what might be. He did not want to care for Libby McGinnis—but he did; and he wanted her. The faster he got her to safety and out of his life, the better off he would be.

The next morning, Wade had a long talk with Libby and Scotty. He explained to them why he had come to Nicaragua and told them he was not here working for the CIA.

"I know that it is my fault that you are in this mess," he said, "and I am truly sorry. I want to get you out of the country as soon as possible. However, now that I have found out that my son is still alive, I have to free him and take him out with us. I hope you understand. I promise you that we will only be delayed a couple of days."

"Why didn't you tell us why you were here?" asked Scotty. "We would have understood."

"To be perfectly honest, I did not trust you. You see, if the Sandinistas found out that I was here looking for my father-in-law and he is still alive, they would surely kill him."

"You don't have a very high regard for the media, do you?" asked Libby, who immediately regretted asking the question.

"No! As a matter-of-fact, I don't care much for the media. But at the same time I would fight to keep a free press." He turned to Libby and asked, "Has Jorge explained to you what has happened to the free press here?"

"Yes, he has; and I am anxious to tell the world about it," she returned.

"How do you plan on freeing your son?" asked Scotty. "If I can be of any help; count me in."

"I'm not sure yet. But I think I'll just walk into the camp and

114

bring him out."

* * *

Later that day while Libby was helping Luisa prepare dinner, Scotty cornered Wade: "Do you want me to go along as backup? I'm a little rusty, but I am a former Marine."

"Thanks Scotty—but I work best alone. You stay here and look after Libby. If anything happens to me, Jorge's people will start you out to Honduras tomorrow. There, you will be met by some American friends of mine and taken home."

"May I ask you a personal question, Colonel?"

"Sure. Only don't call me Colonel—my name is Rich."

"OK Rich. How much do you care for Libby?"

"More than I should, Scotty. A hell-of-a-lot more than I should!"

"You know Colonel, I have always wanted to tell you that I'm sorry for the way things turned out for you after the Rome story. I wish-to-hell I had never taken those pictures!"

Wade put his hand on the cameraman's shoulder. "Scotty, you were only doing what you get paid to do. I have never had any hard feelings toward you."

"What about Libby?"

"What do you mean?"

"That girl has never been the same. She thinks that she is personally responsible for ruining your career and that you hate her for it."

"That's absurd! She was only doing her job. In fact we used her in Rome. She was the distraction I used to get close to the aircraft. It's funny—in Rome I was just doing my job; you were just doing your job; and Libby was doing her job. The truth is we were all pretty damn good at our jobs. It's just that things don't always turn out as you plan."

"Well, someday I hope you tell Libby. Her conscience has been tearing her apart ever since the hearing."

15 _____

That evening, after dinner, as Libby was helping Luisa wash dishes, Wade walked up behind her and whispered in her ear: "Can I speak to you alone?" Without waiting for an answer, he took her by the hand and led her out the door and onto the back patio. The moon had not yet appeared, but the sky was alive with billions of twinkling stars. It was a picture-perfect night for lovers and romance. The small patio was surrounded by a six-foot cement block fence, so the two were hidden from view. Wade still held her hand. He stopped and turned toward her: "I had to talk to you before I left."

She stared up at him boldly and smiled, "I wanted to talk to you, too."

"I just wanted you to know that I never blamed you for what happened after Rome. You were just doing your job—as I was doing mine. I understand your reaction when you saw me shoot that terrorist. It was a horrible thing for you to go through. Just for your information, I did believe that the terrorist was armed; and I really had no choice—I had to kill him. I'm just sorry you had to witness it. I wish we could have met under different circumstances. Maybe you wouldn't hate me quite so much."

Libby's heart melted. The super-soldier, as she used to call him privately, was apologizing to her. She had exposed him to the world; made him into some sort of Nazi-like monster in the public's eye; and helped to destroy his once promising career—and he was apologizing to her! She stammered slightly, finding it difficult to talk to him. "After the tape was aired, things just got completely out of hand. It was as if I was shocked by what happened; I hated you and wanted to see you punished. Later as I found out more about you, I realized I was wrong, but it was too late. Scotty tried to tell me, but I wouldn't listen." Big tears rolled down her cheeks, and she looked up at him and murmured, "I'm sorry for what happened!"

He reached out and wiped away a tear. He was overwhelmed by her confession. It had been a long time since a woman had shed a tear for him, and his lonely heart was filled with emotion. He took her in his arms and pulled her close. Her warm body sent a fire sailing through him and his mouth found hers, waiting for him. They kissed softly at first, igniting the fires; then her arms went around his neck and they kissed long and passionately, feeling the urgent need for each other course through their bodies. Libby felt his strong arms around her like steel bands; and she felt secure in their strength.

All at once, it was as if a dam had burst and they were caught up in the raging waters, being carried away; and they were helpless to fight the swirling current. All their pent up emotions came boiling to the surface. They could not get close emough to one another. Libby felt the electricity tingle through her body; and she knew what she wanted. A new world opened up to her.

Finally, he pushed her back and apologized, "I'm sorry. I shouldn't have done that."

She looked up at him and said hoarsely, "Yes! You should have and I'm not sorry—I need you; and I need your strength!" And she pulled him back to her. He could feel her body trembling against his; and he was lost!

They held each other for a long time—not saying a word; not knowing what to say. But there was really no need for words— Love is a feeling.

When they finally returned to the house, their faces told the story. Scotty knew his two friends had broken through the barrier. It had just been a matter of time before these two strong people found each other. It was preordained! Two belligerants had met on the battlefield of love and conquered one another.

An hour later, Wade was preparing for the most important mission of his life. His uniform and equipment were scrounged by the underground, compliments of the Sandinistas. He dressed in black trousers and shirt and put on a pair of black tennis shoes. Around his head he tied a black scarf, giving him a piratical look. He burned cork from a bottle of wine and darkened his face and hands. His armament consisted of a machete strapped to his back and a Charter Arms 38 caliber undercover revolver. The small handgun was ideal for close-in work at night. His main tool was a pair of heavy-duty wire cutters.

As he was leaving, Libby stepped in front of him and blocked his way. "Be careful!" she said, "and come back with your son." She reached up and pulled his blackened face down to hers and gave him a long kiss, disregarding the others in the room.

He stepped back and took both of her hands in his. "I'll be back." Then he walked past her out of the door. The house was suddenly very quiet.

Libby was overwhelmed by a feeling of emptiness. Scotty walked over and put his arm around her. "Don't worry, he'll be OK. However, I suggest you wipe that burnt cork off your face—you look like a clown."

* * *

Jorge slowed the Isuzu about one mile from the outer perimeter fence of the Youth Camp and turned to Wade: "Good luck amigo— God be with you. I will pick you up here."

Wade opened the door and rolled out into the ditch alongside the road. He lay there for a full minute after Jorge's car disappeared from view; then he crawled under a barbed-wire fence, stood up, and struck off across a small pasture.

A sliver of a moon hung low to the east; and a few clouds had moved in. It was a dark night; Wade was grateful for that. He was accustomed to working at night—and the darker the better he liked it. The darkness was an old friend to this deadly warrior, an old friend whose enveloping blackness protected those who knew its secrets.

Wade's thoughts drifted to his son. He remembered David's first fish, a four inch bluegill. It was a world record as far as the boy was concerned. He insisted his dad take his picture; then he wanted to take the fish home and raise it as a pet. At Fort Bragg, the boy loved to go out to the Holland Drop Zone and watch the paratroopers. One of the last things the family did together was to visit Disneyland. Wade did not know who enjoyed it more: David, Maria, or him. Those were happy days, and Richard Wade believed he had everything a man could want: a beautiful, loving wife; a healthy, happy, bright son; and a job he liked. Sometimes people did not appreciate their blessings until they lost them.

He wondered how much David had changed. Wade knew exactly what political indoctrination meant. The communists were the experts—they had invented it. The political indoctrination of children was a primary communist strategy. That way they did not have to worry about the next generation. Thousands of children were taken from their families in Afghanistan and shipped to Russia for several years of indoctrination and training. On the Isle of Youth, just off the coast of Cuba, over 10,000 third-world children, from Angola, Ethiopia, Nicaragua, and Mozabique, live and study communism. When they return to their homelands, they are trained revolutionaries and hardened communists. Their old beliefs and religions are replaced by the religion of communism and world revolution.

If David had succumbed to this "brainwashing" practiced by the communists, then Wade could be walking into a trap. It was a chance he would have to take!

It did not take Wade long to reach the outer perimeter fence. He found a support pole and climbed the fence easily. A few minutes later, he was at the inner fence on the north side of the main compound. The barracks were dark and only a few outside security lights illuminated the headquarters area. He heard a noise and melted into the blackness of the ground. A non-alert guard came ambling by. He waited until the guard was out of sight; then went to work on the chain-link fence. He wrapped his scarf around one strand of the heavy gage wire; and he cut through with his wire cutters. It was slow, cautious work, but after five minutes he had a small flap inward and crawled inside; then he carefully bent the flap back into place. He crawled slowly on all fours until he reached the shallow ravine; then he moved faster in a low-crouch. When he spotted the tool shed ahead, he stopped and waited, listening for sounds of a trap. He lay dog for a full fifteen minutes before he moved cautiously forward. Mario had done a good job on the sketch! A glance at his watch told him that he was exactly on time.

But David was not there. He moved back up the ravine a few yards and froze into the ground—to wait for a ghost from the dead.

His sharp sense of hearing detected movement to his front; then a form appeared, walking upright, out of the darkness. But it was too tall for David! Wade tensed his muscles to strike. He waited until the figure was right over him; then he quietly whispered, "David?"

The figure above him stopped abruptly; Wade's poised muscles relaxed as the dark figure spoke the most beautiful words the former Colonel had ever heard: "Dad, is that you?"

Wade stood up and his son fell into his arms. They just held each other, not speaking, but patting each other on the back. Wade could feel the tears running down his cheeks; and a great weight lifted from him. He was too overcome with emotion to speak. Finally, the boy spoke: "I knew you would come some day!"

"Yes, son—I'm here; but I thought you were dead. If I would have had any idea that you were alive, I would have been here sooner."

Wade had not lost all of his senses; he realized that this was not the place to hold a family reunion. He pushed his son away and whispered, "Let's get out of here. Follow me."

* * *

Libby, Scotty and Luisa waited anxiously for the return of Wade and Jorge. Waiting for a man on a dangerous mission was new to Libby, and she paced the floor like a nervous cat. Occasionally she glanced at her watch, shook her head and paced faster.

Scotty looked up and said, "Libby, you're going to wear a hole in the floor."

"They should have been back long ago. It's almost daylight," she said irritably.

They heard a car drive into the yard. Libby threw caution to the wind and ran to the door. She opened it and flew outside. She caught Wade as he stepped from the car and embraced him, "Are you all right?" she asked.

Wade was pleasantly surprised by her concern and he hugged her back, murmuring in her ear, "I'm fine—everything is fine. Here, I want you to meet my son."

Libby turned to see a tall, thin handsome young man emerge from the car. The resemblance to his father was clear; but the boy had his mother's dark eyes and hair.

"Libby, this is David! David, Libby McGinnis."

Libby embraced David, smothering him. "I'm glad to meet you Ma'am, he said. She released him and stepped back as Scotty walked up.

"David, this is Robert Scott," said Wade.

Scotty and David shook hands. "I have heard a lot about you both from Dad," said David.

"Call me Scotty," offered the cameraman.

* * *

After a hearty breakfast of huevos fritos, poyo y raz (fried eggs, chicken and rice), David told them his story: When he regained consciousness the morning after the attack on his Grandfather's home, he found himself in the hospital, his head swathed in bandages. As it turned out, the boy only had a minor concussion. An official from the Ministry of Interior told him that rebel gangsters who were former Somoza National Guardsmen had killed his mother, grandfather and grandmother, and then set fire to the house. David had been saved by an alert fireman. David asked the official to contact his father in America, and the man promised to do so.

After he recovered, the boy was taken to a boys' camp several hundred miles from Managua. He repeatedly explained to camp leaders that he was an American; but they insisted that he was a Nicaraguan, therefore not eligible to be sent back to the States. They told him his father was notified but elected to leave the boy in Nicaragua. David knew they were lying. He wrote several letters to the US Embassy, asking them to get in touch with his father— but he never received an answer. His first year he was guarded very closely; then they eased off, apparently believing he was not going to try and escape.

He spent two years in the first camp, then was moved to the Francisco Moreno Special School near Managua. This school was reserved for boys with exceptional intelligence. Recently, David had been informed that he was going to be sent to the Isle of Youth, near Cuba. Since then, he had been planning to escape and join the Contra. He figured that would be the best way to get home. It was just over a year ago that he found out that it was the Sandinistas that killed his mother, grandfather and grandmother, not the Contra. He recognized a high ranking officer that visited the camp as the leader of the gang that attacked Enrique's home.

At this point, Wade put his hand on his son's arm and cut in. "David, do you know this officer's name?"

"Yes sir! He has been to the camp several times. He is a Commandante in the Office of Security. His name is Raul Castro Padilla!"

Libby caught her breath. Colonel Padilla was the officer who had questioned them at the Central Police Station. The cruel bastard who had promised to kill them! She looked over at Wade. His eyes had turned cold; but he did not show any emotion. But she knew that the boy had just pronounced a death sentence for Commandante Raul Castro Padilla. From now on, the Sandinista Colonel was living on borrowed time.

David continued: "I was never treated too badly. I figured the best thing to do was to go along with the program and wait for a chance to escape. I only got whipped twice but was restricted several times; that was for arguing with my teachers about America."

Wade was proud of his son. The boy had evidently not been taken in by the communist propaganda. But when he thought about Colonel Padilla, his heart grew cold. His first urge was to postpone the flight to Honduras; but he realized he had other responsibilities. His first priority was to get his son, Libby and Scotty to safety. Padilla could wait for a little longer—but he was dead! He glanced over at Libby; she was staring at him as if trying to read his thoughts. He put his hand on hers and applied pressure. The gesture of intimacy made them both feel good. Richard Wade was hopelessly in love with the beautiful newswoman. It was comfortable having her near.

"We are leaving tonight!" announced Wade to his charges. "The Honduran border is less than 100 miles as the crow flies and only a few hours by car on the Pan Am Highway. However, according to the underground, the Sandinistas have all the major roads and trails well covered. We would never get through by car, so we are going to have to take the difficult route and walk to Honduras."

He stopped talking and spread a National Geographic Map of Nicaragua on the table in front of them; with his finger, he traced their route to freedom: "Tonight, we will cross Lake Managua in a fishing boat; then we will move generally north paralleling the Pan Am Highway, passing near the towns of Jicaral, Rio Grande, Pueblo Nuevo, Condega, Somoto, and Ocotal. We'll cross the border here, south of El Parisio. It's only a few hours drive from there to Tegucigalpa. There will be some American friends who will meet us at the border. The FDN will furnish us guides from Lake Managua to the border; and Jorge's people will provide us with clothing, arms and equipment for the journey."

Wade turned to Libby and put his hand on hers. "I'm sorry we have to take the rough way out, but it's the only alternative we have now. Jorge told me that the Sandinistas have placed a price on your head. I don't tell you this to scare you—I will get you out!" His eyes told her he was speaking the truth.

He folded the map and stood up. "Now, I suggest we all try and get some sleep. We'll be leaving here just after dark."

David was too excited to sleep. He lay on the bed in what had been Wade's room and thought about better times ahead. Actually, he was happy now. He did not care where he was as long as he was with his father. Finally, he closed his eyes and slept the innocent sleep of a newly freed soul.

16 _____

Wade lay on the cramped couch with his eyes wide open. He was too excited to go to sleep; he was keyed to a nervous pitch. His son was alive, and his son was with him. He felt like he had been born anew. Then there was Libby. He was in love with the beautiful redhead, and he wanted her with every fibre of his being. When he kissed Libby the afternoon before, it awakened a fiery hunger in him. Every time he thought about her, and it was often, he broke out in a cold sweat.

He heard a noise and looked over to see Libby enter the room. She walked over and knelt by the couch; she leaned over and kissed him gently. "Don't you think you would be more comfortable in my bed?" she murmured. "I cannot sleep because my entire body is aching for you—I love you!"

A warm sensation flowed through him, and he reached up and pulled her across him. He wrapped his arms about her and crushed his hungry mouth to hers. An electric current arced between them and their passions welled. Libby ground herself against him as if she was trying to feel every part of him. She felt his hardness against her pubic mound and whimpered with the delightful sensation of it. She felt the hard strength of his lean, muscular body and a delicious warmth coursed through her. Wade moved his mouth to her ear and nibbled; then Libby heard those three magic words: "I LOVE YOU!"

Libby shivered with a delightful feeling that was new to her, and she spoke from her heart: "I love you—more than anything else in the world! And I want you to make love to me tonight—now! I cannot wait any longer!"

The spot between Libby's legs ached with hunger, ached for his touch. She was surprised at her own boldness but she could not help herself. She writhed against him, no longer in control; then she moaned, "Oh my Lord—I can't believe it!"

She surged strongly against him, driving him back into the couch; her hips moving faster, grinding herself against his hardness; her legs spread gripping his body; and her love, her tensions, and her need poured from her in a surprising climax.

She lay for a moment, her body trembling and her breathing uneven. She whispered in his ear, "I want you so much it hurts!" She pulled herself away from him and stood up, straightening her clothes. Then she reached down and took his hand. "Come with me!" she ordered.

They walked into her room, hand-in-hand. She closed the door behind them and slid the lock in place, then she stepped into his outstretched arms. They enfolded her and the two lovers embraced tenderly as their lips closed together. They stayed that way for a long time. Finally, she pushed away from him and stepped back and began unbuttoning her blouse. Her eyes never left his; they were bold, green and sensual. Wade watched hungrily as he started working on his own shirt. Libby was not wearing a bra and her perfect breasts sprang free and proud. For a moment, he stared at the beautiful white breasts, poised, waiting to be touched. Wade took one step forward and cupped them in his hands; while his lips sought hers. He ran his fingers over the hardness of her nipples, and Libby shut her eyes and enjoyed the wonderful sensations that ran through her burning body.

When she could not stand the need any longer, she stepped back and slipped out of her slacks. She placed her thumbs in the elastic band of her panties and wriggle them down to her ankles, and stepped free. Wade savored the magic moment, and desire poured through his veins. Libby was even more beautiful than he imagined. Her marblesque body was perfectly proportioned. Her long, sensuous legs reached up to a small patch of red hair. Her skin was almost flawless except for a few freckles here and there. The sight of her alluring nakedness sent a rushing current of power through him. He removed his trousers, and they stood naked together. Libby admired his lean muscular body. His stomach was flat and knotted with muscle. She reached out and tenderly ran her fingers over scars left by Achmed's cigarette burns.

"I know now what has been bothering me about you."

He looked at her puzzled and asked, "What?"

"Love! I've been in love with you all along and just would not admit it to myself. I think Scotty knew."

Wade took her by her hand and guided her to the bed. They lay down together, and he wrapped her in the warmth and strength of his arms. He slowly pushed her away and ran his hands over her breasts, and they became wonderfully alive to his touch. She reached down and touched him and it sent a blaze of desire through her body; matching the desire her touch sent through him.

Libby moaned aloud as she felt the spasms of orgasm begin again. Her body moved to his touch, finally, she lost control of her senses and was plunged into a world of total joy. Her legs straightened and her body shook, She covered his mouth with hers and her tongue searched deeply. Then she came in a glorious instant of ecstasy. But the moment was not over; Wade moved down between her legs and invaded her with his tongue. Her tender agony continued and she squirmed against him. Libby grasped the back of his head, holding him to the moment. His probing tongue was working magic, and her body was vibrating with pulsating electricity as her orgasms seemed to come one after another, like gigantic waves crashing on the shore. She finally cried out in sheer joy and ecstasy; then she went limp and lay in silence, not believeing what was happening to her.

Wade moved upward and hovered over her. He leaned down and kissed her gently. Their were tears of passion in her eyes, and her body trembled with a myriad of wonderful sensations. But she still had not had her fill of him. She wanted his strength to invade her totally. Libby's eyes widened and she gasped as she felt the initial joy of penetration. He moved slowly as she took more and more of him. She surged against him matching his increasing fury. She felt the raw power and strength of the man; and her emotions commenced to wind into another orgasm. Libby moaned with a sense of complete abandonment: "Oh now! It's now—My darling! Don't stop! Don't ever stop! OHHH!"

Wade's own passions were mounting, and her moving, writhing, body sent flashes of lightning through him. The two lovers came together in one gigantic wave of sensations that left them breathless and exhausted.

The new lovers lay together for a long time basking in the aftermath of their newfound passions. Their bodies were drenched with perspiration. Wade opened his eyes to find Libby looking at him. Both knew that this had been the best ever—the very best. They both spoke at the same time: She said, "You are magnificent!" He said, "You were fantastic!" Then they laughed together. "I have never, never, NEVER, met anyone like you! I've never felt like that before!" she murmured with joy in her eyes.

"And I have never met a woman like you!" he returned.

He finally disentangled himself from her and climbed out of bed. He grasped her hand and pulled her up; then he led her into the bathroom. They showered together under the tepid water. They kissed, and soaped, and hugged and touched one another. After awhile, they turned the shower off and, without drying, they tumbled into bed. Libby climbed on top and looked down at him. "I'm going to make love to you now!"

He began to move against her. "Relax!" she commanded, "I want to make love to you."

Wade closed his eyes and savored the pulsating tightness that engulfed him—and the troubled world went away. After awhile he opened them and looked at his love. Her eyes were closed, but there was joy on her face. His passions soared and he reached up and grabbed her arms and bent her backward. At the same time, he thrust upward. Small animal-like sounds came from her, and they moved violently together. The two lovers became lost together in the wonderful dimension of their sexual pleasure; and they soared upward, higher and higher to a peak of sexual climax.

Libby collapsed on top of him, whispering words of love and joy. She was crying now from sheer happpiness, and the muscles of her legs and abdomen quivered uncontrollably from the violent orgasm.

They lay like that for a long time, mutually secure and happy in each other's arms. Finally, they fell asleep to dream of love and the joys of one another. They had been joined together as a man and a woman should be—and their worlds would never be the same.

17 _____

When Libby awakened, she automatically reached out for Wade, but she found his spot empty. She lay there and stretched, feeling a warm glow course through her. She could not help but smile when she thought of him—the man she thought she hated but had found out that she really loved. She had arrived in Nicaragua, safe and secure in her own little world; then she was thrust abruptly into a world of pain, violence and death. She was shown a different Nicaragua, not unlike Nazi Germany in the late '30s; and finally she was brought into a new, wonderful world of love, passion and fantastic sex. She wondered if her liberal colleagues back in the States would understand—then she realized she did not care whether they did or not. She wrapped her arms around Wade's pillow and hugged it.

The door opened and Wade walked in. Libby had to look twice. His beard was gone, replaced by a black mustache, and his brown hair was black. Except for his gray eyes, he looked like a Latino. She stared at him with a puzzled look on her face.

He came over and sat down on the bed. Libby pulled him down over her. "I had a wonderful time last night," she confessed.

"So did I, beautiful lady—the best ever; and I love you!"

"I love you, too!"

Wade broke the news to her gently, by handing her a pair of scissors and a bottle of black hair dye.

"Oh no! Must I?"

"Yes. I'm sorry, but you must. That beautiful red hair of yours stands out like a beacon."

She climbed out of bed and moved into his arms. "Whatever the master desires," she purred.

"Did you sleep well?" he asked.

"The best sleep of my life," she answered.

"Me too!"

In a few minutes, red-haired Libby McGinnis had disappeared. In her place was a beautiful, curvaceous, green-eyed, raven-haired lady. She walked over to Wade who was lying on the bed and asked, "Wanna make love to a brunette?"

* * *

That evening they prepared for their journey. They all wore green Sandinista Army jungle fatigues rounded up by Jorge's people. Libby crammed her now short black hair up under a fatigue cap. Scotty and David carried AK-47 Kalishnikov assault rifles. Wade carried a short barreled 12 gage pump shotgun, his favorite weapon for night and thick jungle. Three fragmentation grenades hung on his shoulder harness; and a fighting knife was tucked in his left boot. A machete was strapped to his back.

Libby was startled to see young David carrying a weapon. Scotty spoke in his defense, "Hell Libby, he taught me today how to use this damn thing. But I think I still prefer the old M1 Garand."

David smiled. "I trained once a week with the militia; so I am very familiar with the AK-47."

Wade walked over and handed the female reporter the small Charter Arms 38 caliber revolver. "Here stick this in your waist band."

Libby held it in her hand and looked at it. "I don't know how to fire a gun. I don't think I could use it if I had to."

"Well let us hope you never have to—but I want you to carry this for you own protection," said Wade. Then he spent several minutes showing her how to load, aim and fire the small handgun.

They bid farewell to a tearful Luisa and jammed themselves in Jorge's Isuzu. There were tears in Libby's eyes, for she had become very close to Luisa. Jorge's wife was a charming lady who had captivated her new American friends. Her last words to Libby were "Your Colonel is a good man. He will take you to safety. Come back someday and visit us—in a free Nicaragua."

By the time they reached the small unnamed village on the lake, it had started raining, a slow steady drizzle. Wade was thankful, because they were less likely to run into a Sandinista patrol on such a miserable night. They were met by two silent men who did not introduce themselves. After bidding Jorge a quick goodbye, they loaded into a small wooden fishing boat. Libby and David crawled under a piece of heavy canvas, and she spent the next two hours getting acquainted with David. The boy was not afraid; he was excited about the adventure ahead; and he was full of questions about his father and what was going on in the United States.

They reached the other shore without incident, and quiet, eager hands helped them from the boat. Wade dug four already filled rucksacks from the boat and distributed them to the Americans. Libby noted with relief that hers was the smallest. They were joined by four men carrying weapons and packs. One introduced himself as Sergeant Pedro Gonzalez of the FDN, and the three men with him were members of his squad. He told them that his squad would escort them to the first rendezvous.

Without another word, the Contra moved off single-file into the darkness. The four Americans latched on. It was not long before the terrain abruptly changed, and they found themselves climbing a steep trail. It was difficult going because the rain had turned the ground into slick mud. Libby found herself on all fours as much as she was upright; and she often found herself climbing back up where she had just slid down. Whenever she fell, either Wade or David was by her side providing assistance. The rest stops became more frequent as the night wore on and the terrain became steeper. By dawn, Wade had one arm about her, helping her up the slick, steep slope. Shortly after sunup, they arrived at a deserted shack and they all staggered inside. Three of the Contra dropped their packs and headed back outside to provide security. Pedro, the leader, started a fire in the mud-brick fireplace and began cooking the basic diet of the Contra: frijoles negras (black beans and rice).

The newswoman was exhausted from the climb. Every fibre of her body ached. She had muscles hurting where she did not even know she had muscles. Scotty simply sagged back against one wall of the hut and moaned. The cameraman was well past fifty, but he had always considered himself in good shape for his age. However, at this moment he felt as if he were well past one hundred.

Wade addressed them all: "Take your boots and socks off and let your feet dry out. I'll give you some foot powder; there should be a change of socks in your packs."

The former Colonel strung a blanket he had taken from his pack across one corner of the hut; then he took Libby by the hand and pulled her behind the screen. I hope he doesn't want to make love, she thought.

"Take those wet clothes off and I'll dry them." He handed her a camouflaged blanket. "Wrap yourself in that."

While Libby was stripping off her soggy clothes, Wade checked the packs to see what Jorge had stuffed in them. There were changes of clothing for each American, extra socks, soap, toothbrushes, sacks of black beans and rice, a bottle of antibiotic capsules, several cans of meat and beans, camouflaged blankets, three fishnet jungle hammocks and extra ammo. His pack also contained three hand grenades. All the items were precious hard-to-come-by supplies for the underground. Wade vowed to pay Jorge back, with interest.

Libby walked out from behind the screen with the blanket draped around her and announced, "Where is a Holiday Inn when you need one?"

Wade took her clothes and draped them near the fire. The beans and rice tasted delicious to the hungry Americans. When they finished, Wade ushered Libby behind the screen. He removed a bottle of clear liquid from his pack, poured it on his hands, and began to massage her battered feet. Libby just lay back and enjoyed. Then he removed her blanket and massaged her body. Although totally exhausted, she thought his manipulations were delightfully sensual. "You sure know how to take good care of a lady!" she whispered. "We must do this again sometime when we are alone."

"We will!" he promised.

She smiled and fell asleep, feeling warm all over.

* * *

Libby woke up and checked her watch; it was 4 p.m. Her now dry clothes were laying beside her. She dressed and exited her screened area to find Pedro sitting by the fire drinking a cup of coffee. He poured some in a tin cup and offered it to her. The thick sweet coffee hit the spot. "Where is Colonel Wade?" she asked.

"He is on security. Did the Senora sleep well?"

"Yes, thank you. I feel almost human again."

Libby found out that Pedro was 27 years old and from Leon in Chinandega province. He and his wife Maria had three children. Pedro was condemned as a counterrevolutionary for objecting to food rationing, civilian repression, and state agriculture policies. "Just like most of us fighting in the FDN, I am a campesino," he said.

"I would prefer to live in peace and be left alone to farm my small piece of land. But the Sandinistas now tell you what you can and cannot grow on your land. As bad as he was, Somoza never did that. Before, you could sell what you grew to whomever you wanted and buy your supplies from whomever you wanted. Now, you must sell your corn and beans or whatever you grow to the State Agriculture Cooperative, at a very low price; and you can only buy sugar, salt, flour and other things from the state, at a very high price. The campesinos were hoping things would be better after Somoza. Instead they are worse."

The Sandinistas finally confiscated his small farm and arrested Pedro. He showed Libby the scars on his fingers where the finger-nails had been pulled out by the roots.

"We are fighting together for what we believe in; for a Nicaragua free of political indoctrination; for a democracy and a free country—like yours," said Pedro, proudly "We would rather die then let our children grow up in a Marxist, atheist Nicaragua!"

* * *

That evening, they ate another filling meal of black beans and rice before heading on up the mountain. By midnight, they had crossed over the top and were headed down the other side. Libby could not decide which was worse: falling up a mountain or falling down a mountain. It was clear night and the track was dry so the walking was easier. By morning, they had reached level ground and soon entered the thicker vegetation of the jungle. They continued until mid-morning before they stopped to rest and eat. After wolfing down her food, Libby wrapped herself in her poncho liner and soon fell asleep.

Libby was jostled from a deep sleep by Pedro. "Hurry Senorita! We must go quickly. A Sandinista patrol—she come!"

Within a few minutes, the Contra soldiers had moved their charges out on the trail and were shepherding them along quickly. Libby caught up with Sergeant Gonzalez. "Pedro, where is Colonel Wade?"

"El Colonel come soon—he go back to delay the piracuacas."

A few minutes later, the afternoon calm was shattered by an explosion followed by the chattering of small arms fire.Then there was silence. Pedro and his group continued on for two more hours, then halted for a long break. Pedro warned them not to get too comfortable, because they might have to move fast at any time.

It was here that Libby became acquainted with the youngest of the FDN squad. She was shocked to find that Julio Lopez was only twenty-one, yet he had been fighting since he was twelve. He hardly looked more than fifteen now. Julio Lopez Florian was from Ocotal, in northwest Nicaragua's Nueva Segovia province. He and his wife Xiomara have a 2½ year-old son. Julio joined the Sandinistas to fight against Somoza in 1976, when he was 12 years old. His brother had cooperated with the Sandinistas and was caught and tortured by the Guardia. Julio took part in several battles during the successful revolution. However, by December 1982, Julio began cooperating with the FDN. In the three years since the Sandinistas had seized power, Julio saw the piricuacos (mad dogs) increasingly lie to the people. They promised to have free elections and democracy. Instead, a friend of Julio's who worked for a radio station in Ocotal had his ribs broken by the Sandinistas for objecting to certain government programs. In March 1983, Father Ephraim Salcedo was saying mass in the church at Ciudad Antigua when a group of Sandinista soldiers marched in, called his sermon mierda (shit), and physically ripped off his vestments. Finally, Julio began secretly distributing Contra Literature and passing on information after a fellow Sandinista soldier bragged to him over a beer about an incident in Masatape on May 8, 1983. This soldier and his comrades shot seven women who refused to let their sons be drafted into the militia.

Soon after, Julio's brother Bartholomew—the one who had been tortured by Somoza's men for working with the Sandinistas—got into a public argument with a Sandinista officer. When Bartholomew criticized Marxism as anti-democratic and accused Sandinista rulers of not living up to their promises, the officer called him an antisocial reactionary, pulled out a revolver, and shot him dead. It was then that Julio fled to Honduras to join the fight with the Contra.

Wade joined them a few minutes later. He chatted briefly with the four Contra in Spanish, then sat down with his fellow Americans. "It was only a small patrol," he stated matter-of-factly.

Libby did not have to guess at the patrol's fate—she knew! Since leaving Jorge's, Wade had completed a reverse metamorphosis. He was again operating in the familiar violent world of his, where the survivors are tempered like steel and strong men learn to endure.

As they moved out again, Libby studied the man she loved. He moved through the jungle like a cat, while the rest of them, including the four Contra, sounded like a herd of elephants. He was at home; his every sense was attuned to the environment; and he was a deadly coiled spring ready to destroy anyone who got in their way. There was no doubt in her mind that Colonel Richard Wade would get them safely to Honduras. He might have to wipe out the entire Sandinista Army, but he would get them through. She felt safe and secure under his protection. She also noticed that he was clearly in command. The four Contra recognized Wade's unusual abilities almost immediately.

Young David was constantly by Libby's side, helping her whenever she needed it. Finally, against her protestations, he took her rucksack and slung it atop his own. The boy was made of steel like his father. He actually seemed to be enjoying their ordeal—as if it were a Sunday afternoon hike and picnic. His constant good spirits flagged hers.

During one of the stops, Scotty sat down by Libby and watched her looking at the two Wade's with admiration. "How does it feel to be in love with two men at the same time?"

She looked at him and smiled, "It feels fine! But you are wrong. I'm in love with three men!"

"You are some lady, Libby McGinnis! I'm very proud of you. I couldn't have picked a better partner. And we are going to wow them when we get back home."

"Indeed we are," she leaned over and kissed him on the cheek, "my very best friend!"

Scotty nodded his head in Wade's direction, "Do you think you can tame him?"

"I don't want him tamed—I like him just the way he is."

"Well, the only advice I can give you is don't try to change him."

"Why would I try to do that?" she asked.

134

"I know you, Libby. You are a very strong-willed woman. You are used to having things your own way; and I don't think you will with Wade. He's as strong-willed as you are. Just remember when two stones meet, they create sparks."

She laughed, "And those sparks often create fire!"

They stopped just before sunup and worked their way into the thick jungle at the side of the trail and set up camp. Wade decided against a fire, so they had to settle for cold meat and beans from a can. Wade strung a jungle hammock for Libby, and she was soon fast asleep.

Wade and David stayed awake and had a long father-son talk. "I'm very proud of you son; you are holding up well."

"I feel fine, Dad. I like it out here in the jungle."

"I have always felt at home in the jungle," returned his father. "The jungle will treat you well if you don't try to fight it."

David's next statement did not surprise his father. "I want to join the Contra and fight the Sandinistas."

"I understand David, but not yet. I want you to go back to the States and finish school. Then we'll see."

Wade changed the subject. "What do you think of Libby?"

"I think she's great!" answered his son. "Are you in love with her?"

"Yes, I am! Is that OK with you?"

"Yes, Dad! I think its fantastic."

"I never thought I could care for another woman again. Your mother was my one great love. I did not think there would be another—and I really did not want to find another. But I have! I'll always love your mother."

"I know that, Dad. I understand. It has been seven years."

Wade explained to David how he and Libby met. He talked about Rome, the Senate Hearings, the media stories and about his resigning from the Army. He discussed his mission to Nicaragua and how he happened to meet Libby and Scotty again.

"What about grandpa?" asked David. "Are you going to get him out?"

"Yes son. If he is still alive, I will get him out."

18

Robert Hunter looked across his desk at his friends: Tom Patterson, Director of the Civilian Military Assistance, and Rene Marcel, Hunter's Chief of Security, and announced, "I have just received a message from Jim (Jim Turpin, Deputy Director of CMA, who was in Honduras heading a CMA training team, working with the FDN). Colonel Wade is on his way out; and he has the ABN team and his son with him. The Sandinistas are throwing in everything they have to stop them; they don't want the news people to get out and tell their story to the world. 380 (code name for the FDN field comander) has dispatched two companies into Nicaragua to meet Wade and escort him and his party to safety.

"Miss McGinnis is a credible reporter, and she will able to do us a lot of good. The liberal press will have to tell her story. If we can get her to testify before Congress, it might be just the thing we need to get the Aid Bill passed."

"What can we do to help?" asked Patterson.

"I think everything possible is being done," answered Hunter, "but I do think we should fly to Honduras and be there when Wade and his party arrive. Besides, I would like to visit your new refugee camp."

CMA was in the process of establishing a refugee camp near the Nicaraguan border in Honduras. The camp which was only six weeks old had already swelled to over 4,000 refugees: people who had exercised their one remaining freedom in Nicargua—they voted with their feet— they walked out! Patterson's CMA volunteers ran the camp and a small medical clinic. Each month, CMA shipped over $50,000 worth of clothing and medical supplies to the refugee camp. The shipping bill was paid for by Robert Hunter, who also purchased some $3,000 worth of antibiotics and medical supplies each month. The camp staff consisted of CMA members, who worked for no pay. CMA had a long list of volunteer medics and doctors who where anxious to donate a few weeks of their time each year to help fight communism. Hunter considered the taking care of refugees and FDN families the highest priority, and perhaps the ultimate key to stemming the communist roll in Central America. From 1979 to 1986, over 300,000 Nicaraguans have fled their homeland. A simple comparison would be having 1 out of every 15 Americans leave the United States. Americans do not understand the desire for freedom the Nicaraguans have, because our freedom has never been taken from us. Unfortunately, if it ever is— Americans may not have a place to flee to!

MINISTRY OF INTERIOR BUILDING
MANAGUA, NICARAGUA

Commandante Raul Castro Padilla pounded his desk furiously and roared, "I cannot understand why they can't be found! They must be stopped! That woman must be killed!" He glared at his staff, menacingly, hoping to find some answer. But no one spoke up. They all knew that the Commandante had a propensity for over-reacting. The perplexed Padilla turned to his Intelligence Officer and lowered his voice. "Go over again for me the major incidents in the last 24 hours."

A short, swarthy officer stood up. "As I said earlier Sir, there have been only three: A small unit of Contra attacked an Army outpost at Bana. We suffered one casualty. Then Doctor Amador's ambulance was located on a secondary road, leading to Costa Rica. Because of that, we have been concentrating our forces along the Costa Rican border. And finally, we have a four man patrol missing north of Lake Managua in the vicinity of Monatombe."

Colonel Padilla stood up and walked over to a large map on the wall and studied it intently; then he began talking, more to himself than anyone in particular. "This American Colonel is a very clever man. Now what would I do if I were him?" He began tapping the map with a pencil, then it suddenly came to him: "That's it!" He turned and faced his staff and announced, "Finding the ambulance was too easy, because it was a ruse. They wanted us to find it. It's what the Americans call a 'red herring'! This Colonel Wade has a way of making people disappear—perhaps even a four man patrol." Padilla turned and began punching the map with his finger. "Here! Right here! Our American Colonel is walking out. He is going north over the mountains. He's heading straight north for the Contra lines. And he is smart, because he has chosen the most difficult terrain. I want everything we have to concentrate from Lake Managua, north to Ocotal and Somoto. I'll bet he is making for the Contra base camp near El Pariasio." Padilla walked over and stood in front of his Operations Officer. The man came to attention. "Jose," said the Commandante, "I want contigency plans for a special team to infiltrate Honduras and kill the woman if she gets across the border."

"Si, Commandante."

Padilla turned and addressed the group: "I am going to fly to Somoto to and take personal command of the search."

* * *

Wade awakened to the sound of helicopters sweeping the trail. He gathered up his party and moved deeper into the thick jungle. For the remainder of the day, helicopters and light airplanes flew low over the area looking for the Americans.

That evening, just before dark, Wade called the group together and announced, "We have to stay off the trails. We are going to move cross-country and it's going to be rough."

All that night, they hacked and picked their way through the almost impenetrable jungle. By daylight they had only traveled a few hundred yards. Wade called a halt and had a short meeting with Pedro and his men. He realized, at this rate, it would take weeks to reach friendly lines. Their food and bodies would give out long before they made it. According to Pedro, they were supposed to rendezvous with a larger Contra force the following morning. Wade made a difficult decision and announced it to his fellow Americans. "We simply cannot hack our way through this jungle. A few miles from here is a trail that will lead us to our rendezvous with an FDN unit. So we are going to move to that trail and follow it. It will be very risky, because I have a feeling the Sandinistas know approximately where we are and where we are headed—but I don't see that we have any other choice. When we get to the trail, I'll move on ahead and scout. One of Pedro's men will lag behind and provide rear security."

They moved out in the early afternoon and struck the trail just before dark. "Give me five minutes before you follow," whispered Wade and he disappeared up the trail.

The American soldier moved cat-like, his every nerve alert for danger. This was his element, and he knew he was a match for any man in it. Around 2300 hours his neck hairs alerted him—he knew he was not alone. It is a strange but true phenomenon that a man like Wade could feel the presence of danger. It was an instinct for survival that had saved his life many times. He silently dropped to the ground and crawled cautiously forward. He stopped and listened. Up ahead, a friend whispered to a friend. A cramped foot moved: a cramped body shifted to a more comfortable position. Wade pinpointed his targets: two men, one to the left side of the trail about 20 yards away, and the second, ten yards on further. His hand slid to his boot. He grasped the knife and moved it up to his mouth. He inched forward, slowly moving toward his victim—then he reached out. One hand covered the unwary soldier's mouth while the other plunged the knife into the man's throat. There was a muffled gurgle; and one foot kicked the soft earth; and the jungle floor drank the blood.

Then there was a whisper from the rear: "Que pasa, Daron?"

Wade rose to a low crouch and moved toward his second target. Too late, the soldier realized that the approaching figure was not his buddy, Daron. Instead it was death—quick, silent and permanent!

Wade moved on a few yards and heard voices off to the left side of the trail. He investigated cautiously. Approximately 30 yards off the trail, he found a camp of sleeping Sandinista soldiers. The camp was quiet except for an occasional snore or a body shifting in sleep. Two soldiers were awake and talking in low voices on the other side of the camp. Wade could not gage the size of the unit, but he estimated 30 to 40 men. He crawled back to the trail and headed back to meet his friends.

Libby was awakened from her walking stupor by the sight of Wade motioning to them. They gathered in closely and Wade whispered, "There is an enemy unit ahead, so be very quiet."

They waited until the rear security man caught up, then Wade led them out slowly. A few minutes later, Libby stumbled over something lying in the trail and fell forward. She rose to her hands and knees to stare in the open eyes of a man with his throat cut. The horrible sight was too much for her; she put her own hand over her mouth to stifle a scream—but it was too late, and the night quiet was broken by a muffled scream.

A voice called from the Sandinista camp, "Que pasa?"

Wade yelled to his party, "Go like hell for 500 yards then slow down and wait until I catch up. Go now!" Then he turned and charged toward the Sandinista camp yelling, "CONTRA! CONTRA!"

He figured surprise and confusion were his best allies now. He ran to the perimeter of the camp and laid his shotgun against a tree. He removed two hand grenades from his shoulder harness and pulled the pins. He tossed one to the right side of the bivouac area and the other to the left, trying to space them several yards apart. He hoped they would not bounce off a tree and come back at him. That was one problem with tossing grenades in the jungle. The camp was up and moving now, and men were milling about. As the two grenades exploded, Wade stood up and fired nine rounds of 12 gage buckshot into the confused mass of soldiers. There were more screams in the jungle now—screams of injured and dying men. Then the confused soldiers did just as he figured and hoped they would do. They began firing in all directions, including at each other. Wade turned and ran back to the trail. He stopped long enough to pick up one of the dead guard's AK-47 and ammo pouch. As he turned to run up the trail, he ran into a wide-eyed, disbelieving Contra soldier, who had remained behind to provide him cover. Wade grabbed him by the arm and turned him up the trail. "Come on amigo—let's vamoose!"

The firing continued for 5 minutes; and by that time, Wade had caught up with his friends.

"Who are they firing at?" asked Scotty.

"Each other!" answered Wade. He turned to Pedro. "They'll be following us soon. I'll stay behind and slow them up. You go on to the rendezvous."

Libby came over and took him by the arm. "Aren't you going with us?" she asked.

"You go on with Pedro. I won't be too far behind." He took her in his arms and whispered, "You have been magnificent the last few days. I'm sorry you had to go through all this."

"Finding you has been worth it," she returned. "And be careful. I don't want to lose you now."

David walked up and announced, "I'm going to stay with you, dad."

Wade put his hand on his son's arm. "Thanks David, but I want you to go wtih Pedro and take care of Libby. Will you do that for me?"

"Yes Sir," the boy agreed, reluctantly.

After the group departed, Wade knelt by the trail and opened his pack and removed two hand grenades. He hooked one on his harness; he straightened the safety pin on the other so that it could be easily pulled out. He removed a small roll of black tape from the pack and taped the grenade to a tree by the side of the trail. He took a coil of thin wire and tied one end to the safety pin and the other to a tree on the other side of the trail, making a trip wire about 5 inches above the ground. Satisfied with his body trap, he slung the pack over his shoulder and strode off up the trail. His burden was heavier now with the AK-47 and ammo pouch, but he knew that come daylight he would need the longer range of the assault rifle.

Ten minutes later, he heard the grenade explode and he smiled grimly. Let them come! Follow me and die! He was a man fighting for the only two people in the world he loved; but he was not the average man: he was a fighting machine and an expert killer of his fellow man; and he knew more Sandinistas were going to die this night.

Up ahead, Libby was almost out of steam. Scotty and David each had a hold of one of her arms, dragging her along. She was not only worn out physically; she was ashamed and embarrassed because she gave them away on the trail. When she saw Wade charging toward the enemy camp, she thought he had gone crazy. Then all hell broke loose. She could not visualize what had gone on back there.

Pedro finally called a short break, and Libby collapsed to the ground. The four Contra huddled together and began talking about her Colonel. She could not speak fluent Spanish, but she knew enough to understand what they were saying. With obvious respect, they called him a man of death—a killing machine. The young one,

Julio, who had stayed behind, said that Wade had attacked and destroyed an entire Sandinista platoon.

Every muscle in Libby's body cried for relief. She shivered with total exhaustion. She looked over at Scotty, who was about in the same condition and said weakly, "If I get out of this alive, I'll never go camping again."

The situation was so ridiculous that they all had to laugh at her statement. Then a muffled explosion to their rear wiped the smiles off their faces. Scotty shook his head and addressed David: "I sure as hell wouldn't want to be chasing your father through this jungle at night. I almost feel sorry for those soldiers back there."

* * *

The former Commander of the Delta Force knelt by the side of the trail and waited. His friends should be nearing the rendezvous area; so he had to hold the Sandinistas that were dogging his trail. He knew that when daylight arrived, the helicopters would be out in force. He heard his pursuers coming; he waited until the point man was a dead target and squeezed off one round. The man clutched his chest as he pitched backwards. The soldiers behind him opened up and sprayed the jungle. Wade sprinted away, lugging the rucksack over one shoulder. He moved about 200 yards and stopped to take up another delay position. Just before daylight, heaven blessed them and it began to rain. As it grew light, heavy dark clouds roiled low over the jungle. At least they did not have to worry about choppers for awhile.

Wade uncoiled some more wire and tied it about waist high across the trail—but he did not rig it with a grenade. Instead, he tied part of his scarf to it, in plain sight. Then, he backed into the bush about 10 yards and waited. The point man spotted the wire and the scarf fragment just before he reached it and froze. He turned and signalled to the men behind him. Two men came forward and warily began searching for the grenade they believed attached to the trip wire; the main body stayed back about 30 yards. Wade pulled the pin from a grenade. He allowed the handle to fly off and counted to three; then he tossed the grenade at the feet of the soldiers saying, "Here it is—catch!"

There was a mad scramble; but it was too late and all three soldiers were cut down by the blast. Wade fired a full 30 round magazine into the force behind, scattering them in all directions.

But these were well-trained soldiers. They recovered quickly and automatic fire began chopping the trees around him. A machine gun opened up and found his range. Bullets zipped past like angry hornets; and they cracked as they broke the air about him. Something hit him in the left thigh and spun him to the ground. At first his leg was numb, then a burning throbbing pain began. He looked down to see dark red blood bubbling out of his leg. He cursed himself for staying in the area an instant too long—he should have known better. He lay there trying to regain his senses. He heard movement and realized they were closing in on him. He grabbed his one remaining grenade and pulled the pin. He tossed it out on the trail, and when the grenade exploded he rose to his feet and tried to run. He only got a few yards before he fell sprawling on his face. This was as far as he could go; he would have to make his stand here. He removed his scarf from his neck and cinched it tight around his upper thigh. He inserted a new magazine in the AK-47 and prepared to meet his enemy.

* * *

Pedro finally called a halt at a point where two trails crossed. "This is the rendezvous," he announced. "We wait; our friends will come soon."

They waited there as the sounds of Wade's battle increased. David stood up and said, "I'm going back and help Dad."

Scotty stopped him. "No! You stay here with Libby; I'll go back."

Pedro had already dispatched one of his men on ahead to meet the Contra unit. He walked over to where Scotty and David stood. "Julio will go with you." He motioned for the young Contra and issued some orders in Spanish. Julio took off back down the trail towards Wade's firefight, with Scotty puffing along behind.

They had only been gone a few minutes when a line of camouflaged soldiers came streaming into their position. The leader talked briefly with Pedro, and then he sent a group of men toward Wade's position. Libby noted that the leader of the Contra unit had his left arm missing.

He walked over to her and in perfect English introduced himself as Commandante 36. "We are happy you are safe, Miss McGinnis. My Commander, Enrique Jiron, sends his compliments."

Libby was shivering from the cold rain. Commandante 36 removed his field jacket and draped it over her shoulders and smiled:

"The rain is good—it keeps away the Russian helicopters."

The firing increased as the Contra joined the battle; then it stopped and the jungle returned to silence. A few minutes later, a tired-looking Robert Scott returned with several Contra, carrying a make-shift stretcher. Libby sensed who was in the stretcher, and she ran over. Richard Wade lay there with his eyes closed. "Oh no!" she gasped. She reached and stroked his face, fearing the worst.

Wade opened his eyes and smiled weakly. "Wipe that worried frown off your face. I'm only a little bit shot."

A Contra medic bent over Wade and started working. The bullet had entered the fleshy part of the thigh and passed through without breaking any bones. The bullet had evidently been armor piercing, because the exit wound was not much larger than the entrance wound.

Commandante 36 left one platoon behind as rear security and moved the rest out. A short while later, Sandinista artillery began crashing into the jungle behind them.

19

The Contra column force-marched for two hours before turning off the main trail onto a small, almost imperceptible path. By midday, the rain stopped and the clouds rolled away, to be replaced by Sandinista helicopters and airplanes. The feared Russian M-24 Hind helicopters began pounding the main trail with rockets. At times the battleships of the sky commenced their firing runs almost over the heads of the Contra unit.

"We cannot fight the Russian helicopters," explained Commandante 36. "When they come we have to run and hide like scared rabbits."

"What about portable ground-to-air missiles like the redeye or stinger?" asked Scotty.

Commandante 36 laughed sarcastically, "And where would we get them, Mr. Scott? Your own Congress voted against giving us money or defensive weapons. We don't have enough money to buy them on the international market—they are very expensive. A few months ago, we carried four Russian Sam 5's (shoulder fired ground-to-air missiles) into Nicaragua with us. One day we were attacked by three Hind helicopters. We stayed and fought. Three of the four missiles would not fire, and I lost eight men. The fourth fired properly, and we shot down one Hind. Incidentally, there were two Cuban pilots flying the chopper; we found their bodies and identification." The Commandante's eyes turned sad. "I have lost many good men to the Russian helicopters. If we only had a few good missiles, we could defend ourselves. We must have them before we can start a general offensive."

Libby became a moving nurse. She forgot her exhaustion and sore muscles and looked after Wade like a trained Florence Nightingale. She and David never left the former Colonel's side.

* * *

It was not a general offensive, but things were suddenly active throughout Nicaragua. Fearing that the Sandinistas would marshall their forces in order to stop Wade and the ABN news team from reaching safety, Enrique Jiron, the FDN Field Commander in Honduras, radioed his subordinate commanders in Nicaragua and ordered them to step up operations, with special emphasis on attacking isolated military outposts and military convoys. He also sent three companies across the border to attack Sandinista units around Jalapa and Somota. He hoped this stepped up activity by his forces might relieve some of the pressure on Commandante 36.

* * *

The rescue column moved through the rugged hills and thick jungle for two days; and on the third, several horses miraculously appeared. The American's feet received a much needed rest. Wade was relieved, especially for the FDN soldiers who had taken turns carrying his stretcher. He could not straddle his horse, so they tied him on side-saddle. David refused to ride, saying he wanted to walk with the soldiers. Wade admired that; if he had not been wounded he would have walked with the troops.

The Contra soldiers impressed Wade. They were a mixture of Campesinos, Miskito and Misura Indians and a few former students. The only professional soldier in the company was Commandante 36. He had been a sergeant in the National Guard before the revolution. The ages of the Contra ran from 16 to 45—and they were all in excellent physical condition. They practiced outstanding light and noise discipline; and he especially noted that they took good care of their weapons. Most of them carried AK-47s, because this

146

weapon was easy to purchase on the international gun market at a fairly cheap price. However, a few still carried old German Mausers and US Carbines. The thing that impressed him most about the Contra was their dedication to the war against the Sandinistas.

* * *

FDN HQS
CAMP LAS VEGAS, SOMEWHERE IN HONDURAS

Libby and David sat outside her hut and watched the FDN recruits marching on the parade ground below. The Americans had been at Las Vegas for five days and were scheduled to depart for the United States the following day. When they arrived at the Contra camp they had been greeted by the FDN field Commander, Enrique Jiron, and four Americans: Robert Hunter, Tom Patterson, Jim Turpin and Rene Marcel. Libby and Scotty were treated as heroes by the Contra. Scotty reveled in his new found fame, but Libby was still a little wary.

Wade had become an overnight legend for his actions in Nicaragua. The escape from Managua and the running jungle battle was a major victory for the FDN. The former American Colonel was taken to the small FDN field hospital, which was poor by American standards; but it was clean and the doctor and nurses seemed quite capable, although overworked and understaffed. Libby was surprised to see three American medics working in the hospital. She found out that all were former Army medics and were full-time paramedics in the States. They were not receiving any pay for their services. All three were members of Tom Patterson's Civilian Military Assistance Group.

Libby's accomodations were spartan; but they were a major improvement over the preceding week. And compared to the way the Contra soldiers lived, they were palatial. In fact she was living in the VIP Quarters. VIP or not, she had to share the same basic food fare as the Contra—black beans and rice.

Libby and Scotty were surprised by a special gift from Robert Hunter: a video camera! "Just in case they wanted to do a story on the FDN."

The ABN News team set to work immediately. Enrique assigned an unforgettable character as their guide and interpreter. Pecos Bill was aptly nicknamed, with his drooping mustache, cowboy hat and affinity for horses. Pecos was a graduate of Texas A&M and served a stint in the US Marine Corps. His father owned a cattle ranch in Nicaragua, before it was confiscated by the Sandinistas. So Pecos Bill not only looked and acted like a cowboy—he was one. The Freedom-Fighter had a seven year old daughter in Miami that he had not seen for six years. When the Sandinistas took over Pecos Bill's ranch, his father protested and was thrown in jail as a counter-revolutionary. He died from mistreatment. Pecos himself was arrested and beaten by the Sandinistas but escaped before he was sentenced.

Many of the FDN soldiers that Libby interviewed were mere children, who should have been in school or playing with toys rather than guns: Antonio was a small, young boy not much bigger than the AK-47 he carried. Antonio was 13 years old. In 1983, his mother complained about food shortages and said in public that the Sandinistas were ruining the economy. In response, Sandinista soldiers broke into their home. One soldier shot Antonio's baby brother in the shoulder, while another stepped on the baby's right hand, breaking it. They threatened to kill Antonio's mother and her entire family if she made any more "reactionary" complaints. Antonio's father went into hiding while the rest of his family fled to Honduras. His father had recently joined them; and now, father and son were fighting with the Contra.

Another Contra she talked with had been a student in a high school in Managua. He and a group of his fellow students protested the Marxist rhetoric being taught by the Cuban teachers in their school. The Sandinistas broke up their meeting, beat them up and killed two of their leaders. The young students, fearing that he would be next, contacted the FDN who helped him escape.

Most of the soldiers she interviewed had similiar stories: "San-dinista soldiers arrested my father because he spoke against the government—I never saw him again." "They tortured my father because I did not report to the Army." "They killed my father." "They took away our land." "I was arrested and tortured." "They poured sand in my father's eyes." "I ran away from the draft." "If I have to fight, I would rather fight the Sandinistas." "The Sandinistas have betrayed our revolution." "Things are worse now than under Samoza."

Libby met Simba, 26 year old leader of the Creoles (Nicaraguan Blacks) and was surprised to find that the first group of people to take up arms against the Sandinistas were the Nicaraguan Blacks.

What was the reason? Racial persecution!

She talked to a group of Miskito and Misura Indians who related stories of rape, torture and murder that made her blood run cold![1] Thousands of these Indians were rounded up and forced to march to "relocation camps." Not only were their homes and lands taken from them but so was their way of life. Libby wondered how this massive relocation, bombing of villages, and mass genocide escaped being covered by the American Press. One leader of the Miskito Indians said he had sent a letter to Jesse Jackson with a list of 250 names of people who had been taken by the Sandinistas and simply vanished from the earth. The Indian leader had some harsh words about Jackson, because the American politican never even bothered to answer the letter.

When she asked about the Jews in Nicaragua, she was told that they had all been driven out; and the Synagogue in Managua was now a social club for high ranking Sandinista officers and their families. "The PLO and Libya are close friends and allies of the Sandinistas, you know!"

Enrique Jiron, the popular, charismatic, FDN Field Commander, was a well educated Nicaraguan from a wealthy family. He was a Colonel in the National Guard and attended college and the US Army Command and General Staff College in the United States. During the last years of the Somoza regime, Enrique was the Nicaraguan Military Attache in Washington, exiled there by Somoza for trying to start reforms in the Guardia. After the revolution, he was not arrested by the Sandinistas, because even they agreed that he was an honorable soldier and did not participate in any of the excesses of the Somoza government. Because of his popularity in Nicaragua, the Sandinistas tried to entice him into their fold. However, Enrique was a fervent anti-communist; and he fled the country when he realized the new government was under the control of a small group of dedicated Marxist-Leninists. Trained as an engineer, Jiron was rapidly becoming a guerrilla warfare expert.

"We are fighting for freedom and democracy in Nicaragua," Jiron told her. "The US exported more to our nation than plastiques, chemicals and manufactured materials. You also exported freedom and democracy. We would like to see a Nicaragua free from communism, without outside influence; a western style democracy— like the United States. Our primary tactic is to harass and wear down the Sandinistas. But every time the US Congress hesitates on aid, it makes the Sandinistas believe they can wait us out; time is on their side.

"We do not want American troops fighting in Nicaragua; we want to fight our own war—but we do need help in the form of weapons, ammunition, and supplies, However, you should never doubt that this is your war; because the ultimate objective of the communists is to defeat the last bastion of democracy—the United States of America. If you do not help us with guns and materials now, Americans will pay with blood later. My men realize that they are not only fighting for Nicaragua; they are fighting for America. Don't forget, we are all Americans: North Americans, Central Americans, and South Americans.

"If you think you have an illegal alien problem now, wait until Mexico falls to the communists. Mexico has the largest communist party in Central America and is a nation with major political and economic problems. It could easily succumb to communism. If it does, your country will be flooded with illegal refugees, and many of them will be trained terrorists and drug smugglers."

Enrique paused, then continued, "We know that the communists are heavily involved in drug traffic in the US. Castro is involved; Borge is involved; and Russia is involved. Not only is the US helping to pay for the communist revolution, but the drugs are weakening the moral fiber of your nation. Americans better wake up to the communist menace in Central America before it is too late. Tell your people, they should help us now or they might have to fight alone later."

Libby could see that the Civilian Military Assistance Group enjoyed a close relationship with the FDN. Over the last three years, the US based group, financially backed by Robert Hunter and headed by Tom Patterson and Jim Turpin, had provided medics, trainers, technicians, and over $7 million worth of material aid. The FDN went through some dark days when the US stopped aiding them in 1984. At one time, they did not have the money to feed their men, let alone buy arms and ammunition. Hunter gave them a check for $25,000. A convoy was dispatched to Tegucigalpa and brought back several truckloads of food. You can buy a lot of black beans and rice with $25,000.

CMA kept 10 to 20 volunteers in the field with the FDN. They did not participate in combat operations; they were medics, doctors and trainers in communications, small arms, weapons repair, mechanics, aerial delivery, etc. The CMA people with the FDN did not receive any pay; the organization tried to pay their

150

transportation to Central America and give them $50 a month to buy food, but this was not guaranteed. Patterson told Libby that they had more volunteers wanting to come and help the FDN than they could financially support. CMA's members in the States collected supplies, clothing, foodstuffs, and money and provided information and education programs for the American public. CMA printed a bimonthly newsletter that went out to over 10,000 people, including the members of Congress.

Robert Hunter was a unique individual. He was obviously wealthy and a major supporter of both the FDN and CMA. Hunter was a handsome man in his late thirties who exuded the same quiet confidence and capabilities that Wade demonstrated. In many respects the two men were much alike. The Memphian understood the area and the growing communist problem in Central America. He was not a raving, "Let's kill a commie!", conservative. He was an intelligent, well-informed conservative who acted on his convictions rather than simply talking about them.

Libby asked him why a wealthy businessman, who could afford all of the pleasures of life, was involved in this dirty little war in Central America. His answer was short and to the point. "I want to help stop the spread of communism in Central America."

Hunter explained that during his travels he had seen what communism is doing to nations like Angola, Mozambique, Cambodia, Afghanistan and Ethiopia and the havoc the Communist sponsored wars of liberation are causing in Central America.

"I just want to do everything in my power to stop the communists before they get to our borders," he said. "and if you don't believe they are coming—then ask them!"

He continued: "The Contras are not reactionary 'Somocistas'; they represent a genuine peasant rebellion against a totalitarian regime of Marxist fascism that is similar to the crazed fanaticism of China's Cultural Revolution. And I have a genuine affection and admiration for the men and women in the Contra who are risking their lives—voluntarily and without pay—to fight against Soviet-Cuban imperialism and for the freedom of their homeland. And we Americans should not view Central America with tunnel vision. There are eight anti-Soviet guerrilla wars being conducted in the world today. In Nicaragua, Angola, Mozambique, Ethiopia, Afghanistan, Laos, Cambodia, and Vietnam, there are thousands of men and women who have joined liberation movements to fight the Marxist governments that are chaining their countries. The opportunity is there now for the United States to support these movements and stop communist expansion in its tracks. And, why not? Russia has supported the communist guerrillas throughout the world for years."

Hunter believed that Nicaragua was the key in Central America. He explained that if the communists succeeded in consolidating their base in Nicaragua, they would then be able to continue to export their revolution throughout Central America; and ultimately we would have a communist nation on our border. "Mexico is a ripe prospect for the false promises of communism," he said.

* * *

Libby's thoughts were interrupted by the figure of Richard Wade hobbling up the hill on crutches. He sat down beside her and took her hand in his. "Well, you will soon be back in the land of K-Mart and Taco Bell."

"Yes," she answered, "an experience like this sure makes one appreciate the good old USA. However, I must admit," she winked at Wade, "it certainly had its good moments."

"Yes," he agreed, "it sure did. By the way, in a few weeks David and I are going down to the Cayman Islands. Why don't you come with us?"

"Oh, I don't know. You two need to be alone for awhile to get reacquainted; and I have a lot of things I have to do."

"Come with us, Libby," echoed David.

Wade looked at her with a soft smile on his face and said softly, "Libby I love you! You are a part of my life now—an important part. I—We want you to come with us."

Libby felt a warmth flow through her. She really did not want to be apart from Wade for one moment. His admission of his love in front of his son touched her deeply. He had seemed so distant the last few days that she feared she had lost him. She smiled and kissed him on the cheek, "Of course, I'll come—I love you too!" Then she kissed David on the cheek, "Both of you!"

A few minutes later, an astute David excused himself and went to his tent. Libby looked at her love and said, "Do you want to come inside? I want you to make love to me!"

"Yes—I want to; but I'm afraid I won't be worth much with this

game leg."
She stood up grasped his hand, and pulled him to his feet and whispered, "We'll improvise!"

Note 1. "In several villages I talked to people who had witnessed the arbitrary killing of Miskito civilians by Sandinista military forces. Many of these killings occurred during one of several Sandinista military invasions and occupations of Indian villages. Some of the villagers were arbitrarily shot when the government soldiers first invaded the villages; others were killed during the weeks of occupation, confinement, torture and interrogation. For example, it was reported to me by several different firsthand sources that one man was nailed through his hands and ankles to a wall and told he would remain there until he either confessed to being a "Contra" or died. He died. His widow, dressed in black, and others in that traumatized village are filled with grief and anger over this and other atrocities committed during their forced confinement under a reign of terror by several hundred Sandinista soldiers. Other Miskito were killed by forcing their heads under water to extract confessions of 'counterrevolutionary' activities. Two older men, 60 and 63 years of age, were threatened with death unless they confessed to involvement with 'Contras'. They, too, were finally killed in the course of these same events. "Throughout my notes and tape recordings are descriptions of such killings in village after village in the Atlantic Coast Indian Region. Descriptions were given to me by wives, daughters, mothers, and other relatives and villagers. The occurrence of arbitrary killings of Miskito civilians appears to be widespread. A pattern is readily seen. Miskito men and women are accused of being Contras, tortured or threatened with death unless they confess, killed, and then reported as having been Contras, if, indeed there is any report at all."

Statement by Professor Bernard
Nietschmann to the Indian Law
Resource Center, October 3, 1983

153

20

Several miles away from Camp Las Vegas, in a secluded hut, Lieutenant Alvaro Baldizon and his five-man special unit waited for their "contact" to report. Baldizon and his men were wearing Honduran Army uniforms—but they were not Honduran soldiers. They were a special Sandinista attack squad who were in Nicaragua on a "killing" mission.

Lt. Baldizon's "contact" was a Nicaraguan, loyal to the Sandinistas, who had infiltrated the Contra several months ago. In the espionage vernacular, he was known as a "mole" or an agent planted in the enemy fold with orders not to surface until called upon. Baldizon, himself, had sneaked into the Contra camp several nights ago to contact the spy.

The Lieutenant owed his loyalty to Commandante Raul Castro Padilla. The young officer had received his special training in Cuba and Libya and was well suited for his mission in Honduras. Baldizon and his squad crossed the border into Honduras two nights before Wade and his party reached freedom. His orders were to assassinate Libby McGinnis, if she made it to FDN headquarters. His primary plan was to use the Contact. He had instructed the Contact to kill the female reporter as she slept.

The Lt. heard a noise outside the hut and looked up to see the Contact walk in. "Did you kill her?" he asked.

"No!" returned the man. "I could not get near her because of the heavy security. And tonight, she sleeps with a man. She is leaving for Tegus tomorrow morning."

"Damn!" puffed Baldizon. "That's disappointing!" However, he had planned for this. "We will have to go with our alternate plan." He stood up and looked at the Contact. "You return to the rebel camp and revert to your role. We will no longer need you on this operation."

* * *

They loaded into three open jeeps for the six hour ride to Tegucigalpa. Hunter, Pecos Bill and a driver were in the first; Libby, David, Wade and a driver in the second; and Patterson, Scotty, two guards and driver in the third. They did not expect any trouble because the Honduran army patrolled the road between Las Vegas and the capitol. Nevertheless, they carried AK-47s loaned to them by Enrique Jiron. They had hoped to fly to Tegus by helicopter; however the "Lady Ellen," the FDN's one and only helicopter, was down with maintenance problems. Rene Marcel had gone ahead to Tegus to make arrangements for the flight home.

* * *

Lieutenant Alvaro Baldizon stood by the cab of the "borrowed" Honduran Army truck which blocked the narrow dirt road, as one of his men peered into the engine compartment as if he were trying to make repairs. The Lieutenent's other men were close by: two in the bushes by the side of the road and two in the back of the truck. One man by the side of the road carried an RPG-40 grenade launcher; the others were armed with AK-47 assault rifles. The man with the grenade launcher was to pick out the vehicle with the American woman inside and destroy it. Baldizon sighted the three jeeps coming and signalled to his men.

* * *

The driver of the lead jeep spotted the Honduran truck stalled on the road and stopped. He climbed out of the jeep and walked

155

unsuspectingly toward the Hondo soldiers. The other two jeeps stopped behind.

Hunter climbed out of the jeep to stretch his legs. A sudden movement in the bushes to the side of the road caught his eye, and he instinctively yelled, "AMBUSH!"

Wade was just starting to climb out of his jeep when Hunter gave the alarm. He immediately reached in and grabbed Libby by the hand and dragged her out. David came tumbling after her—just as a hail of automatic weapons fire raked the vehicle. The unfortunate driver slumped forward against the steering wheel, and the blast of the jeep horn joined the rising crescendo of gunfire.

Hunter was already swinging into action. Lt. Baldizon leveled his AK-47, but Hunter was faster. His first burst caught the Lieutenant in the chest and drove him back crashing against the truck. He bounced off and dove face-down on the dirt road. Baldizon's mission of murder was over for him.

Wade pushed Libby and David down into the ditch by the road— just as an RPG rocket smashed into their jeep, blowing it to smithereens.

The driver of the lead jeep turned and tried to make it back to the vehicle and his weapon; but he was cut down by fire from the Hondo truck. Hunter moved quickly. He dove for the ditch to the right of the road. He landed hard and rolled up to a fighting position. His second burst killed the soldier who had been leaning into the engine compartment.

Wade came into action, comcentrating his fire into the bushes on the opposite side of the road. One man stood up, screamed and pitched forward across a rock.

Pecos Bill was out of the lead vehicle and kneeling by the jeep. He began concentrating his fire on the Hondo truck. Patterson and the Contra guards were out of their vehicle and firing into the thickets on both sides of the road.

The dirt kicked up in front of Hunter's face as he began receiving fire from the Hondo Army truck. He raised up and, on full automatic, fired the remainder of his thirty round magazine. The combined firepower of Pecos Bill and Hunter commenced to disintegrate the truck. Hunter ducked back into the ditch and ran forward, reloading as he moved. He was soon behind the truck. He raised up firing. His burst caught the remaining ambusher in the side. The man danced about in the bed of the truck like a puppet on a string. The dying soldier spun and danced off the truck.

He landed hard and kicked his life away in the dirt. As the firing stopped, Hunter spotted the other man lying in the back ot the truck.

It was suddenly echoingly quiet, and everyone just stood looking around as the Contra guards began a quick search of the area. If there were other ambushers, they had fled the scene. The Sandinistas' last chance at Libby McGinnis had failed.

Wade walked up to where Hunter was surveying his carnage. Wade, the professional warrior, looked at the businessman with obvious respect. Hunter had sensed the ambush, given the alert, and fought like a demon. If it had not been for Hunter's quick actions, Libby and David would be dead—blown to oblivion by a Russian rocket. Wade had one more reason to settle the score with Commandant Raul Padilla. He patted Hunter on the back and said, "Good show! You saved our ass! I owe you a big one!"

Libby watched the two strong men shake hands; and she knew that Robert Hunter had a friend for life. Scotty walked up behind her and put his arm around her shoulders. "Are you all right?"

Libby, who was standing with her arm around David, nodded. "Yes—but I'm ready to go home. I have had enough excitement for my next two lives."

About this time, a Honduran Army convoy arrived on the scene in a cloud of dust. They searched the bodies of the dead ambushers, but were unable to identify them. The Hondos then gave them a military escort to Tegucigalpa and they arrived without further incident.

* * *

Thirty minutes after the Americans checked into the Maya Hotel, Commadante Raul Castro Padilla was informed. He immediately picked up the phone and broke the bad news to Nicargua's Minister of Interior, Tomas Borge. Borge contacted his Chief of Propaganda and within minutes the government of Nicaragua released its first official story concerning Libby McGinnis and Robert Scott— "wanted criminals!"

* * *

Wade found a message waiting for him at the desk at the Maya hotel. He waited until he was alone to read it:
"I AM IN ROOM 208." HOWARD

Howard was the code mane for Wade's CIA contact in Miami. He was the man who gave the former Delta Force Commander, code named Barracuda, his "Special Assignments."

Wade went straight up to 208 and knocked on the door. Howard let him in and shook his hand. "Well Colonel, you have been a very busy man. Why didn't you notify me of your plans? We might have been able to assist you."

Wade looked at his contact, with a hard glint in his gray eyes. "I told you people long ago that I am an independent operator. The mission in Nicaragua was a private one."

Howard smiled. "I understand you found your son. I'm happy for you. Actually, we are very pleased with what you did down there. First, we're happy you got rid of Doctor Death; now if Congress will only listen to Miss McGinnis, maybe we can get the Contra Aid Bill passed."

"Did you know about Amador and what he did?"

"Yes," answered Howard, "we have known about the Snake Doctor for several years. He was a real evil bastard. Did some horrible things in Angola. Killed one of our top agents last year. We want to pay you for him."

"No! Killing the doctor was my pleasure. My personal pleasure." Wade changed the subject. "There is a favor that you people can do for me. See if you can locate Enrique Salazaar."

"Your father-in-law?"

"Yes."

"We heard rumors several months ago that he might still be alive; and we have tried to locate him—but so far no luck. I can try to put some more emphasis on it."

"By the way," interjected Wade, "is Robert Hunter one of your people?"

"No, but he has some contacts at the highest level. That's about all I know about him."

Howard walked over to his dresser and poured two glasses of vodka, then dropped in a few ice cubes. He handed Wade one of the glasses. "By the way, Richard, you have to keep your name out of the papers on this one. You know, national security and all that stuff, especially if you plan on going back into Nicaragua."

"I don't know if it can be done. Libby McGinnis is a pretty independent lady."

"Well old buddy, we'll have to give it a try. Anyway, we are glad that you are alive—and that you found your son. Do you plan on working with the Contra again?'

"I might—any objections?"

"No! Not at all. In fact we could discuss a salary."

"No! No way. I don't want any pay. Right now this is a personal matter."

"OK," returned Howard, "have it your own way. Now, how about giving me a quick rundown on what happened down there."

"Howard" was more than satisfied when Wade left. The former Army Colonel was doing exactly what the Agency wanted. However, it would have been nice to have Wade on the payroll. Much easier to pull the strings that way.

A few minutes later, "Howard" knocked on Libby's door. When she opened it, he introduced himself as James Harbone from the US State Department. He showed her his credentials as proof. She invited him in.

Howard took her hand and said in a most dignified voice, "Miss McGinnis, we are very pleased that you are safely out of Nicaragua. Mr. Wade explained a little of what you have been through. That must have been a horrible experience."

"Thank you, Mr. Harbone. I appreciate your concern."

"Miss McGinnis, I would like to talk to you concerning a matter of utmost national security." He paused to let his words sink home, then continued, "The story of what happened to you in Nicaragua and what you saw and learned about the government there is very important and must be told to the American people—and the world. It's especially critical at this time when Congress is considering aid to the Contra. And coming from someone of your stature and credibility, it will have a major impact on public opinion and the Congress. However, we are going to ask you not to mention Colonel Wade."

So that was it, thought Libby. The real purpose of the State Department man was to get her to keep quiet about Richard. Another thought occured to her: Wade has been lying about his mission to Nicaragua. She spoke back with a slight hostility in her voice, "And may I ask why you don't want me to mention Colonel Wade?"

"Well, Miss McGinnis, I cannot go into details of course; but the Colonel has done some rather sensitive work for the government, and we prefer to keep him as anonymous as possible. I assure you, it is very important that you not talk about him."

So, thought Libby, Richard is this assassin that Colonel Padilla mentioned. Somehow, the word "assassin" made her skin crawl. "I'm not in the habit of being censored by the US government, Mr. Harbone. So just give me one good reason why I should not talk about Colonel Wade."

"Well, to begin with Miss McGinnis, it could be dangerous for him and his son. Then there is Wade's father-in-law. If Enrique Salazaar is still alive, the publicity about the Colonel could get him killed. And finally, publicity about the Colonel could make him useless to us in the future."

Libby's Irish temper was rising to the boiling point; but she had to admit to herself that Harbone's arguments were sound. She cooled down a bit and took a deep breath before talking. "All right, I'll do everything I can. Do you have any suggestions on how I should handle the matter?"

"Let us just consider this scenario: A man calling himself Robert Alford helped you escape; however, he disppeared in Managua. Just stick to that story and everything will be fine."

A few minutes after the man from the State Department departed, Libby's phone rang. She had put a call through to the States earlier to her boss in New York. She picked up the phone and answered, "Libby McGinnis."

On the other end was a familiar voice—her boss, Ralph Fairchild. "Libby girl, is that you? Are you all right?"

"Yes, Ralph, it's me and I'm fine. I'll be home tomorrow, and I have one hell-of-a-story."

"Yes I know! It just came in over the wires. You are going to be tomorrow's headlines."

Libby was puzzled. "What are you talking about?" she asked. "I have not released any story yet."

"It just came over AP wires a few minutes ago. The Nicaraguan government claims that you and Scotty are CIA agents. They say they have irrefutable evidence. What did you get involved in down there?"

The connection was bad, but Libby understood what Ralph had said. "That is all a bunch of bullshit!" she exclaimed. "I hope you are not going to use any of that crap."

"Well, we need to get your story—that's for sure. Where have you been? We tried every way to find you. Some guy from the State Department called and said you were alive and that you would be home soon. What was that all about? You had us worried sick."

The phone connections were beginning to get worse and Libby

had to yell into the phone, "I didn't get myself into anything. I was arrested for no reason at all. Scotty was tortured! They were going to murder us and blame it on the Contra."

"What did you say about the Contra trying to murder you? I can't hear you!" Fairchild's voice was weak and distorted.

Libby repeated what she'd said, but the line went dead. In frustration, she said, "Shit!" and slammed down the phone. She would be home tomorrow; then she could get this straightened out.

21

The restaurant at the Maya Hotel was jammed full of customers—yet it was surprisingly quiet. This would seem unusual if one did not know the scenario and cast of characters. The talk was low and usually in whispers, as if everyone wanted to keep their conversations from others—and they did. Tegucigalpa was a mini-Cairo of World War II, where more secret agents, mercenaries and Walter mitty types congregated than in any other city in Latin America. At one table sat four Americans wearing guyubara shirts— obviously CIA. At another sat three men wearing less expensive guyubara shirts—obviously KGB. At still another sat three Latinos wearing guyubaras—Honduran Secret Agents. At other tables sat less nondescript men, most of them wearing guyubara shirts, making them very suspect. Whenever someone new walked into the room, eyes glanced up to see if they could figure whose side he was on—or perhaps to admire his guyubara shirt.

Wade noted that Libby was unusually quiet through dinner; something was bothering her. He was puzzled by her cool and distant attitude. She talked about her phone conversation with her boss; so Wade figured that was her problem, until he reached across under the table to take her hand and she pulled it away. He walked her to her room with anticipations of a wonderful night of love, but that was not to be so. She unlocked her door and walked in, followed by Wade. As soon as she closed the door, she turned on him with fury in her eyes: "You have been lying to me and I want to know why!"

Taken by surprise and shocked by her attack, Wade asked, "Libby, what are you talking about?"

"You lied to me about Nicaragua and why you were there!"

"I didn't lie to you. I went there in search of my father-in-law."

"That's a bunch of bullshit! You went there to kill someone for the CIA! You are that assassin that killed the PLO man in Cypress, the one that Padilla talked about, aren't you?"

Libby was looking at him with disgust on her face, as if she was seeing something evil. Her look tore the guts out of him. He shrugged his shoulders. He couldn't think of anything to say. He just stood there watching her with a hurt, dumbfounded look on his face.

"I was paid a visit this afternoon from the US State Department and ordered not to mention your name in my story. The man said it was a matter of national security. I don't like to be muffled, and I don't like the man I love lying to me. At least you could have told me the truth!"

"Libby, I did tell you the truth!"

"Then why did this Harbone character tell me to keep my mouth shut where you were concerned?"

Wade knew that Harbone must have been "Howard"; and he could understand the strong-willed Libby's abhorrence to attempted censorship. Then all she had to do was to put it together, and it added up to Wade working for the CIA.

Libby looked at him with a fiery challenge in her green eyes. "Do you want me to leave your name out of the story?"

Now, Wade's stubborn defensive mechanism was turned on, and he glared back at her, "Yes! I think that would be best for all concerned."

Libby's temper boiled over. "Do you want me to forget you, as if you—we—never existed?" she snapped back.

"No, of course not! I love you. I don't want to lose you."

"Well, if you love me, then let me tell your story. Maybe if the truth came out it would help you get back into the Army, and you could continue your career. Don't you want that?"

"No! I do not want to go on back into the Army at this time."

"But you want to go on fighting and killing, don't you? I think you enjoy killing. You are very good at it, you know. I understand one thing for sure; you enjoy violence and killing more than you love me!"

Wade was hurt to his soul. He had to admit there was some truth to what she said. He was a soldier; he had been a soldier his entire adult life; and the violence and killing were a big part of that life. He could understand why a lady like Libby would look at him with disgust.

Libby continued; there were tears in her eyes now. "You are going back into Nicaragua aren't you? You are going back to fight with the Contra?"

"Yes I am. I thought that you understood that," he returned evenly.

Libby had wanted him to say, "No! I want to stay with you." She wanted him to take her in his arms and tell her he would change his life and never leave her. She asked one more question; and she already knew the answer. "You are going back to kill Padilla, aren't you?"

"Yes! I am.'

"Why? Why do you have to kill him? Is revenge that important to you? Why can't someone else kill him?"

"I have to—that's all. I thought you understood."

"Well, I do not understand." she sobbed. "Just get the hell out of my life and leave me alone. I don't want to see you again!"

Just before Wade spun on his heels and walked out of the room, Libby saw tears in his eyes. She stood there feeling a hollowness develop in her stomach and a cloud of loneliness settled over her. She stood there waiting for him to return; then she realized he wouldn't. She had a sudden urge to run after him—but she did not. She tried to sleep but could not. She paced the floor and cursed herself for being such a silly fool. She realized that Wade was the last person in the world she should have vented her anger and frustrations on. Way down deep she knew who he was and what he was—and she loved him all the more for it. Again, she cursed herself for her self-righteous stupidity.

Early the next morning, she met Scotty in the restaurant having a cup of that thick sweet mud that the Central Americans call coffee and that he had come to like so well. He took one look at her red eyes and knew something was wrong.

"What's the matter with you? You look horrible!"

"I made a terrible mistake last night," she confessed.

He sat his cup down and gave her his attention. "What did you do?"

She explained the events of the day before and how she had jumped on Wade. "I just couldn't help it—everything just seemed to build up, and I felt like I was going to explode. I don't want him to go back to Nicaragua and get hurt again, or worse. I want him with me."

Scotty put his hand on her arm and said quietly, "Libby, we have been through a lot in the last two weeks. It is just natural that you feel anxieties. But, I warned you not to try and change him. The man is rock-hard. He can be broked but not bent, and you would not want him broken. In many respects you two are very much alike. If you want Richard Wade, you are going to have to take him like he is."

"Yes, I know you are right; and I do love him. In fact I can't visualize a life without him now. I just hope he will understand and forgive me for losing my temper. Have you seen him this morning?"

"Honey, I thought you knew. He's gone! He and David stopped by my room to say goodbye."

"Where did they go?"

"I do not know. He said he would see me in a few weeks in the States."

"Damn!" she exclaimed. "He didn't even give me a chance to apologize. At least he could have brought David by to say farewell. That man is so infuriating."

"Well, what did you expect? A few minutes ago you said that you told him you never wanted to see him again."

"I did—but I didn't mean it!"

"Lord Gawd Almighty!" exclaimed Scotty. "Save me from prideful people."

* * *

Hunter leased an executive jet for the flight home, and they flew in luxury and comfort. Hunter could tell that something was wrong with the beautiful newslady. She was nervous and fidgety and seemed on the verge of bursting into tears—a far cry from her usual confident and poised self. He thought that Wade and Libby were in sinc, and he envied the former Colonel.

Libby relaxed a bit as she upped her quota of Bloody Marys,

and she finally turned to Hunter and asked, "Why does a man like being a soldier?"

He realized that Wade and Libby had evidently had an argument. He thought for a moment before answering. "I don't know for sure, but I believe it is a combination of factors: Patriotism is one, and adventure and excitement to a certain extent; I guess for glory, too, and challenge. I guess it could be considered the ultimate sport. I do know that once the smell of gunpowder gets into your blood, it is difficult to get it out. I know that I have always wanted to be a professional soldier."

"You like Richard, don't you?" asked the newswoman.

"Yes I do. He is one helluva soldier and man. I believe if it had not been for that Rome mess, he would have been a General Officer by now. I think it's our country's loss."

"You are aware of the part I played in that, aren't you?" she asked.

"Yes—but you cannot blame yourself. You were just doing your job. Some of our liberal Congressmen were out to get the Administration, and Wade just happened to be a convenient scapegoat."

"Yes. So everyone tells me, including Richard—but I still feel guilty, and I know that every time Richard looks at me he remembers Rome."

"I don't agree with you. I believe that every time he looks at you he sees a wonderful, brave lady—the lady he's in love with."

"There are times when he's very gentle; but I have seen him fight. He turns cruel and hard, almost like a machine."

"That is why he is still alive; that is why he is good; and that is probably why you and Scotty are still alive. I happen to think that Richard Wade could be and do anything he wants to. It just so happens that right now he wants to be a soldier, and he is a man with a mission."

Libby felt at ease talking to Hunter. "I have always hated violence and war. I grew up anti-war, anti-Vietnam, anti-Nuc, and anti-military. I have always considered myself a staunch liberal. Richard Wade is the epitome of everything I have always hated. Now the man has turned my world around. I am even in favor of aiding the Contra."

"Sometimes the truth can make a conservative out of a liberal, Libby."

"Do you think I have become a conservative?"

"I don't know. But I think you are moving in that direction."

"My Gawd!" she smiled. "Before long I'll be wanting to reopen the Vietnam War."

Hunter laughed at her. "Oh, I don't think you will go that far. But I do believe that you understand what's going on in Central America and why we must stop the communists. And you can do a lot of good for us."

"Yes! I want to help; I'll do anything I can."

"Just tell the truth. Just tell what you saw and heard in Nicaragua and Honduras. Be honest about your feelings toward the Contra. Tell your story on TV; tell it to the newspapers. Come to Washington with me and tell it to our politicians. I will gladly cover your expenses in Washington. I think people will listen to you; and I believe you can change the mind of some of the Congressmen who voted against the Contra Aid Bill. There are some, though, that will never change their mind."

Libby was confident that ABN would allow her to do a TV special, using her Contra tapes as background. She was also sure that the major newspapers would give her front page coverage.

They stopped in Memphis to drop off Hunter. Rene Marcel would escort them the rest of the way to New York. Hunter's secretary, Michelle, met them at the plane with a copy of the Memphis Enquirer. Hunter glanced at it and shook his head; he handed it to Libby. The first thing that caught her attention was a picture of herself on the front page with headlines that blared

ABN NEWSWOMAN ACCUSED OF BEING CIA AGENT

ABN newswoman, Libby McGinnis, and her cameraman, Robert Scott, are wanted by the Nicaraguan Government on charges of murder and espionage. Nicaraguan authorities said today, "The two American newspeople conspired with confessed CIA agent Robert Alford to assassinate a top government official. The three alleged spies were arrested and escaped from custody, killing two policemen, stealing an ambulance and kidnapping a 64 year old doctor. The elderly doctor's body was found in a roadside ditch beaten to death." According to a Nicaraguan spokesman: "This horrible, brutal murder of a helpless old man was entirely uncalled for." The fugitives eluded a nationwide search with help from the Contra rebels. Their whereabouts at this time are unknown. A spokesman for ABN declined to comment, saying that ABN is confident that Miss McGinnis and Mr. Scott are innocent of the charges.

By the time she finished reading the article, Libby was almost frothing at the mouth. She lost her ladylike demeanor and spat out, "Those sons-of-bitches! How could they print those lies. That is the biggest bunch of bullshit I have ever read." Hunter scanned the article again and shook his head. "Well, our liberal press has done it again. They have taken half-truths, inuendos, and one side of the story and made them a front page sensation. The communists are masters at disinformation, and our press is so gullible, they love it." He turned to the fuming newslady, "Libby, you have to get to New York and call a press conference. You have to refute these allegations."

Libby was shaking with anger and frustration. "What about the government? Will they help me?"

"Sure," he returned. "They will tell the truth and say you are not a CIA agent—but no one will believe them. Much of the press will insinuate that it is just another government coverup. People will believe that. It is strange, but the American people tend to believe the media more than they do a responsible government official. It's sad that we have come to that."

"This article reads as if Scotty and I are criminals rather than the victims. Poor kindly old doctor Amador, indeed. I should have killed the old evil bastard myself—I'd feel better now."

Libby said farewell to Hunter with a promise to meet him in Washington and a promise from him that he would make some calls and try to help her get the truth printed.

At one point during the final leg to New York, Libby turned to Scotty and remarked, "It's all a plot you know—he's finally getting even with me."

Scotty looked at her, a puzzled look on his face. "Who's finallly getting even?"

"Richard. Can't you see it? The same thing is happening to us that happened to him after Rome. Everything is being twisted. And they did not even print his real name in the article. I wonder why they called him Alford rather than Wade."

"Well, at least we know how Wade felt," mused Scotty. "Don't worry Libby; we'll get this straightened out. Everything is going to be fine. I'm more worried about you and Wade getting back together. Don't let your pride get in the way. If you want him, call him and tell him. I'll bet you he will be on the first available plane to New York."

22

It was late in the afternoon in New York when Libby and Scotty walked into the office of Ralph Fairchild, Director of Newsprogramming, American Broadcasting Network. Fairchild, a balding, middle-aged, overworked and under-exercised executive type stood-up, walked quickly around his desk and gave Libby a warm embrace; then he moved to Scotty and shook his hands. He was back behind the protection of his desk and seated in 12 seconds. He leaned forward and slapped the top of his desk and roared, "Boy, are you two ever a welcome sight for sore eyes. I have been worried sick about you!" He noticed Libby's short black hair. "What have you done to your hair?" he asked.

The cordialities over, Libby lay the Memphis newspaper on Fairchild's desk and asked, "Ralph, have you seen this story?

"Hell yes! You two are front page news. Great publicity! But what the hell did you two get yourselves into down there?"

"This story—it's all a bunch of bullshit!" exclaimed Libby, angrily. "How could you allow this trash to by printed?"

"There wasn't anything I could do. It came over AP wires."

"Don't give me that—you could have stopped it and you know it. You just wanted the publicity! You could have at least made a little stronger statements on our behalf. ABN spokesman declines comment—My Lord Ralph! Surely, you had more to say than that," Libby shot back.

"Yes. I admit I thought the publicity would certainly not hurt ABN. Regardless of that, I thought it best to say as little as possible until you two returned. Now calm down and tell me exactly what happened down there."

Libby gave Fairchild a quick version of their adventures in Central America, carefully avoiding talking about Wade.

When she finished, Fairchild leaned back in his chair and shook his head. "A remarkable story! That was a terrible experience. I'm just thankful that you two are safe and sound. The Nicaraguan government must have been misinformed."

"They were not misinformed," said Libby, wondering if she had gotten through to Ralph. "They knew exactly what they were doing. I'm trying to tell you they were going to murder us and blame it on the Contra."

"That's awfully hard to believe, Libby. Perhaps they were just trying to frighten you to get at the truth. What proof do you have that they were going to kill you?"

"Proof? What do you mean proof? My Gawd Ralph—this is me, Libby McGinnis! You know I'm not lying! What's wrong with you?"

"Of course I know you are not lying. I'm just playing the devil's advocate. It will just be the word of you two against a legitimate government."

"A legitimate government, my ass!" bellowed Libby. "They are just a bunch of Nazis!" She stopped her tirade and tried to calm down. "I have a great story, and I have some tapes we made of the Contra in Honduras, interviews with Contra soldiers. They are good; Scotty did a great job. And they tell the true story about what is going on down there. Ralph, I want to do a TV special to explain what happened to us down there and to show what is really happening in Nicaragua. The truth will scare the hell out of you and the American people. It will be a great program—I guarantee it."

Fairchild picked up a pencil and tapped his desk with it. He had known this moment was coming and he dreaded it. He spoke very calmly, carefully measuring his every word, "Libby, I'm sure you have some good material, but I don't think this is the right time for a special—maybe later."

Libby was dumbfounded by his statement. She could not believe she heard him say no. "It has to be now, not later. It has to be before Congress votes on the Contra Aid Bill."

"That is why we cannot do the program now," said Fairchild. "We don't want to be accused of playing politics or trying to influence the vote."

Scotty had been sitting quietly, willing to let Libby speak for both of them, confident that she could handle Fairchild; but he could not stand the obvious "freeze-out" any longer. He stood up and said angrily, "Damn it, Ralph! How can you treat Libby like this, after all she's been through. And I'm the one they tortured! This is not politics. This is the awful truth about what the communists are doing there; and the American people have a right to know the truth. And since when haven't we been playing politics at ABN? What you are really saying—but you don't have the guts to come out in the open about—is that good old liberal ABN is officially against the Contra Aid Bill; and you are not about to do anything that may help to get it passed—even if you have to give up the best story of the year."

Fairchild took Scotty's blast quietly and re-counted the fingers on his left hand. Finally, he said, "You two have been through a lot, and I'm sure you are tired and edgy. Why don't you take a few weeks off—with pay of course—rest up."

Libby's Italian temper flared: "Ralph, you mealy mouthed bastard! This is the best story of my life, and I have gone through hell to get it. If you don't put me on the air, you can take this job and shove it!"

Fairchild did not want to lose Libby. She was a great newswoman, but he already had his marching orders. He could not look her in the eyes as he spoke, "I'm sorry you feel that way, Libby. I'm just doing my job as I see fit. If you change your mind, your job will be waiting for you."

That ripped it for Scotty. He reached across the desk and grabbed the Director by the shirt, dragging him up across the desk. He brought Fairchild's face up close to his and bellowed, "You son-of-a-bitch! I ought to smash your face in. This lady is the best you have, and maybe the best in the business; and she has the best story you will ever get. If she goes, I go, too." He slammed the surprised Fairchild back in his chair and turned to Libby. "Girl, this place smells like Sandinistas—let's go get a drink!"

* * *

171

By the time Libby reached her Manhattan Apartment, she was exhausted from the trip; wrung out from her confrontation with Fairchild; and more than a little intoxicated from the Martinis at Sardis. Libby had decorated her apartment carefully to reflect her personality and taste; and in the past, she always looked forward to coming back to her nest. But not so this night. She found her nest filled with a gnawing loneliness, and her thoughts were filled with Richard Wade. Her body ached for the want of him; and after her treatment by those she thought were her friends, she needed his strong arms about her. She constructed herself a very dry vodka martini and toasted the mirror. "Richard Wade, I need you!" Then she sat down at her vanity and addressed her image in the mirror, "Libby McGinnis—you look like hell." Then she did something she had not done for a long time. She stood up, walked over to her bed, sprawled across it face down, and had herself a good cry.

She was snapped out of her self-pity by the ringing of the phone. A man identifying himself as Bob Leppert, Managing Editor of the Washington Times and a close friend of Robert Hunter, was on the other end. He said that Hunter had explained some of her experiences in Nicaragua; and he asked her to wrote a series of articles about Central America. "We'll start you off on the front page," he promised.

* * *

TEGUCIGALPA, HONDURAS

Wade and David had just returned to their room at the Maya Hotel, after spending the day at the FDN safehouse in the suburbs of the Honduran capital. Wade was unaware of Libby's troubles. He figured that she would be welcomed with open arms by ABN and would already be working on her TV special. Wade had spent the day with Alfonso Caldera, the President of the Nicaraguan Democratic Forces, discussing an operation that he and Hunter wanted to conduct. They desired to train a group of FDN volunteers and attack the oil refinery and storage depot near Managua. Hunter would provide the financial backing for the operation. The two Americans believed the FDN needed to strike a high-impact, highly-visible blow against the Sandinistas. There were many American Congressmen who were against the Marxist regime, but they did not believe the Contra were a viable fighting force. This was in part because they did not understand that the FDN was fighting a guerrilla war. Many Americans believed that because the Contra were not taking and holding ground in Nicaragua, they did not have a chance to win. These Congressmen had been led to believe, especially by the one-sided media, that giving money to the Contra would be a waste—like pouring water down a drain.

Hunter and Wade chose the oil refinery and storage depot because it was the only major oil refinery in Nicaragua. Secondly, over 80 percent of the nation's oil reserves were stored in the depot. If they succeeded, the Nicaraguan economy would be devastated, and the Sandinista war machine would grind to a sudden halt. It would take months before the country could recover.

Alfonso explained that he had been wanting to conduct a high-impact operation, but his organization simply did not have the money or special equipment. The meager FDN treasury was kept near-dry, just trying to feed and supply their growing Army. The FDN leader said the oil refinery was the number one target of the FDN. Its destruction would be a major blow to the Sandinistas and, at the very least, give the FDN an opportunity to build and extend its influence within Nicaragua. He had some reservations about the plan because the oil complex was the most guarded installation in Nicaragua; and it was secured by Cubans. However, even though the undertaking would be risky, he agreed to it in principle.

The plan called for Jim Turpin, who had just resigned his position with the CMA, to select 70 FDN volunteers and begin a special training program in physical fitness, marksmanship and demolitions, while Hunter and Wade continued planning.

* * *

Libby had her press conference the next afternoon—but it was almost a total disaster. Evidently the media was not very interested in her denial, because only six reporters showed up. They listened to her politely as she synthesized her adventure in Nicaragua, denied the charges, and denounced the Marxist government of Nicaragua.

That evening, her story appeared in a few newspapers across the nation; but only the Washington Times felt it important enough to put on the front page. The rest buried it somewhere on the fifth or sixth page. ABN Evening News gave her story a full 30 seconds of air time.

She contacted the three major networks and offered to appear on any of their programs; but none of the three were interested. Libby knew her old news agency had put the word out on her, and there was no use fighting any longer in New York City.

* * *

Libby McGinnis attacked Washington, DC with a vengeance. She wrote a five page document and sent it to every member of Congress; she ran off copies of her tapes and distributed them to liberals and conservatives alike; she met personally with every Congressman or Congresswoman that would see her; and her story appeared daily in a series on the front page of the Washington Times. Within three weeks, the once liberal Bostonian newswoman, turned conservative, had become the toast of conservative Washington.

Hunter spent a week in Washington introducing her to some of his acquaintances. She was especially surprised one morning when Hunter took her into a small conference room in the Inter-American Defense Council Building, and the Vice President of the United States greeted her. After the introductions, Hunter said, "The Vice President wants to hear the whole story; and in this case, you can talk about Richard Wade!"

When she was finished, the Vice President asked her several questions, then had to hurry on to another meeting.

Libby found out that conservatives love to have breakfasts. Before long, she was making the rounds speaking at conservative breakfasts. After two weeks in the Capital, she began to see the bubble that was conservative Washington: Conservatives meet with other conservatives and usually have conservatives as guest speakers. Everyone tells everyone else what they want to hear and they all agree. All the conservative groups print newsletters and information letters and send them to each other and they all read them and shake their heads and say. "That's true! That's right!" It is a classic example of the old choir-preaching-to-the-choir syndrome. And millions of dollars are spent in these endeavors. She remarked to one conservative group that the liberals were a lot better organized in that they did not try to sell other liberals—they tried to sell the general public.

Libby came to the conclusion that it was not the Congress who made our laws and governed our nation—it was all the little people that worked in the Congressmen's offices. The politicians were too busy trying to keep their jobs and stay in Washington to worry about

174

the day-to-day grind of running the country.

It seemed to her that everyone in Washington was a little monkey running around in a circle, grabbing for the tail of the monkey in front. Some catch the tail; some do not. But even when they catch the tail of the other monkey, they do not know what to do with it. So after awhile, they let go—so they can try to catch it again.

Libby talked to several liberal Congressmen and came away talking to herself, wondering how she could have ever called herself a liberal. For some reason they all reminded her of Jimmy Carter. Then she realized that Congress was still suffering from "Carter-Itis."

After leaving a lengthy meeting with former UN Ambassador, Jeane Kirkpatrick, Libby had to agree with Hunter. Kirkpatrick would make a good Presidential or Vice Presidential candidate. Hunter said, "Do not be surprised to see her on the next ticket."

She took an immediate liking to Congressman Robert Dornan, the champion conservative in Washington. Dornan assured her that he would do everything he could to get the Contra Aid Bill passed.

Libby left Washington wondering who was really running the nation—and how. She also left with a good job. CNN hired her to become a member of their TV news crew. However, the fiery woman, now a redhead again, left her impact on Washington. A few weeks after she departed, Congress approved the Contra Aid Bill by a narrow margin; and many conservatives gave Libby the credit.

Scotty landed a new job, too, with CNN.

23 _____

Wade and David spent two weeks on Grand Cayman Island, getting reacquainted. However, his second day there, David almost drowned. His father had told him, "Before I teach you to SCUBA, I want you to learn to snorkel."

David was wearing a face mask, rubber fins on his feet and a snorkel for the first time. He became transfixed by the underwater beauty of Eden Rock Reef, by the trumpet fish riding on the back of the Nassau Grouper, by the myriad of Blue Parrot fish feeding on the gray coral beneath him, by the gently waving purple sea fans, and by his own feeling of weightlessness as he swam above the corridors where shafts of brilliant light filtered through the fingerlings, zoanthids, and gorgonians. He was having a wonderful time in a new—and as yet undiscovered—world, when, without thinking, he dove underwater to take a closer look at the vast beauty below him. He forgot to hold his breath; and his snorkel, mask and mouth soon filled with warm, salty sea water. He gasped and jerked his mask off and battled his way to the surface, where he struggled to get his breath. His mask fell out of his hand and sank. He was scared because he seemed unable to catch enough air. He went under again and struggled back to the surface. His chest began to hurt and he panicked.

A strong hand grasped his shoulder and a calm voice said, "OK son, take it easy. Just lay on your back and float. You won't sink." Wade gently guided his embarrassed son back to shore.

A week later, David was diving to 120 feet with his father! For the rest of their stay, the boy shared a new and wonderful undersea world with his father; and Richard Wade had finally found a diving partner.

The warm sea water worked its magic on Wade's leg, and it was soon as good as new—as he proved by returning to his old habit of running two miles every morning. David began to fill out as he put solid muscle on his thin body. He told his dad that he wanted to play American football. That was a wish his father readily understood. The boy also said he had a secret desire to go to West Point and become a career Army officer like his father. Although flattered, Wade was not sure he wanted his son to be a soldier. He decided that when the time came it would be David's decision.

They returned to Memphis, and David enrolled in Calumet Military Academy, Robert Hunter's High School Alma Mater. The school maintained high academic standards and had a fair-to-middlin football team.

Wade and Hunter completed the plans for the Nicaraguan operation before returning to Honduras. Wade hated leaving his son, but the boy understood. "Don't worry Dad. I'll be fine. I will miss you but I know you have to go back. I'm half Nicaraguan too, and I want to see Nicaragua free."

* * *

The 70 volunteers for the raiding force that Jim Turpin selected all came from an FDN unit called the COE or Commando Operations Especial. This special unit, formed in 1984, was made up entirely of combat veterans of raids and ambushes deep inside Nicaragua. It was the unit that had attacked and destroyed the Sandinista garrison at Condega in a daring night raid, three months earlier. The COE was the only unit in the FDN to have undergone airborne training. Turpin and several CMA airborne experts had conducted the course.

After introducing his volunteers to Wade and Hunter, Turpin turned to the new arrivals and bellowed, "They are damn good soldiers, and they want to fight Sandinistas! All they need is equipment and a mission."

Hunter reached up and put his hand on the shoulder of the 290 pound giant. "I think we can take care of both of those requirements, my cuddly friend."

Wade set up a series of practical application tests to see where the emphasis on training should be. He found the volunteers weak in two areas: marksmanship and demolitions. This was understandable because the FDN was critically short of ammunition and explosives. The Contra trainees only fired five rounds of ammunition during their basic training phase—then they went to war. Bullets were a precious commodity in the FDN. A shooter cannot even learn to zero his weapons with five rounds. In comparison, American basic trainees fire several hundred rounds during the marksmanship phase of their training.

Rene Marcel had been busy during a shopping trip to Israel and South Africa; and miraculously, weapons, ammunition and equipment for the special force began to appear: new FAL and AK-47 assault rifles, Heckler and Koch MP5A3 submachine guns, 84mm L14A1 Carl Gustav antitank rocket launchers; American M-60 light machine guns and several boxes of the new British Limpet mines.

Robert Hunter was a skilled marksman, having graduated from several special schools including the FBI marksmanship course. He and Rene Marcel set up a basic marksmanship course for the volunteers, similar to the US Marine Boot Camp Course. The volunteers, who for the first time had good weapons and plenty of ammunition, were soon squeezing off the much desired, tight (you could cover them with a quarter), three round shot groups, on the 25 meter range. From there, they moved to a special assault course with cardboard pop-up human-type targets.

When the raiders reached a satisfactory stage of training, Hunter began conducting all of the training at night. He introduced them to two special items of equipment they would be using on the raid: battery powered night vision goggles which increased their night vision 100 per cent up to 80 yards and turned night into day and infrared (redeye) laser-scopes. These small battery powered scopes attached to a weapon and cast a red dot on the target. The size of the dot depended on the distance to the target. At 100 yards, the size of the dot was about the size of a quarter. The weapon is zeroed so that the strike of the bullet coincides with the red dot at a given distance. The weapon does not have to be aimed—just turn the laser on, place the dot on the target, and fire.

Wade and Turpin taught the demolitions course. One of the main weapons for the impending raid was to be the British Limpet mines. These mines could be attached to a target and with a twist of the bezel on top, one could activate the timer and detonator. The Limpet's internal design caused the mine to explode like a shaped charge, so the bulk of the explosion was directed toward whatever it was attached to. During the Falkland Islands War, British frogmen sunk an Argentine destroyer with two of these deadly little mines, or "boogers" as Turpin called them. He would say, "You stick this little booger on the helicopter about here, give it three clicks to the left, then move your ass out of the area!"

Although he was an experienced, skilled soldier, Jim Turpin's greatest asset was his outstanding rapport with the Contra. They had genuine affection for the giant from Memphis, Tennessee, and had given him the code name of "Sailor," because they said he reminded them of Bluto in the Popeye cartoons.

Turpin was one of the many Vietnam Veterans that still believed they had a war to win. He used to say, "We won the battles and lost the war." He hated communism and was well aware of the communist threat in Central America. He was afraid that if the communists were not stopped in Nicaragua, we would have to fight them someday along our southern border. In many ways, Turpin was a maverick. He had tried to cross the border into Nicaragua several times to fight with his Contra friends; but each time he was stopped by Enrique Jiron, who did not want to see any more Americans killed fighting with his forces.

Jiron had reluctantly agreed to allow Hunter and Wade to conduct the raid. He approved primarily because his forces needed the weapons and equipment Hunter promised. He also agreed that it was time to strike a major blow against the Sandinistas; and he did not have the resources to do it.

Wade selected fifteen men and gave them a special course in silent killing techniques. He taught them how to cover the mouth of your target with one hand and stab downward into the right shoulder at the base of the neck, cutting the subclavian artery and causing almost instant death; how to cut a man's throat by inserting the point of the knife into the left jugular vein and moving your arm sharply to the right; and how to use an ice pick and jab it into the small soft spot at the base of the skull, causing almost immediate death. He showed them the use of the wire garotte which had both a cutting and choking effect. Then he introduced them to a new weapon for the raid: the modern version of the ancient cross-bow. It was made out of tubular steel, had a stock and looked like a short rifle. The sighting system was a small penlight laser scope that put a small red dot on the target. It was zeroed so that at 25 yards the eight inch dart would strike center-red-dot. The darts that they would be using on the mission were built to collapse in the center and break a small glass vial, releasing a curare-cyanide solution that caused very quick death.

The last item of equipment that Wade issued to his special killing team were 22 caliber, Hi-Standard automatic pistols with silencers. These small caliber weapons were deadly, silent little "boogers" when working up close.

Wade and Hunter finally decided that their raiding force was ready. They whittled the number down to sixty. The two leaders left Turpin and Marcel to continue the training and left Nicaragua. Hunter flew back to Memphis to take care of some business problems, and Wade went on to Grand Cayman for a couple weeks of solitude and scuba diving. Hunter was to join him in a few days.

24

Libby's new apartment in the quiet suburbs of Atlanta still lacked some of the charm of her old home in New York but it was beginning to reflect the personality of its new occupant. After the hustle and bustle of New York and ABN, the slower-paced Atlanta and more relaxed CNN was a distinct relief for the newswoman. Libby had taken over as the anchor person on CNN's evening news. She also made spot appearances during the day, giving highlights of the national and international news.

She had just returned to her office after doing the 7 p.m. News when she was called to the phone. It was Robert Hunter. "Congratulations!" he said. "I just caught your newscast; you are really very good. I was impressed."

"Thank you, kind sir. And how are things with you? Do you have a scoop for me?"

"No. Not at the moment. But how would you like a private interview with Alfonso Caldera?"

Libby took the bait like a voracious barracuda. Her new boss had been after her to get an interview with the FDN leader. He kept saying, "With your contacts in the FDN, it should be easy. I would like to hear what he has to say about the passage of the

Aid Bill and how he intends to use the money.'

Libby did not hesitate. She said, "I would love to! Just name the time and place.'

"I figured you would. It is all laid out. There are tickets in your name at the Northwest Orient desk in Atlanta. Your flight leaves at 9 a.m. tomorrow. You will be in Grand Cayman at 2 p.m. Caldera's brother, Mario, will meet you at the airport. I have made reservations for you at the Holiday Inn."

The Cayman Islands! Richard! Libby's heart stopped a beat. She hesitated, then asked hesitantly, "Where is Richard?"

"Oh, he is still down in Honduras," lied Hunter. "I haven't seen him for several weeks."

"How is he? Do you know?"

"I understand he is fine. He brought David here before returning to Honduras, and the boy is going to school."

Libby felt a stab of disappointment and a pang of relief when she heard that Wade was not in the Cayman Islands. She had not heard from Wade since that night in Tegucigalpa. Much to her chagrin, he took her at her words. She almost tried to contact him several times—but her hurt pride stopped her. Scotty, a nag and her perpetual conscience, told her in no uncertain terms that "she was a damned, spoiled, stubborn, stupid fool!" And those were the kind words.

Libby did not ask the Memphis businessman what Alfonso Caldera was doing in the Cayman Islands. She figured it was none of her business.

Libby thought for a moment. She was positive her boss would want her to go; and he could easily find a stand-in for her on the show. A few days in the sun might be fun. "All right! I'm sure I can make that."

"Good!" returned Hunter. "Have fun and enjoy the sun."

The single conspirator, Robert Hunter, hung up the phone and smiled. He flipped his intercom switch, alerting his secretary: "Michelle, call Wade in Grand Cayman and tell him I'll be arriving on the 2 o'clock flight tomorrow."

"You do not have reservations," she said. "Do you want me to make them?"

"No. I'm not really going; just tell him I am. It's a joke."

With a puzzled look on her face and wondering if her boss had flipped his lid, Michelle picked up the phone.

GRAND CAYMAN ISLAND, BRITISH WEST INDIES

Richard Wade sipped his rum punch and watched the Northwest Orient DC-9 touch down on the runway. He glanced at his watch. It would take Hunter at least 20 minutes to clear immigration and customs—he had plenty of time to finish his drink.

Twenty-five minutes later, Wade stood outside customs waiting for his friend. He was not prepared mentally for Libby McGinnis to come walking through the door, though the beautiful redhead had constantly been on his mind. He had found himself thinking of her more as the days passed. The feel, the touch, the smell of her was imprinted in his memory. But her last words, "Get out of my life—I don't ever want to see you again!" kept gnawing at him like fingernails on a blackboard.

Wade's heart jumped into his throat when her spotted her, and a flood of emotions swept through him. There was no place to run, and she was walking straight toward him.

Libby sighted Wade and felt a shiver of excitement. He was wearing a flowered sport shirt and tennis shorts, and his body was bronzed by the sun. From a distance, he looked a lot like Tom Selleck. He was blocking her way, so there was no way to avoid him. She wondered if Hunter knew Wade was here. She walked up and stopped three feet from him. She had to swallow before she could speak. "Hello Richard, I thought you were in Central America."

"I was. I just arrived here a few days ago. What brings you here?"

"I'm here to interview Alfonso Caldera."

Wade knew that the FDN President was in Miami. He was beginning to suspect something was up. He suddenly realized that he and Libby were the victims of one of Robert Hunter's intrigues. There was a Hunter in the woodpile somewhere. "Alfonso is in Miami."

"Are you sure?" asked Libby, a puzzled look on her face.

"I'm positive—but maybe he is coming here and I don't know about it."

"What are you doing at the airport?" she asked.

"I'm supposed to be picking up Hunter. But it looks like he isn't on the plane."

They both realized that they'd been had by the Memphis businessman. Neither knew what to do or say next. Finally, he reached for her luggage, asking, "Where are you staying?"

"At the Holiday Inn."

"I'll run you over there."

On the way to the hotel, they chatted in a strained, very formal manner: "How is your leg?" "It's fine." "How do you like your new job?" "How is David getting along—does he like school?" "Maybe Alfonso got delayed." "Maybe Hunter was delayed." "Maybe he'll be on tonight's plane." "Maybe they'll come in together." "Maybe there is a message at the hotel."

There were two messages at the hotel, one for each of them:

"LIBBY. ENJOY YOUR WEEK ON CAYMAN. ALFONSO WILL MEET YOU IN MIAMI ON RETURN FLIGHT. YOU AND RICHARD BELONG TOGETHER. ENJOY EACH OTHER. ENJOY. ENJOY. —HUNTER."

"RICHARD. TAKE CARE OF MY GOOD FRIEND, LIBBY. SHE NEEDS YOU. YOU NEED HER. ENJOY EACH OTHER. ENJOY. —HUNTER."

Libby folded her message, stuck it in her purse and announced, "It's from Robert, Caldera has been delayed."

Wade folded his message, stuck it in his pocket and announced, "Mine's from Robert too. He's also been delayed."

They did not say a word during the elevator ride and short walk to her room. At her door, Wade asked, "Would you like to go to dinner this evening?"

Libby nodded and said quietly, "Yes, I would like that very much." There were butterflies sailing around in her stomach.

"OK. I'll pick you up at six. We don't want to miss the sunset. It's at 6:20 today."

"I'll be ready."

Libby found an iced bottle of Dom Perignon Champagne in her room, and she knew it was from Hunter. She decided that a drink was exactly what she needed, so she popped the cork and poured herself a glass. She quickly downed two unladylike glasses and began to feel her anxieties ebb. She lay down on the bed and closed her eyes. Hunter had planned this whole escapade. He had given her a chance to get her man back. And now that she had that opportunity, she did not know what to do or say. She made the right decision; she decided to play it by ear and follow her heart.

She suddenly jumped out of bed and opened her suitcase. She rifled through her clothes, but she could not find anything to wear. On an impulse, she decided that she had to find a dress shop.

* * *

Libby studied her reflection in the mirror. The taxi driver took her to a local boutique, and she purchased a bright, multi-colored, silk cocktail dress. It was backless to the waist and had a slit up one side to just above the knee. The dress was a little more daring then she usually wore; but it seemed to fit the island mood. She paid too much for the dress; but again, that seemed to be the right thing to do. Satisfied with her looks, she dabbed a bit of Emile de Paree perfume in a few strategic locations. Libby was as nervous as a young girl going on her first date; and this was, actually, her first date with Richard. She glanced at her watch—it was only 5:30. It seemed unfashionable to be ready a half hour early. She both dreaded and anticipated Wade's arrival. She poured herself another glass of champagne.

Wade knocked at her door promptly at six. She opened the door and he walked in. For a few seconds, he could not speak—he was struck dumb by her beauty.

He was wearing white slacks, flowered sport shirt and a white tropical dinner jacket. He looked as if he had just stepped off the set of Miami Vice. "That is a beautiful dress!" he offered, breaking the strained silence.

"Thanks, it's just something I had along. Would you like a glass of champagne, compliments of Robert Hunter?"

She poured him a glass and refilled hers. He touched his glass to hers and said, "To Robert Hunter. A good friend. Wherever you are." They drank, then he asked, "You do realize that we've been had by Robert, don't you?"

"Yes, I do. Are you sorry?"

His eyes held hers closely. "No. I'm not! What about you?"

"I'm not sorry either!" Wade changed the drift. "We can see the sunset from your balcony."

She followed him out, and they looked across the beach into the turquoise blue waters of the Caribbean. There was hardly any wave action, and the water was smooth as glass. "It's breathtakingly beautiful!" she proclaimed. "You have mentioned the sunset twice today. It must be a big deal here."

"It is. See all those people down there?"

Clusters of tourists, in various states of undress and sobriety, some twisting camera dials, stood in little groups on the beach and around the outside bar, watching the sun go down. Soft calypso music played in the background; and without realizing it, most of the sun-watchers were swaying to the island rhythm.

"They are all waiting to see the Green Flash," announced Wade.

"The Green Flash?"

"Yes, the Green Flash. It is a legendary phenomenon of the West Indies. They say if you watch very carefully, you may see a green flash just after the sun disappears over the horizon."

"Have you ever seen it?"

"Nope. Not yet—but I will someday."

They watched the sun in silence. It sank and sank and was finally gone. Wade turned to her. "Did you see it?"

No. Did you?"

"No!"

Down below, someone bellowed, "The Green Flash! See it? See it? A perfect Green Flash!"

Some said they saw it. Some said they did not. On all accounts they agreed it was a perfect sunset.

Wade took Libby to the Verandah Restaurant at the Holiday Inn. They were met at the door by a distinguished looking Maitre d' complete with black beard and tuxedo. "Good evening, Mr. Wade. Table for two?" he said, with a slight Italian accent.

"Yes Romano, please."

"This way please; follow me." He led them to a table near the window and held the chair for Libby. "We have crab claws tonight, Mr. Wade. I know you like them. Can I get you a cocktail?"

"Bring us a bottle of Dom Perignon, please."

"Yes Sir—right away," Romano turned and hurried away.

"What a nice man," remarked Libby.

"Yes, he is. And a good friend, too."

"Do you eat here often?" she asked.

"Yes. This is my favorite restaurant. There are many great eating places here—but I love fresh fish. Here they serve grouper and snapper caught the same day. And when they have Caribbean crab claws, they are delicious."

They feasted on escargot, conch chowder, crab claws and grouper filets washed down with chilled French Fume Blanc. The champagne, wine and delicious food—but mostly the wine and champagne—went straight to Libby's head and put her in a bubbly, talkative mood. After awhile she realized that she was monopolizing the conversation and apologized. "Excuse me, I didn't realize I was talking so much—it must be the chanpagne. But this is the first time I have felt this good since . . . ." She stopped, realizing she was about to say, "Since I was last with you."

She hurriedly changed the subject. "I cannot understand the dialect these islanders speak; what is it?"

"The local speech is a mixture of American-Southern drawl, Scottish lilt and Jamaican idioms delivered very fast. One thing to watch for is the tendency to pronounce 'v' as 'w'. On dads de trut mon—dads de trut!"

Libby laughed. "OK, mon."

"That's how the island got it's name, you know."

"What do you mean?"

"They say Christopher Columbus was walking with one of his men along Seven Mile Beach, and he asked the sailor what he thought of the island. The sailor answered, "It's OK, MAN!"

"Not really?"

"No. Probably not; but it sounds good."

"Ok, mon, what's next?"

"Well mon, next we gone donce to de Barefoot Mon."

"I have heard a lot about him since I arrived. Does he always go barefooted?"

"Yes. I guess so; I've never seen him with shoes on. He is very popular in the islands. His real name is George Nowak. He was born in Germany. His mother married a US serviceman, and they moved to America when he was 12. He grew up wanting to be a country western singer and beach bum. He went to Nashville but did not make the big time so he came down to the Caribbean. Down here he soon found out that the people wanted to hear the island songs and music; so he learned from the natives and soon developed his own unique style. He's been on the island for 16 years and now has quite a following."

After dinner, they moved into the Wreck of the Ten Sails Night Club, and Wade ordered two Remy Martins. They sat down and let the music settle their meals. The couples on the dance floor rolled their hips in a step that was not the rhumba or the samba. The Barefoot Man sang:

"WELL I ASK MY LA-DY WHAT SHOULD I DO

TO MAKE SHE HAP-PY TO MAKE LOVE. SHE
SAID THE ON-LY THING I WANT FROM YOU IS
A LIT-TLE PIECE OF THE BIG BAMBOO. SHE
WANT THE BIG, BIG BAMBOO, BAMBOO. OH LA,
LA, LA, LA, LA, LA, LA, LA. WORKING FOR
THE YAN-KEE DOL-LAR."

Next, the band began playing a Reggae. Libby started to feel the
music. She looked over and smiled. "It has a nice beat."

Wade stood up, took her hand and began pulling her to the dance
floor. She protested saying, "I can't."

"Sure you can! It's all in the knees—just like taking a Sunday
afternoon stroll to music."

By the time she had wriggled through the Reggae and another
calypso, Libby was really getting into the West Indies dancing.
Finally they sat down, and she gave Wade a puzzled look and said,
"You really are quite a good dancer!"

"Does that surprise you?"

"Yes, frankly, it does. I just did not think you were the type." Libby
was seeing a new side of Wade—the romantic and gentle side—
and she liked it. "You really love this island, don't you?" she asked.

"Yes. I do. Each time I come here it's like being born again.
It refreshes me and gives me peace."

The band played a slow song, and Wade took Libby's hand and
guided her to the dance floor. Once there, she floated into his arms;
and an electric current of emotions flowed between them. She felt
the strength of his arms and a warm fire coursed through her veins.
She whispered in his ear: "I'm sorry for what I said in Tegus—
I—I—really didn't mean it! I've been so miserable without you."

He hugged her, and she dropped his hand and placed her arms
around his neck. "And I have been lost without you!" he confessed.
"I love you—more than anything else in the world."

Her mouth came up to his, urgently and demanding and the whole
world disappeared as they kissed in the middle of the dance floor.
A current of mutual desire welled up between them; and she rubbed
against his leg, trying to put out the fire that was blazing between
her legs. She pulled away from his mouth for just an instant to say,
"Do you have any idea what you do to me?"

Wade felt the blood surge to his loins, and he pulled her even
closer.

And the band played, and the Barefoot Man sang:
    "THIS IS MY IS-LAND IN THE SUN, WHERE MY

PEOPLE HAVE TOILED SINCE TIME BE-GUN.
THO I MAY SAIL ON MANY A SEA, HER HOPES
WILL AL-WAYS BE HOME TO ME. OH, IS-LAND
IN THE SUN WILLED TO ME BY MY FATHER'S
HAND. ALL MY DAYS I WILL SING IN PRAISE
OF YOUR FORESTS, WA-TERS, YOUR SHINING
SAND."

The song finally ended, but Libby and Wade were oblivious to everything but each other. After awhile, Wade realized that people were staring at them, and he gently pushed Libby back. He glanced up at the Barefoot Man. George had a knowing smile on his face; and he winked at the American. "We'd better sit down before we get thrown out," whispered Wade.

"If you don't get me out of here and up to my room where we can be alone," whispered Libby, "I'm going to rape you right here! Then we will get kicked out, for sure.'

Her hand clung tightly to his as they walked out of the bar. Someone at one of the tables turned to his wife and said knowingly, "Honeymooners!"

Once inside her room, they fell into each other's arms. Libby's passions soared. "When you touch me," she said hoarsely, "I lose all control of my senses."

Wade's hands caressed her body; he moved to her lower stomach and rubbed gently. She ached, hungrily and she moved her body against his touch. Her mouth sought his; her tongue pressed through his lips looking for the warmth of his mouth. She felt herself coming! And she trembled as she moaned in his mouth. Her fingers dug into his shoulders. She gasped and stepped back, not believing that just his touch had caused an orgasm. She quickly wriggled out of her dress, her eyes never leaving his. Wade peeled out of his clothes. The two lovers left their clothes lying where they fell in two heaps on the floor and moved into each other's arms. "Now Richard! I have to have you now! I want you now!"

Wade swooped her up in his arms and carried her to the bed. As he lay her down, she kept saying over and over, "Now! I want you now!" Without further preliminaries, he rose above her. Her eyes widened and she gasped as she felt the initial shock and joy of penetration; then there was only pure ecstasy. Her hips moved furiously and she moaned with sheer delight. They made love fiercely, violently, hungrily, lips together, bodies smashing against each other. Libby cried out in her pleasure, and they spent their emotions in one gigantic wave of sexual sensation that left them weak and exhausted. They lay in each other's arms, trying to catch their breath. It had been brutal, almost animalistic; but, at the same time, it was what they both needed.

After the initial sexual frenzy of passion, the two lovers had showered together and settled into a night of sweet and tender lovemaking. It was almost daylight before they fell asleep in each other's arms.

Wade awoke the next morning, feeling a special glow. Libby slept on her side with her left leg lying across him; her long red hair tumbled over his chest and shoulders; her left arm clung to his neck. It was a comfortable feeling. There was still a faint aroma of Libby's perfume in the air.

* * *

In the days that followed, they basked in the warmth of their rekindled love. They became a carefree loving couple. They acted like newlyweds alone in an island paradise. They hiked along Seven Mile Beach; they snorkeled in the warm, clear waters; they "skinny-dipped" at night; and they pretended to be Burt Lancaster and Deborah Kerr and made love on the beach. And, oh how they made love! They found it impossible to keep their hands off each other. They were both amazed at the waves of virility that swept through them, again and again.

And they left the island together, the Island of Sun—their Island of Love. And when they parted in Miami, they parted with a kiss and a promise of a future together.

* * *

When Wade returned to Memphis, he sent Hunter a dozen red roses, with a note attached:

"ROBERT. THANKS FOR THE WONDERFUL
WEEK ON GRAND CAYMAN! WE ARE
ENGAGED! RICHARD."

Michelle read the note and shook her head. She was right; her boss had flipped his lid.

25

FDN HEADQUARTERS SOMEWHERE NEAR
THE NICARAGUAN BORDER

A group of men sat around the conference table at Enrique Jiron's headquarters: Alfonso Caldera, FDN President; his brother, Mario; Commandante Jiron; Robert Hunter; Rene Marcel; Jim Turpin; Pecos Bill; Commandante 36; and Richard Wade. With the exception of President Caldera, the others knew the plan for Operation Trojan Horse by heart. This briefing was for the FDN leader.

Wade stood up: "Mr. President, Operation Trojan Horse will be conducted in three phases. During Phase I, Commandante Jiron's forces will increase their activity along the border. We believe this will cause the Sandinistas to reinforce their border installations at the expense of troop strength in Managua and also increase convoy activity throughout Nicaragua.

"Mr. Hunter's ship, the Spanish Doubloon, left Jamaica several days ago. It will sail through the Panama Canal and up the west coast of Central America to El Salvador. Hunter's Marine Archeological Research Foundation has a legal contract with the El Salvador government to search for a Spanish galleon that wrecked off the Amapolo Point in 1635.

"Four days before the raid, Mr. Hunter, Pecos Bill and I will parachute into a small pasture outside of Managua and linkup with the underground. During the next three days, we will reconnoiter the objectives and make final coordination with the underground. We have been in almost daily contact with Jorge Dunn, and his people have everything ready on their end.

"During Phase II, the Spanish Doubloon will move to the Honduran Coast and pick up the raiding force. It will be a tight squeeze with the troops, their equipment and rubber boats; but the journey is short. The ship will move to a location off the coast of Nicaragua, and the raiders will be ferried ashore by RB-15 rubber landing boats. The RB-15's will return to the Spanish Doubloon, and the ship will slip back up the coast to international waters, near Honduras.

"We will pick up the Strike Force which will be wearing Sandinista Army Uniforms, at the beach; and using Army trucks and drivers furnished by the underground, we will convoy to an abandoned warehouse a few miles from the coast. There are so many military convoys moving about in Nicaragua that one more should not draw much attention.

"On D-Day at 0100 hours, we will attack two targets near Managua. The main attack will be against the oil refinery and storage tanks at Salan. The diversionary attack will be against the MIGs and HIND helicopters at the Managua Airport. Both of these targets are guarded by Cuban Infantry Units. We are fortunate that several of our commadoes are familiar with the targets, and two members of the underground work inside the oil refinery.

"Pecos Bill and ten men will conduct the diversionary attack. He is familiar with the airport, as he used to base his private airplane there. His group will infiltrate the airfield complex and get as close as they can to the MIG's and helicopters—then they will attack the parked aircraft with Carl Gustav rocket launchers, inflicting as much damage as they can before withdrawing.

"The main attack will be against the oil refinery and oil storage depot." Wade uncovered a scale model of the target and explained how the attack was to be conducted. He finished by saying, "We have used this scale model in rehearsing the troops."

Alfonso Caldera asked a few questions; then, satisfied, he brought up a point: "I want to keep the civilian casualties to a minimum. I do not want any unnecessary killing of Nicaraguans."

"We plan to keep civilian casualties as low as possible, Mr. President," returned Wade. "The 12 to 8 shift has only a few civilian workers. A large group comes in at 4 a.m. to load tanker trucks—but it should all be over by then. And if all goes well, they won't need to come to work."

"It is a bold plan, Colonel Wade. Are we ready for such an undertaking?" asked the FDN leader.

"Yes sir. We are as ready as we ever will be," answered Wade. He paused to see if the President had any more questions or comments; then he continued: "During Phase III, we will convoy to the coast and rendezvous with the rubber boats. We'll be back in Honduras the next day. If anything goes wrong during the movement to the coast, we will split up into small teams and Escape and Evade to known link-up points with guerrilla units."

Wade sat down and a general discussion ensued. At one point, Alfonso asked, "Has the underground found out anything about your father-in-law?"

"No sir! Nothing.'

"I'm sorry! I'm afraid I fear for the worst for my old friend." Then the FDN leader changed the subject: "Colonel Wade, since your wife was a Nicaraguan, we consider you a Nicaraguan. So from now on you are commissioned a Colonel in the FDN and your code name will be Commandante 480."

* * *

MINISTRY OF INTERIOR
MANAGUA, NICARAGUA

Commandante Raul Castro Padilla wrote some notes on a yellow legal pad, then returned to reading the papers in front of him titled, "PLAN FOR THE INFILTRATION OF AGENTS INTO THE UNITED STATES AS ILLEGAL ALIENS."

The PLO had established a special school on terrorism in the outskirts of Managua in 1985. The money to run the school was furnished by Libyan strong man Muammar al Khadafy. The plan called for infiltrating graduates of the school through Mexico and across the US border. Once in America, these agents would organize cells and await instructions to turn their newly acquired terrorist skills loose on the Americans. Padilla thought the plan a good one; however he wanted to expand its scope to include Costa Rica and Guatemala. These two nations would have to fall before the revolution could commence the final assault on the United States' soft underbelly, that porous 1900 mile border between the US and Mexico. There was plenty of time; the American penchant for apathy and deceiving themselves was on the side of the revolution.

Padilla glanced at his watch—it was almost 6 p.m.; his driver would be waiting. He tossed the plan into his hold box, stood up, put on his fatigue cap and strode from the office. His car, a 1983 Mercedes-Benz, was waiting for him in front of the Ministry. He climbed into the back and the car sped off. His home was in the north suburbs, a large Spanish-style mansion complete with swimming pool and tennis court. It had once belonged to a cousin of Somoza. Now it was his—spoils of a successful revolution.

The Commandante made a sour face when he thought of his wife, Felicia, waiting for him at home. When he met her during the early days of the revolution, she was young and pretty and full of fire; but now after four children and too much good food, she was fat and slovenly, and he could not stand that course black hair that covered her arms and upper lip. One of these days, he thought, he was going to send her back to her village where she belonged and move his young mistress, Lolana, into the big house with him. Ah, Lolana, she made him feel like a young man again!

A SECRET AIRFIELD, SOMEWHERE IN HONDURAS

Wade made a last minute check of Pecos Bill and Hunter. Wade was a Master Parachutist with over 500 jumps to his credit—so this was old hat to him. But Pecos Bill was new to the game, with only 10 jumps, and five of those were in the last week. Hunter was an experienced jumper; but he had never made a night jump behind enemy lines.

There were certain things about Hunter that were an enigma to the former Colonel. Hunter was a successful businessman—he did not have to risk his neck. Wade was a professional soldier; danger was a way of life. Pecos Bill was fighting to free his country; so he had a reason to risk his life. But Hunter had very little to gain. Wade had always assumed that Hunter would back the venture financially but would not get involved in the actual operation; but he assumed wrongly. Hunter had insisted on going on the assault. And since he was paying for it, he had the right to go. Wade also felt that Hunter had a lot more pull in Washington then he let on.

They finally climbed into the obsolete PV-1 Neptune, the only multi-engine airplane in the FDN inventory; and after some cracking and sputtering, both engines started. They were soon winging their way toward the Nicaraguan border.

The pilots were old hands at dropping supplies to the guerrilla forces; but this would be the first time they dropped paratroopers inside Nicaragua. During the practice jumps in Honduras, they put their jumpers on target every time.

The Neptune flew across the border at 200 feet to avoid radar

194

detection. Ten minutes from the Drop Zone, the plane climbed to 700 feet. Five minutes from the DZ, a red light next to the door went on. A crew member slid the door open. Wade gave Pecos Bill and Hunter the signal to hook up; then he hooked his static line to the steel cable running down the center of the aircraft and moved to the open door, with the other two jumpers right behind him. Wade looked out, and a warm blast of air smacked him in the face. In the distance he could see the lights of Managua. Just ahead, on the low horizon, he spotted the unmistakable winks of a strobe light. He turned and gave thumbs-up to his fellow jumpers, then assumed a good jump position: hands outside the door, one foot slightly ahead and knees bent.

Robert Hunter was sick at his stomach and needed to go to the bathroom. He had a sudden moment of regret and asked himself, "What the hell am I doing here? What am I trying to prove?" He began to wonder if he would ever get to sail his boat through the blue Caribbean again.

The light near the door turned green and Wade propelled himself through; then Pecos Bill disappeared into the blackness. Hunter found himself falling through the air before he even realized he had exited the aircraft. He kept his body tight, chin down, hands tight around his reserve. When he reached the end of his 15 foot static line, the chute commenced to deploy. It opened with a pop, and he felt as if he had stopped in mid-air. As all paratroopers do, Hunter breathed a sigh of relief when he realized the parachute was open. He reached down and undid the tiedowns to his cargo pack, and it fell free to hang below him on a 12 foot bunji cord. He reached up and grabbed his rizors as the black hole below him that was the ground came up fast. He put his feet together and bent his knees. Then the ground was there, and he hit bone-jarring hard and rolled to his right. He hit his Capewell quick release, and the parachute floated free. He lay there trying to get his wind back. When he opened his eyes, two men were leaning over him. He hoped they were friends!

* * *

One hour after exiting the aircraft, the three raiders were safely hidden in the root celler behind Jorge Dunn's home, eating—of all things—black beans and rice.

Early the next morning, they took off in the back of a dilapidated van to take a look at the oil refinery. They were unable to get any closer than four blocks because the area was cordoned off by roadblocks. Jorge parked the van in an alley, and they entered the back door of a four story apartment building and climbed the stairs to the roof. From there, they could get a good view of their target. The oil refinery and storage complex covered an area the size of four city blocks. It was surrounded by two 12-foot-high chain-link fences 50 feet apart. The perimeter was well illuminated by floodlights every 100 feet. There were two entrances, one on the south and one on the west; and each was guarded by a cement blockhouse with a sand-bagged machine gun emplacement on top. There were guard towers in between the two fences, every 250 feet. Machine gun jeeps patrolled the perimeter at irregular intervals. Inside the complex were 12 large storage tanks, several warehouses, the refinery, quarters for the guards, loading docks and several maintenance buildings.

It was going to be a tough nut to crack. The outer shell was too hard for a direct assault; so they would have to peel it from within, and that is exactly what they intended to do. The plan was bold and risky—but the rewards were worth it. They spent all that day and night atop the building, studying the complex and watching the comings and goings. They returned to Jorge Dunn's early the following morning. Pecos Bill spent the day with an old friend, looking over the airfield.

* * *

D-DAY PLUS ONE

Big Jim Turpin knelt in the bow of the lead RB-15 and searched the shore with his night vision goggles. The water was choppy, and the boats were making painfully slow progress. He placed a metascope up to the goggles. A metascope detects infrared light. And there it was, dead-ahead, a steady blinking red light.

The landing went off without a hitch; and two hours later, all 60 commandoes, happy to be out of the cramped quarters of the Doubloon and with steadier stomachs now that they were out of the small pitching rubber boats, were safely in the abandoned warehouse.

26

Roberto Dominguez drove his 5000 gallon oil tanker with skilled and experienced hands. He had been a truck driver for over 20 years and he liked the feel of the big rigs. He treated his truck like a big, strong, lovable lady who moved responsively to his gentle, loving touch. He pulled up to the first roadblock and stopped, like he always did, and produced his papers. A guard glanced at the papers and waved him through, as they always did; and with a whoosh of air as the brakes released, Roberto's oil tanker rolled on down the street. Two blocks further, he repeated the process at the second roadblock. Roberto approached the south gate of the refinery complex slowly and shuddered to a stop short of the cement blockhouse. A Cuban guard came over and checked his papers and ordered him to follow the jeep to the loading area.

Roberto released his brakes and followed the jeep through the two gates and into the compound. Once inside, they made a couple of turns, and Roberto stopped his rig behind a line of driverless oil tankers. This was a daily routine for the Nicaraguan truck driver. Roberto delivered oil to several Army installations in the Managua area. Each morning at 10 a.m., he picked up his filled tanker and started on his deliveries. Every night he returned empty and parked

197

his truck in the loading line, where the early shift would start filling the trucks at 5 a.m. He glanced at his watch. It was 11:30 p.m. He was a little later than usual; but he often got delayed. He climbed out of his rig while the two Cuban guards conducted a cursory inspection of his tanker. Then he hopped in their jeep, and they drove him back to the gate. From there he walked across the street to the parking lot, climbed in his car and drove to pick up his family. They were going on an ocean voyage.

* * *

One hour later, the top hatch of Roberto's oil tanker cracked open; then it opened slowly and a man's head appeared. After determining that there was no one in the area, Richard Wade crawled cautiously out of the tanker and dropped to the ground. The former US Army Colonel was dressed in black fatigues and carred a Heckler and Koch MP5A3 submachine gun or "Hockler." His head and face were covered by a black mask and a kit bag hung from one shoulder. Nine men, dressed and armed similarly, followed the American out of the tanker.

Wade and his team had spent two hours in a false compartment at one end of the tanker, crammed in like sardines and breathing Self-Contained-Underwater-Breathing-Apparatus (SCUBA). Although there was probably enough air in the tanker to last them for the two hours, they could not take the chance so they opted for the SCUBA gear. Wade did not believe in taking chances. He and his team were the key to success on this operation.

The raiders moved up along the line of trucks and in between two warehouses and stopped. Wade signalled, and four of the men moved out toward the oil storage tanks, their bags of deadly Limpet mines over their shoulders. Then, with a nod from their leader, three men moved off to the west. Their mission was to go to the west gate and, when the lights went off, they would kill the guards and secure the gate. The other two stayed with Wade. Their objective was to silence the radio and Command Post, then to knock out the lights. The CP was located in a small cement-block building next to the power station. Wade's group moved off cautiously; when they were about 50 yards from the CP, they stopped and melted into the blackness of the ground. Up ahead, Wade could see two Cuban guards just outside the Command Post. He glanced at the luminous dial on his watch; it was 12 midnight. He did not want to make his move yet; he needed to give the other men time to sow their Limpets of destruction and Hunter's group time to get into position.

A few blocks away, an Army convoy was moving along Avenida de Paz. When the convoy reached the road leading to the Airport, the last vehicle left the convoy and turned into the Airport Road. The convoy looked like many other convoys that were going hither and yon on the roads that night, except this convoy was different. For one thing, two men were lying atop the canvas on each truck—men that looked like strange creatures from outer space, with their night vision goggles and crossbows.

The convoy rolled up to the first roadblock and stopped. Commandante 36 sat in the front seat of the lead vehicle, holding a 22 Caliber Hi-Standard pistol with silencer in his lap. A Sandinista soldier poked his head in the cab and asked for convoy papers. Commandante 36 was about to shoot the soldier when a black-clad figure dropped from the top of the truck and a hand went across the soldier's mouth and a knife flashed. At the same time, there were several snapping sounds as crossbows went into action and four Sandinista soldiers crumpled into the pavement. Hunter, in the second vehicle, was amazed at the quick and quiet efficiency of Wade's crossbowman. Several men jumped out of the back of the second truck and replaced the dead men; and the convoy rolled on. Hunter reached for the pocket-sized GE radio in his tunic and spoke two words: "First Base." There was no answer, only two audible clicks signalling that Wade had received the message.

Sergeant Alfredo Garcia, one of the "Cuban Volunteers" in Nicaragua, put out his cigarette and ordered his men to look sharp when he spotted the convoy approaching his roadblock. He was not alarmed; apparently the convoy's papers had been in order or they would not have been passed through the first roadblock. It was not unusual for convoys to come to the refinery at night to "gas up." When the lead truck stopped, Sgt. Garcia casually walked toward it.

* * *

After receiving Hunter's message, Wade shut his radio off, and he and his men began inching toward the Cuban guards. When they were within 20 yards, Wade turned and motioned for one of the men to join him; then he reached down to the bag that hung from his shoulder and removed the already loaded crossbow. He signalled to the Contra next to him to take the guard on the right and slowly rose to one knee, bringing the crossbow up to his shoulder. He glanced to the right to see if his companion was ready; satisfied, he switched on the laserscope. The red dot fell on the Cuban's chest, so he raised it to the base of his throat. There were two snaps, and both guards tumbled back against the blockhouse and crumbled to the ground. Wade was up and running before the bodies hit the ground. He opened the door and rushed inside the blockhouse, reaching for his silenced 22. He found the Duty Officer asleep in a bunk and the radioman dozing next to his radio. He let his companions silence the two Cubans, while he destroyed the radio and tore out the wires of the telephone. He was out the door and headed toward the power plant in a matter of seconds. He pushed the door open and scared the hell out of two civilian workers. "Be quiet and you will live!" he said, in Spanish.

* * *

Sgt. Alfredo Garcia was about five feet from the lead vehicle when he heard a snapping sound and something struck him in the throat with a tremendous force, knocking him backwards. He felt himself falling and he tried to cry out, but no sound came. He turned to his left and fell to the pavement. A strange icy feeling shot through his body; then the black veil of death closed his eyes. Alfredo Garcia would soon go home to Cuba—in a wooden box. It was all over in a matter of seconds at the second roadblock. As the convoy pulled out, Hunter spoke into his tiny radio again: "Second Base!" This time he received an answer from Wade: "Power station secure; standing by to douse lights."

* * *

Seventy yards away from the power station and across a vacant lot was the main Cuban troop barracks. It would be from this building that immediate reinforcements would pour, once the attack began. Wade turned to his two companions: "Get outside behind the retaining wall and cover the troop barracks. Put your goggles on; I'm going to be turning out the lights soon."

The lead vehicle in the Contra convoy rolled up to the gate and stopped. The installation perimeter was lit up like a city. Hunter

200

put the GE radio up to his mouth and whispered, "OK, turn the lights out."

By this time, Wade had learned the working intricacies of the power plant from the two more-than-cooperative civilian operators. First, he shut off the emergency back-up generator; then he shut off the main power switch from the city power. The installation was suddenly swathed in blackness!

At the main gate, the Contra commandoes poured from the trucks, and the quiet night was awakened by the sound of gunfire. The defenders, who were temporarily blinded, were no match for Contra, who had been enclosed in the backs of the trucks, wearing their night vision goggles. Within seconds the lead vehicle was through the first gate and had smashed through the second. Jim Turpin and a group of Contra leaped from the lead vehicle and began working their way down the perimeter fence toward the west gate. Turpin spotted the first guard tower and took a Carl Gustav from the nearest Contra gunner. He dropped to one knee and sighted his target. The guards in the tower were still nightblind and confused. They were not firing yet, because they could not see any targets. Turpin squeezed the trigger, and there was a whoosh of hot air as the rocket left the chamber. A split second later, the guard tower was blown into smithereens! Turpin handed the Carl Gustav back to the gunner, reluctantly. He would have preferred to keep it. His team moved on toward the second guard tower.

Commandante 36 and Rene Marcel dismounted their group at the front gate and began working to the east around the perimeter fence toward the oil refinery, destroying the Cuban positions as they went.

* * *

Wade could hear the crescendo of gunfire at the front gate. Then the door of the troop barracks swung open and one soldier came running out. He ran about ten steps before two red laser dots found him and a burst of gunfire nailed him mid-chest. He performed a French pirouette and died. He was followed by two more soldiers. Wade knelt at the door of the power plant and raised his Hockler. The two men joined the first. The troops inside the barracks realized that the front door was not the best way out. Windows opened and automatic gunfire began searching for Wade and his two companions. A group of Cubans escaped through the back door, and they joined the firefight. One of the Contra, the young man named Jose, screamed and flew backwards, never to rise again!

Hunter's truck continued through the complex. They off-loaded near the Power Plant and joined Wade's battle. One round from a Carl Gustav entered a window of the troop barracks and exploded inside, causing the roof to buckle. Another went in through the front door, and the building collapsed in upon itself; and the firing stopped.

Small fierce battles raged through the complex as Nicaraguans killed Cubans; and Cubans killed the people they were ostensibly there to help—Nicaraguans. Finally, only a few pockets of diehard Cubans were resisting. Marcel and his team were busy placing explosives in the oil refinery, while Wade, Hunter and Commandante 36 established a temporary Command Post near the demolished barracks. Three of the four men that had moved out earlier to attach the Limpet mines to the oil storage tanks reported in, saying they had accomplished their mission. The fourth man did not return. When Marcel reported that the refinery was rigged for detonation, Wade decided it was high time for them to load up and move out. They only had a few minutes before the entire complex turned into Hell-On Earth! However, things do not always go as planned. One of the oil storage tanks on the far end of the complex suddenly exploded! A huge fireball rolled into the sky and the night turned into blazing hot day. The commandoes had to take cover from the burning debris that rained down on them. Wade did not know what caused the Limpet to detonate prematurely; he had set them all to go off ten minutes from now. However, one did expode, and now there was danger of sympathetic detonations of other Limpets by fires that were raging throughout the compound.

Commandante 36 came running over and announced, "Turpin just called and reported that armored personnel carriers and tanks are approaching the west gate."

Wade thought fast. His force was in grave danger of being trapped in an exploding inferno; the armored force had to be delayed, and Turpin's small group did not have sufficient firepower to hold them long. He spotted a small 2000 gallon oil tanker parked nearby and sprinted over to it. On checking, he found the truck full of gasoline. He yelled to Hunter, "We have to go out the way we came in. Get the men loaded and haul ass! I'll delay the armor." Without another word, he climbed into the cab of the tanker and started the engine. He pressed the accelerator and the truck jumped forward. Wade headed toward the west gate.

The Contra commandoes began piling onto the trucks, carrying their dead and wounded with them. Suddenly the compound was shaken by another explosion, and a smaller fireball rolled upward from the vicinity of the west gate. A few seconds later, Jim Turpin and his men came running up to the trucks. Hunter stepped out to meet them. "Where's Wade?" he yelled.

A very excited Jim Turpin stopped and tried to get his breath. "He's had it!" gasped the giant. "He crashed the oil tanker into a tank at the gate. I didn't see him get out. It's like a blast furnace over there!"

Hunter's body became numb. Wade was indestructible! He couldn't be dead. "Was he in the truck when it hit?"

"I think so. I didn't see him jump out." returned Turpin.

Commandante 36 put his hand on Hunter's shoulder. "We have to get out of here; the whole place is going to go up in a few minutes!"

Rene Marcel could see that Hunter was about ready to take off for the west gate. He put his hand on Hunter's arm, restraining him, and said, "It is too late. We have to get out of here now."

"No!" said Hunter. "I'm not going without him."

Turpin nodded to Marcel, and they grabbed Hunter by the arms and started to force him into the truck; but they were stopped by a "YO!"

They turned to see Wade running toward them. Hunter broke away long enough to shake Wade's hand and say, "We thought you had been killed!"

Wade smiled, "So did I. I jumped just in time! Boy it is hot over there, and it's going to get hot here in a couple of minutes. Let's haul ass!"

The convoy pulled out and roared through the front gate. It stopped long enough to police up the Contra at the two roadblocks. When they were about six blocks from the refinery, a rumbling sound began behind them. At first it sounded like an approaching freight train, then it began to crack like thunder. Wade stopped the convoy so the raiders could watch the results of their handiwork. A series of fireballs rolled skyward and combined into one gigantic, fiery, belching mushroom. If they had not known better, they would have thought that an atomic bomb had been dropped on the refinery. When the burning debris started falling around the convoy, Wade ordered the convoy to move out.

Pecos Bill and his team were well behind schedule. They had just cut their way through the fence at the southern perimeter of the airfield and were slowly worming their way toward the parked aircraft when they heard the first explosion at the oil refinery. They had found the initial movement much slower than anticipated, because the area was crawling with Cuban soldiers. At one point they were held up for twenty minutes while two jeep crews stopped, talked and smoked cigarettes. Pecos Bill was not fooling himself; the delay was serious. Once the fireworks started, it was going to be difficult for him and his men to get away. He decided to throw caution away and ordered his men to get up and run. In a few minutes, they reached the end of the runway; and up ahead about 100 yards, he could see the Russian MIGs. He halted his team and told them to load. He moved behind each gunner and assigned them a target. When he was sure they were ready, he said: "FIRE!"

There was a series of whooshes as five rockets left their tubes. Four were direct hits, and the MIGs exploded in blinding flashes. The fifth rocket ricochetted off the concrete runway and exploded harmlessly in the air.

"Come on. Follow me!" yelled Pecos Bill, and he took off running towards the HIND helicopters across the runway. Lights were coming on all over the airfield and bouncing vehicle headlights could be seen in the distance. There were sporadic burst of gunfire as the confused Cubans began firing at anything that moved or looked like it was moving. Once across the runway, Pecos Bill again lined his five gunners in a kneeling position. Again, he walked to each gunner and assigned them a HIND helicopter; then he said grimly, "OK—Gawd Dammit! Don't anyone miss this time! Fire when you are ready!"

They were all on target this time, and five of the feared Russian Mi-24 HIND helicopters exploded and burst into flames and the airfield changed from night into day. "Let's go!" screamed Pecos, sprinting back across the runway.

Several gun jeeps were bearing down on them with all guns blazing. One of the gunners stopped to do battle with the oncoming jeeps, but he lost it in a hail of gunfire. Then providence played a hand, and several jeeps coming from the opposite direction got into a firefight with the jeeps coming down the runway; a mini-war between friends ensued. This confusion gave Pecos Bill and his men the respite they needed to make it back to their hole in the fence; but there was no way they were going to get back to their hidden truck!

* * *

The Contra convoy soon reached the main avenue and mixed in with the dozens of other convoys on the road. Ambulances and fire trucks, with their sirens blazing, were all headed toward the blazing refinery. After turning off the main road, they only ran into one roadblock, which was taken care of in short order; and in less than two hours, the Contra raiders were piling off their trucks on the deserted beach. The RB-15s which were waiting offshore were called in, and the troops began loading. The underground drivers took off with the trucks to ditch them and resume their secret lives.

Commandante 36 walked over to where Jorge Dunn, Hunter and Wade were standing and announced, "I'm worried about Pecos Bill. He should have been here by now."

The Commandante had no more than gotten the words out of his mouth, when two taxi vans came bouncing along the beach. The Contra still on shore spread out and took up firing positions. The lead taxi stopped with a jolt and out crawled Pecos Bill, holding a beer in on hand and dragging a young woman with the other. There were sounds of laughter and singing from inside the taxis. Pecos Bill stood there with a big smile around his drooping mustache and announced, "We were cut off, so we did the only thing one can do in Managua—we hailed taxis! These ladies thought the revolution had come, and they wanted to celebrate with us!"

As Hunter and Commandante were about to load in the last RB-15, Wade put his hand on the Memphian's shoulder and announce, "Bob, I'm not going with you!"

Hunter turned to the former Colonel with a puzzled look on his face, "What do you mean, you're not going with us?"

"I still have a couple of loose ends to tie up here before I can leave. Our contract is finished."

Hunter knew it was useless to argue with Wade. "Well, if it has to be. I wish you good luck."

The two friends shook hands, and Hunter climbed into the boat. He left Wade standing on the beach next to Jorge Dunn.

27

Commandante Raul Castro Padilla had a dark frown on his troubled face as he read the first reports from the previous night's Contra attacks on the oil refinery and airfield. He really did not need the reports on the former, as he could look out his window and see the smoke billowing skyward from the still blazing refinery. Under his breath, he cursed the Cubans. First, they said they had to use their pilots to fly the new HIND helicopters because, according to the Cubans, "the Nicaraguan pilots could not be trusted!" Then they had to bring in Cuban troops to guard the airfield; and finally they insisted that Cuban troops had to secure the sensitive and valuable oil refinery. Not that Nicaraguan troops could have prevented the disastrous attacks—it was just the pompous attitude of the Cubans that he did not like. Although he had great respect for Castro and the revolution, Padilla did not love the Cubans. They were literally running every echelon of the Sandinista Government. Every unit in the Army had its share of Cuban "Advisors," and some battalions were actually commanded by Cuban Officers. There were eight Cuban Advisors in the Security Office alone!

The destruction of the oil refinery and storage area, the best defended installation in Nicaragua, was a total disaster for the

Sandanistas. Over 90 percent of the petroleum reserves had been destroyed in one night! The nation and the military would be forced to come to a standstill; and the economy might take years to recover. It would take months before a new refinery could be built and the Russians could bring in sufficient oil to get things moving again. And the Cubans would probably use this as an excuse to bring in more men and tighten their control of the Sandinista government. Padilla groaned as he thought about having to face his boss, Tomas Borge, when the Minister returned from surveying the damage— the "Old Man" would be hell to live with for awhile.

Padilla picked up a copy of the "Official News Release" that was to be given to the media at a news conference at noon and scanned it again:

> "Contra rebels made two attacks last night against public facilities in the Managua area, inflicting minor damage, while suffering heavy casualties.
>
> "Thirty-three rebels were killed by security forces at the Salan Oil Refinery. The Contra rebels managed to destroy three small oil storage tanks and inflict minor damage to the refinery, before the survivors were driven off.
>
> "Thirteen more Contra rebels were killed by alert Security forces at the International Airport, as they attempted to infiltrate the facility. Two private airplanes were damaged."

Colonel Padilla got up and walked to the window. In the distance, heavy black smoke covered the western horizon. He shook his head and mumbled to himself, "They'll never believe that release."

It was really too late for an "Official News Release" anyway, because the "cat was already out of the bag"! In fact, by 10 a.m. most of the international media had already wired or phoned their stories home. Their sources were their own eyes and many of the hundreds of firefighters, medics and soldiers that had been working at the target areas. And these "sources" also reported that they did not see any Contra bodies.

A blind man could see from downtown Managua the massive flames and smoke from the refinery. It was clear to all that the oil refinery and storage tanks had been destroyed.

The Sandinistas tried to hide the facts of the terrible devastation from the world—but this time, they were unable to hide the truth.

* * *

ATLANTA, GEORGIA

When Libby McGinnis heard the reports coming in from Nicaragua, she knew instinctively that Wade was behind the attacks. And she reported the story that night with a great deal of personal satisfaction and pride.

Later that same night, Libby received a long distance phone call from Robert Hunter. Her first question was, "Is he all right?"

"Yes!" answered Hunter. "He's fine, but he stayed in Nicaragua. He said he had some loose ends to tie up."

"Yes, I knew he would stay," said Libby, her statement surprising Hunter. Libby was silent for a moment. She realized that Commandante Padilla's days were numbered.

"Do you have your tape recorder on?" asked Hunter.

"No!"

"Well turn it on. You are about to get an exclusive from an unnamed reliable source."

* * *

That evening, Libby started her news broadcast by saying, "Today I talked to one of the Contra officers who was on the raid in Nicaragua which completely destroyed the Oil Refinery and Oil Storage Depot at Salan and destroyed five Russian-made HIND helicopters and four MIG jet airplanes at the International Airport. According to my source, who I happen to know personally and whose word I consider above reproach, the Contra . . . ."

* * *

Achmed Ben Abdullah, Khadafy's gift to the Sandanistas, walked out of the Central Police Station at 7 p.m. He hummed to himself as he swung into stride for the 10 minute walk to his apartment. He only lived a few blocks from the Station so it was his custom to walk to and from work.

The Arab enjoyed living and working in Nicaragua. The Central American nation was very different from the spartan life of Khadafy's strict Muslim Libya. For one thing, here Achmed could have a drink of liquor any time he felt like it; and Achmed felt like having a bottle of scotch every night.

The large Libyan was a true Paleolithic mesomorph. He was a brute who enjoyed his craft. He derived a sensual pleasure from inflicting pain on his fellow human beings. These days, his Sandinista friends gave him plenty of pleasure. His business had especially picked up since the crazy Cuban Doctor had been killed.

A van parked along the side of the street did not draw Achmed's attention nor did he take special notice when a man got out of the van and started walking toward him. But he did take notice when the man stopped, blocking his way, and said quietly, "Achmed old friend, it is good to see you again!"

The Libyan stopped abruptly. He did not recognize the voice or the man. "Hello?" he said.

The figure stepped closer, "Don't you recognize me, Achmed?" Then recognition hit Achmed's dull mind and he blurted, "The American Colonel?" At the same time, he went for the pistol on his hip; but it was too late. The Arab never saw the foot that struck him in the testicles! He groaned as the sharp pain climbed into his groin, and he doubled up. The second kick caught him on the jaw and his lights went out. When Achmed regained consciousness, he found himself bound to a wooden chair and sitting in the center of an empty warehouse. He heard a noise and looked up to see the American Colonel walking toward him. Wade stopped in front of his prisoner and addressed him: "Salam ah-leikum, Achmed. I hope Allah gave you good dreams."

The American drew a knife from his belt and stepped forward. The Arab cringed, expecting the worse. However, Wade did not cut him; instead he slashed the bonds, freeing the Libyan, and stepped back. Achmed sat there rubbing his wrists and trying to figure what the American was going to do next. He considered jumping the American immediately and killing him, but something held him back. He looked around the warehouse, but he did not see anyone else.

Wade noticed Achmed looking around and said, "That's right, Achmed. There is no one else here. We are alone! Just you and me. And I'm not armed." He threw the knife across the room.

The Arab gathered a little confidence and looked at his captor. He outweighed the American by 50 pounds and was at least a head taller. Achmed spent two hours a day lifting weights, so he knew he was stong. The Americn did not look that strong. He stood up and flexed his muscles.

"Achmed, you enjoy beating up defenseless people. And I

understand that sometimes you even beat them to death. Well, I am going to give you a chance to beat me to death; how do you like that? Does that give you a hard-on, you stupid camel?

The Arab's eyes blazed at Wade with animal-like hatred. "I will kill you, American dog!"

Wade laughed out loud, "You are something else Achmed. Ask yourself why I let you loose. I am going to beat you to death, and you will never lay a hand on me. I still have some scars from your cigarette burns; and those will be the last scars you will give me."

"I'm going to break your neck!" growled Achmed.

"OK, start breaking, you miserable ape." Wade turned his back on the Arab and started walking off.

Achmed roared like a bull and stormed forward. Wade danced aside and turned, bringing his foot high in the air and kicking the Arab in the back of the head. Achmed's head exploded with pain, and he pitched forward. As he tried to stand, Wade did a complete circle and lashed out with a vicious kick to Achmed's mouth. The Libyan flew backward from the force of the blow and lay there stunned. Blood streamed from a broken nose, and he spit his front teeth on the floor. Wade stood patiently as Achmed struggled to his feet.

"Come on Achmed. Get up. I thought you enjoyed this physical stuff," Wade taunted.

Achmed slowly got up from the floor. His head throbbed with pain, and he was choking from the blood running back down his throat. But the American gave him no respite; he moved in and pummeled the Libyan with a series of body blows. Achmed heard his ribs breaking with each smash, and sharp pains ripped through his chest. Wade stepped back, pivoted, and kicked the Arab in the testicles; and the hapless Achmed screamed in pain. He fell to his hands and knees and whimpered like an injured animal. A feeling of despair came over him as he realized he did not have a chance against the American—he was going to die! "Please don't kill me! Please don't kill me!" he pleaded.

"How many of your victims begged for mercy, Achmed? How many? You had better make your peace with Allah now," said Wade, stepping forward and breaking the Arab's collarbone with a vicious karate chop.

Achmed struggled to his feet and stood there swaying and whimpering.

"I once told your friend, Doctor Amador, that there is truth in the old adage, 'He who lives by the sword, dies by the sword!'' said Wade, deciding to finish it off. He stepped forward and struck Achmed with a vicious karate knuckle blow to the upper solar plexis.

The Arab felt horrible pain as his heart ruptured; and he knew it was a killing blow. He fell forward to his knees, vomiting blood. Wade delivered the Coup de Grace with an open hand chop to the back of the Arab's neck. Achmed pitched forward and kicked the floor three times before he left to join his Allah.

28

MANAGUA, NICARAGUA

As usual, Commandante Raul Castro Padilla left the Ministry building at 6 p.m. and walked down the front steps to his waiting Mercedes-Benz. As usual, his uniformed chauffer opened the door for him, then climbed into the front with the bodyguard; and the car pulled out onto the Avenue for the ten minute drive to the home of Padilla's mistress. As usual, the black Mercedes parked in front of a two-story apartment building at 894 Avenida Ruiz, and the bodyguard got out first and held the door open for Colonel Padilla. As usual, the bodyguard checked his watch as his boss disappeared through the front door. As usual, he climbed back into the car and settled in for a little siesta, because his boss would be occuppied with his young mistress until 11 p.m.

At 10 p.m., a man and woman walked by the Mercedes. The man was obviously drunk, and the woman was pulling on his arm and crying hysterically. They stopped near the car; and the man slapped the lady, knocking her to the ground. The driver and bodyguard sat watching the incident, wondering if they should get involved. They did not have to make a decision; because the door on the driver's side was suddenly jerked open, and Padilla's men found themselves staring into the barrel of an automatic pistol.

At 11 p.m., Padilla walked out of his lady friend's apartment building and headed toward his waiting car. He really did not want to go home, but his wife would probably be asleep by now; so he might not have to face her. He felt good, recharged! Lolana always made him feel that way. After a trying day at the office, she was the perfect anodyne for his frayed nerves. She seemed to be able to read his moods and give him exactly what he needed and wanted. Sometimes, she was gentle like a baby deer; other times she was wild like a tigress.

Suddenly, he was startled by a figure that stepped out of the bushes and blocked his way. Padilla's right hand automatically moved and rested on the butt of the revolver at his right hip.

"Good evening, Commandante!" the figure said.

"Who are you? What do you want?" demanded the Sandinista Colonel, in a brusque voice.

"I have come for you, Commandante! You are under arrest for murder and treason!"

Padilla panicked as he suddenly recognized the spectre in front of him, and he clawed for his revolver—but he was an instant too late! The spectre turned; and his foot lashed out, smashing the Nicaraguan Colonel in the lower groin. Padilla dropped his revolver, clutched his stomach and doubled over in pain and shock. The figure moved again, and Padilla's head exploded. He flipped backwards and lay still on the sidewalk.

* * *

Padilla struggled back to consciousness. He had trouble focusing his eyes, because his head throbbed like a trip-hammer. He found himself lying on the cement floor of a small empty room. Sitting next to him was a tin cup of water and a chunk of moldy bread. He pulled himself to his feet, and a wave of dizziness almost sent him back to the floor. He staggered around the room, inspecting his small cell—but there was no way out. He sunk back to the floor and covered his face with his hands. Cold fear ran down his spine, causing him to shiver. He had recognized the American Colonel too late. Now he was in the hands of the madman. He was in the hands of the man who had killed Doctor Amador and, most likely, Achmed. He had not thought much about Achmed's disappearance—until now. Confused thoughts ran through Padilla's head, but he still did not link Wade with the Salazaars.

The door opened and the American walked in. He stopped and looked down at the disheveled Nicaraguan Colonel. "You look like hell, Commandante—guess you didn't sleep well."

Padilla screwed up his waning courage and asked, "What are you going to do to me?"

"Well Commandante, if it was just up to me, I would kill you very slowly. However, you are going to be tried by a People's Tribunal. You know what they are. You guys use them all the time. But before you go on trial, I want to ask you some questions. We know that Enrique Salazaar is still alive, and you are going to tell me where he is being kept."

"Enrique Salazaar is dead. He was killed by the Contras," returned Padilla.

Wade reached down and grabbed the Nicaraguan's shirt and pulled him to his feet. "You are a liar!" exclaimed Wade. "I want you to remember back to that night on August 21, 1980. Do you remember that night and what you and your men did?"

Padilla remembered—but he remained silent.

"Do you remember Salazaar's daughter? Well, I do! She was my wife! You murdered my wife!"

Padilla's blood turned cold, and he felt as if he were going to pass out. Waves of dizziness swept through him, and he began to shake. He could see the hatred in the American's eyes. But how had Wade found out?

Wade could see the animal fear in Padilla's eyes. He shook the Nicaraguan like a dish rag and growled, "That's right, you bastard. The girl you murdered was my wife! The woman you murdered was my mother-in-law! The man you say is dead was my father-in-law; and the boy you beat and imprisoned was my son! Now, where is Enrique?"

"He is dead!" whimpered the defeated Padilla. "He died last month in prison!"

Wade sensed the Nicaraguan was telling the truth. The years of loneliness and mourning poured out of Wade, and he tore into the Colonel with uncontrolled fury. Padilla tried to protect himself from Wade's punishing fists, but he was helpless. Pain—horrible pain— engulfed him. Wade vented his anger and frustration; then he dropped the unconscious Colonel to the floor and covered his own face with his hands and cried. He cried for the first time since his wife's death. He cried for her! It was over for him.

* * *

They held the trial in a vacant warehouse. Raul Padilla was brought before the Tribunal at 8 a.m. The Tribunal was set up according to Sandinista Revolutionary Laws and consisted of one man with legal training and two commoners. The man seated in the center picked up a piece of paper and read:

"Commandante Raul Castro Padilla, you are accused of the following crimes:

"The murders of Enrique Salazaar, Janice Salazaar and Maria Salazaar Wade on the night of August 21, 1980. How do you plead?"

Padilla's face was battered and swollen. He glanced over at Richard Wade and cringed. "I am innocent!" he whimpered.

The Tribunal Chairman continued: "Further, during the months of March, April and May of 1983, in the districts of Cua, Kilambe, Pita del Carmen, and Tigre, soldiers under your command arrested a number of people who were accused of performing counter-revoluntionary activities. A short time later, these persons were found dead. They were . . .

"Efrain Molina—captured in May in the district of Cua. Four days after his arrest, he was found dead in the district of San Pedro.

"Cuto Torrey and Justiniano Cano—summoned to El Cua Command in May, arrested for one hour, and subsequently released. They were murdered on their way home.

"Salome Roderiguez—taken from his home by Sandinista soldiers in the month of March. They took him to the bank of the Cua River where he was machine-gunned.

"In Chontales District on November 28, prisoners were executed by troops under your command. Among them were Genaro Sequeira, Marcario Amador, Elias Flores, Ignacio Raudex, Jose Calero, Isaias Robleto, Herberto Sier, Alfonso and Aristides Miranda."

Padilla sat in his wooden chair, stunned as the list of names continued, names he could not even remember. But the man he feared most, the eyes he could not get away from, was sitting directly in front of him. He could remember vividly what took place in the Salazaar home—and he remembered vividly the pain from Wade's fists. He shivered when he thought about what Wade would do if the American knew he had raped his wife before putting the gun to her head. Padilla quit listening to the trial. He leaned forward and put his face in his hands and cried. He suddenly wanted to talk to a priest.

Raul Castro Padilla was found guilty and sentenced to death.

They did not waste time. A single rope was slung over the rafters of the deserted warehouse and a folding chair was positioned below the dangling rope. Padilla was crying and pleading for his life as they dragged him to the chair. It took five men to put the rope around his neck and stand the Commandante on the chair.

Wade watched with a hollow feeling in the pit of his stomach. He turned and walked out of the room before the chair was kicked out from under Padilla.

Inside, Padilla kicked for 60 seconds before he stopped being an earthly oxygen consumer. Justice was done!

* * *

The following morning, at a cemetary in the suburbs of Managua, there were fresh flowers on the graves in the Salazaar family plot. The stone with David Wade's name on it was gone. A short distance away was a fresh grave and a brand new headstone, on which was chiseled . . .

**RAUL CASTRO PADILLA
"TRAITOR TO THE REVOLUTION"
1940-1986
EXECUTED FOR THE MURDER OF:
ENRIQUE SALAZAAR
JANICE SALAZAAR
MARIA SALAZAAR WADE**

29

FDN HEADQUARTERS, SOMEWHERE IN HONDURAS

When Wade walked out of Nicaragua and arrived at the Contra Camp, he found Robert Hunter waiting for him. The Memphian did not waste time with cordialities. He shook Wade's hand and announced, "I have a jet waiting in Tegucigalpa to take us to Washington tomorrow."

"Not me," returned the former Colonel. "I want to go straight to Atlanta to pick up Libby, then on to Memphis to see David."

"You will get to see them. They are both waiting in Atlanta," said Hunter. "but first we have to go to Washington. The President wants to see you as soon as possible!"

Wade turned to his friend, a puzzled look on his face. "The President wants to see me? I don't understand."

Hunter patted Wade on the back. "Because my friend, we have been working for the President all along. And he thinks it is time he meets you."

Wade was still confused. "What do you mean, working for the President?"

"What I'm saying is that the President knew about the planned raid in Managua, and he gave us his tacit approval. Of course, this must remain our secret; but he gave me permission to tell you."

"I can't believe the President was involved in this," returned Wade.

"Well, he wasn't—officially. It was strictly a private sector and FDN operation. But unofficially he approved it and sanctioned it. He has access to the finest intelligence information in the world, and he knows what is going on in Nicaragua and what will happen if the communists solidify their base there. If he could, he would give FDN whatever help and materials they need. He knows that if the FDN loses, the United States will someday have to send in troops. The President's hands are tied by a liberal Congress still suffering from the Vietnam War Syndrome and a hostile media which has succumbed to the communist disinformation program. It is just too damn bad that the US cannot act in its own self-interests because of the media, the Congress and the Communists. So, you and I have been working for him all along. And I can tell you, he is damned pleased with the results of the raid. I can only assume that he wants to tell you himself."

Wade had always suspected that Hunter was more than he seemed—but he was somewhat surprised to find out that Hunter was working directly for the President. And still being a good soldier, he could understand why Hunter had not confided in him. Wade did not get much time to renew his friendships in the FDN. He departed, promising he would return.

* * *

A black limousine rolled out on the runway at Andrews Airport and picked them up as they stepped off Hunter's private jet. It whisked through the heavy mid-afternoon traffic of Washington and to the back of the White House. A sharp-looking Marine guard met the car and escorted them into a back entrance of the Chief Executive's home.

* * *

The President of the United States stood up as Wade and Hunter entered the Oval Office. He was wearing a dark-blue business suit and looked 20 years younger than his age. The Commander-in-Chief walked around his desk and met them in the center of the room. He reached out and grasped Wade's hand firmly and said, "General Wade, I am very pleased to finally meet you in person; and I'm happy to see you back safe and sound."

Wade noticed the President's mistake of calling him General, but he dismissed it as an executive oversight. "It is an honor to meet you, Mr. President."

The Chief Executive dropped Wade's hand and turned to Hunter and shook his hand. "Robert, I trust you had a good flight?"

"Yes Sir. No problems at all."

The President gestured to two leather chairs in front of his desk, then walked around and sat in his own chair. He put his hands together and leaned forward with his elbows on the desk. "General, I presume Bob has told you that he has been working as a Special Assistant to me?"

"Yes, Sir, he did."

"Well, I want you both to know that your raid in Managua was brilliantly planned and brilliantly executed. Well done! Well done! And it could not have come at a better time. I think we are going to get some help for the Contra now! And God only knows, they need it. I only wish I could tell the world what you two have done— so you could get the recognition you deserve. Unfortunately, we cannot tell anyone for reasons I am sure you understand. Our friends in the press would crucify us. And I know you have experienced that before, General."

Wade noted the President's use of the word General again, and he wanted to correct him. However, Wade was not in the habit of correcting Presidents. So he kept his mouth shut.

The President continued, "General Wade, I have followed your career and life for several years, and I have kept tabs on you since you left the Army. Your assault on the airliner in Rome was brilliant. And my heart went out to you during the hearings when you sacrificed yourself for me and the Delta Force. Believe me son, your personal sacrifice did not go unnoticed. The only mistake I made was not calling you in and telling you—and I apologize for that."

Wade could not believe what he was hearing. The President of the United States was apologizing to him. Wade did not like the fact that he had to give up his career—but he had known what he had to do, both for the good of his country and the Delta Force. It made him feel warm inside to here the President's words.

The Chief Executive paused to let his words sink home, then continued—this time dropping a blockbuster: "I also followed your work in the Agency and was in on selecting you for several of your missions. Bob here did not contact you by chance. We wanted you involved in Central America. Because of your personal ties there, you were a natural. Your resignation from the Army was never accepted! In fact you have officially been carried on Special Duty to the President of the United States."

Wade was stunned! Not even in his wildest imagination could he have dreamed up the scenario being explained by the President. Why, he thought, didn't someone tell me?

The President tried to answer his thought: "I thought it better to keep this from you for awhile, because I did not want the media to find out. I know now that this was a mistake, and I apologize again. But I must admit that everything has turned out for the best."

Wade did not agree. He was angry and almost to the point of telling the President so—but he held his tongue.

The Man behind the desk dropped his final bombshell: "Last week, I sent your file before a Stand-by Promotion Board with a personal letter from me." He stopped and handed Wade a set of official-looking orders, then said, "You have been promoted to Brigadeer General!" The President stood up and reached for Wade's hand: "Congratulations, General Wade!"

* * *

Brig. Gen. Richard Wade left the President's Office with a bag of jelly beans, a new rank, a new assignment, and a new lease on life. What goes around comes around!

The FDN would soon be establishing a "Government-in Exile," and the President was confident that he could swing enough votes in Congress, since the successful raid in Nicaragua, for the US to recognize the new government. Once this was accomplished, the FDN would be eligible for American Aid based on the US Foreign Aid Bill. The President wanted Wade to act as his "Special Assistant" and coordinate the assistance efforts to the FDN.

HOLIDAY INN, GRAND CAYMAN ISLAND, BWI

Brig. Gen. Richard Wade and his lovely wife stood holding hands on their balcony, looking out across the sandy beach into the turquoise waters of the Carribean. Just below them, clusters of tourists, in various states of undress and sobriety, some twisting camera dials, stood in small groups on the beach and around the bar, watching the sun go down. Soft calypso music played in the background;

and without realizing it, most of the anxious sun-watchers were swaying to the rhythm of the island music.

"Look darling!" exclaimed Libby Wade. "They are all waiting to see the Green Flash."

They watched the sun in silence, content in their love and happiness. The sun sank and sank. Down below, someone yelled, "The Green Flash! See it? A perfect Green Flash!"

Some said they saw it. Some said they did not. On all accounts it was a perfect sunset.

Up on the balcony, the two honeymooners watched as the sun disappeared below the horizon—then it happened! A brilliant bright green light flickered through the sky—for them!

It was a perfect Green Flash!

Appendix A

THE STORY OF CIVILIAN MATERIEL ASSISTANCE

On 1 September 1984, two Americans, Dana H. Parker and James P. Powell, were killed by Sandinista forces in Nicaragua. The next morning, a Deputy Director in the Defense Intelligence Agency phoned his condolences on the deaths of what he thought were two CIA men.

"Our two men?" returned the CIA Deputy. "We thought they were your men!'

"Well, if they were not yours or ours, said the DIA Deputy, "what in the hell is the CMA?"

Who were Parker and Powell? What is the CMA? Were they hired mercenaries as some papers claimed? Were they gun-toting, camouflage-wearing, good-old boys, who liked to play soldier on weekends as others claimed? What kind of man would write home as James Powell did and say,

"These people and the Americans I am with make me proud to be here. We are all dedicated to helping these people. They have inspired us with their determination and valor. I am doing what I think is right."

* * *

In November 1984, I was in Central America visiting one of the forward camps of the Nicaraguan Democratic Forces (FDN) or Contra. I noticed several other Americans in the camp working with the FDN. They were all wearing t-shirts with CMA FREEDOM-FIGHTERS emblazoned across the front. I figured these Americans were with the CIA, so I asked one of the FDN officers who these Americans were.

"They are with the CMA," he answered.

"You mean CIA, don't you?" I whispered, with a knowing wink.

"No, I mean the CMA, Civilian Military Assistance."

"What is Civilian Military Assistance?" I asked.

"They are our friends—they are FDN!" he returned.

I remembered reading about the two Americans who had been

killed in Nicaragua several weeks earlier—but like many, I figured the CMA was just another cover for the CIA. And now it appeared that I might have been wrong.

My curiosity aroused, I walked over to one of the CMA medics and introduced myself. His name was Richard Johnson and he was from New Orleans. He said that he was a CMA volunteer, working with the FDN, without pay, and he had been in the country for six weeks.

I returned to the States a few days later having decided to find out more about this CMA bunch. They sounded like my kind of people. I was delayed for several months, because I went into isolation near the beautiful Los Padres National Forest in California to write my second book, THE HEROES WHO FELL FROM GRACE, a true story about the search for American POW/MIAs in Southeast Asia.

In August 1985, while attending the Soldier of Fortune Convention in Las Vegas to plug my new book, I spotted a booth manned by a group of men wearing camouflaged uniforms. Over the booth was a banner which read: "CIVILIAN MILITARY ASSISTANCE." There I met Tom Posey, the Director of CMA, and his Executive Director, Jim Turney. Five minutes later I was a paid member. Since I had some time in-between books, I wanted to get back into the fight against communism. I offered my services to Posey and Turney and told them I had several months to volunteer—and that I was ready to go to Nicaragua and fight or whatever. The two Directors explained what they needed most was someone to reorganize the National Headquarters and publish a Monthly Newsletter—so that is how I became CMA's Director of Operations and Editor of the VICTORY and established a very close association with a Kay Pro 16 Computer.

Tom Posey, the Director and founder of CMA, is a wiry, blue-eyed, intense man with closely cropped hair. He was born and raised in Decatur, Alabama, where his father owned and operated a small produce business. When he was 17, Posey enlisted in the US Marine Corps. In Vietnam, he fought in several tough battles, including Khe San. He spent seven years in the Corps, rising to the rank of Staff Sergeant before he returned to Decatur and took over his father's produce business. He soon became a leader in his community and was elected to the City Council. In his spare time, he coaches Little League Baseball.

Posey has strong convictions about patriotism and the American sense of fair play and justice. He is a staunch anti-communist who firmly believes the communists must be stopped in their efforts to take over Central America. It is difficult for a man like Posey to understand why the American public is so apathetic to the growing communist menace. He states, "The United States and America deserve a victory over communism. We are all Americans—don't forget that—whether we live here, in Canada, Nicaragua or Brazil. We need a major victory over the communists, one in which they can be the ones, for a change, to have to go home and lick their wounds. Since World War II, over 40 countries have fallen to communism; and how many have they lost besides little Grenada? But once they lose a major country such as Nicaragua, other people living under communist domination will see that the communists are our sworn enemies. So I say anything that can be done right now to stop the spread of communism, America ought to do it."

About CMA, Posey says, "We're together to fight communism before it comes to the United States. We've drawn our line, and that line happens to be in Central America. We're offering our knowledge and expertise and what little material support we can to those who need it, who are themselves fighting for the survival of something we believe very strongly in: freedom.

"If the politicians won't let us win, then the private sector must take it in their own hands to do it."

Posey's unique, private-sector approach to fighting the spread of communism came to a head in 1983, when he and four other Vietnam Veterans decided to do something besides talk about fighting the communists in Central America. They chose El Salvador because the Army there which was fighting communist insurgents, backed by Cuba and Nicaragua, was short of field equipment and other supplies. They began collecting what they could: uniforms, boots, field gear, medical supplies, etc. In October 1983, Posey flew to El Salvador at his own expense to ask the government what they needed most and to arrange for the supplies his group had already collected to be sent down. His initial goal was to collect enough supplies to outfit two infantry companies.

Meanwhile, back in Washington, the US Congress finally passed a much needed Foreign Aid Bill that included substantial aid for El Salvador. When Posey and his small band found out about the Aid Bill, they turned their attention to the forces fighting the Marxist government in Nicaragua, the Nicaraguan Democratic Forces (FDN).

Posey's group arrived in Tegucigalpa in January 1984, where Honduran officials discreetly put them into contact with the leaders of the FDN. The Nicaraguan Freedom Fighters, who were trying to fight a war with meager monies and supplies, welcomed Posey's offer of assistance.

Posey returned home and resigned his seat on the City Council so he could devote full time to the growing organization he now called the Civilian Military Assistance.

Posey made no attempt to hide his organization's desire to help in the struggle against the spread of communism in Central America or of his support for the Contra. He placed ads in local and regional newspapers soliciting supplies and money for the anti-communist forces in Nicaragua. As word of CMA's activities spread, their credibility grew. More Alabama Chapters opened and then a few in Tennessee and Georgia. Large amounts of donated and purchased supplies and equipment began to stockpile, and Posey and his men began trucking the supplies to New Orleans and turning them over to the FDN.

It was about this time that Jim Turney, who was to become the Executive Director of CMA, joined the organization. Turney is a huge, 260 pound, muscular man with a thick black beard. Turney owned a surplus store in Collierville, TN, and was one of the leaders of a group called the Phantom Division. The CMA was just what Turney was looking for. He donated most of his stock to the FDN and sold his business so he could devote his efforts to help CMA fight communism. Turney's natural leadership ability and magnetic personality soon began to pay off, and the membership of CMA grew rapidly. He soon established CMA's National Headquarters in Memphis, TN.

Jim Turney graduated from Kingsbury High School in Memphis and immediately enlisted in the Marine Corps. He was wounded twice during the Battle of Hue City in Vietnam. After a lengthy stay in the hospital, he volunteered to go back to Nam. His Marine Corps career was cut short when he stepped on a booby trap near An Hoa. Two years later, after a series of operations and long hospital stays, he was retired with a medical disability from the Corps.

Turney is bitter about the Vietnam War. He thinks it was the right war at the right time and that we should have been allowed to win it. He does not believe that the war is over. He has dedicated his life to stop the spread of communism and knows that we must hold the line in Central America. He says that communists are not even good when they are dead—but they are more manageable!

In July 1984, Posey and Turney decided that CMA could afford to sponsor a six-man training team which would provide their military expertise to the FDN. The men chosen were . . .

Dana H. Parker, Jr., who was on a leave of absence from the Huntsville, Alabama Police Department. The Green Beret Reservist was a physical fitness enthusiast who could bench press 370 pounds and usually run five miles a day. He finished first in his Special Forces Training Class at Fort Bragg and maxed the Army Physical Fitness Test at the Alabama Military Institute.

William P. Courtney, 43, an Army Chief Warrant Officer and Vietnam Veteran who holds a full time civilian job with the 1st BN, 20th Special Forces Group, Alabama National Guard.

Walton "Cisco" Blanton of Sheffield, AL, another Vietnam veteran who served 10 years in the Army.

Cliff Albright of Memphis, a retired Republic Air Lines Pilot and Vietnam veteran. Albright is a Master Parachutist, Rigger, Jumpmaster and Instructor.

James Powell, a civilian flight instructor who served as an Army helicopter pilot in Vietnam where he was shot down three times. Back problems from his combat injuries have occasionally incapacitated him with excruciating pain.

Louis McKnight, who had been a friend of Powell's since the two went to high school together. The Vietnam veteran helicopter mechanic had recently been a civilian maintenance instructor at Hurlbert Air Force Base in Memphis. McKnight is also a qualified pilot of both single and multi-engine airplanes.

Tragedy struck the group on 1 September 1984. James Powell, Dana Parker, and an FDN pilot, Mario Pozo, were killed when their helicopter was struck by Sandinista ground fire.

The bodies of the Americans were exploited for their full propaganda value by the Sandinistas, who paraded them through the streets of Managua in an attempt to imply connection between the CMA and CIA. Their remains were not returned to American soil for over a month.

As a result of the deaths of Powell and Parker, the CMA had to endure the scrutiny of the government, the press and a largely unsympathetic public, who saw the dead men and their friends not as Freedom-Fighters but as some type of adventurous mercenaries. The term "mercenary" was used with abandon.

The CMA mourned, buried their fallen comrades and got on with the program. In November 1984, Jim Turney arrived in Honduras with the second CMA training team. They spent several weeks working with the Commando Especial Operations unit of the FDN. When the team departed, two medics and a weapons repairman remained behind.

1985 was a busy year for CMA. The organization grew by leaps and bounds. Chapters were established in 35 states and 5 foreign countries. In the beginning, most members were Vietnam veterans; however, as CMA's reputation grew, people from all walks of life joined and/or supported the group. Also, as CMA received more publicity it began to draw the attention of communist and left-wing organizations.

In December 1985, the Director of the Mid-South Peace and Justice Center, a liberal organization which advocates the total withdrawal of the US presence in Central America and which is a "Solidarity Group" which supports the Sandinistas and the communist insurgents in El Salvador, wrote, "The CMA which has been providing assistance to the Contra rebels in Nicaragua should be stigmatized as thoroughly as Khadafy of Libya should be." He continued by saying that the CMA supports terrorists. In a secret meeting, he told his followers that he was not as concerned about the actual supplies the CMA was sending to the Contra as he was about the idea of CMA and the fact that CMA was gaining popularity in a conservative South.

Other liberal groups branded the CMA as Nazis, KKK, CIA, and mercenaries. Mercenaries receive pay to fight for other countries and causes. CMA members are not fighting and certainly not getting paid. CMA membership includes Blacks, Jews, Latin Americans, women, and even a few Democrats. It is easy to see why communist and left-wing groups fear the CMA; all one has to do is to read the CMA pledge:

> "WE ARE NOT GOING TO ACCEPT THE BRUTAL COMMUNIST REGIME IN NICARAGUA, AND WE ARE NOT GOING TO ABANDON THE PEOPLE OF NICARAGUA TO THE COMMUNISTS AS WE ABANDONED THE PEOPLE OF EASTERN EUROPE, CUBA, ANGOLA, ETHIOPIA, AND SOUTHEAST ASIA . . . . THE LINE IS DRAWN!!! . . ."

In 1985, CMA provided over $4 million worth of non-lethal

supplies and equipment to the FDN. These included:

-10,000 uniforms, 4,000 pairs of boots, and 8,000 pairs of socks.

-Field equipment (packs, suspenders, canteens, canteen covers, ponchos, poncho liners, headgear, etc.) for 2,000 men.

-The equivalent of three field hospitals plus three tractor-trailer loads of medical supplies.

-Enough civilian clothes and shoes for 10,000 people.

-Fifteen generators (12 portable and 3 walk-in).

-35 general purpose tents.

-Hundreds of radio batteries, solar battery chargers, classroom materials.

-300 cases of field rations and four truckloads of other food.

Three to twelve men (trainers, technicians and medics) worked with the FDN on a continual basis. However, the most important thing the CMA furnished the FDN in 1985 was moral support. The US government had withdrawn support to the Freedom-Fighters, and CMA showed them that there were still Americans who cared.

In January 1986, Jim Malia went to Honduras to work at FDN HQS. Malia, a retired Special Forces Sergeant with prior experience in Central America, had started out handling CMA supplies in New Orleans. However, because of his skills and leadership ability, he soon took over as supervisor of the FDN warehouse and resupply operations. He headed a small crew of Nicaraguans and CMA volunteers who received, stored and loaded supplies bound for the Contra.

I replaced Malia until CMA could find a suitable replacement. January was a slow month, and only a few supplies trickled to the FDN. These were the remnants of the $27 million in humanitarian aid furnished by the US; supplies and materials collected by the CMA and other private groups; and a few supplies purchased by the FDN with monies donated from the private sector.

It is interesting to note here that the CMA, using the "good-old-boy-network," was able to help the FDN purchase items such as fatigues, ponchos, poncho liners, boots, etc., at a lower price than the US government paid—and often from the same manufacturer or supplier.

My temporary job in New Orleans was not as exalted as it sounds; mostly, I helped to unload trucks, load trucks, move things around in the warehouse, count an awful lot of stuff, and, on a couple of occasions helped to load an aircraft. The aircraft was interesting in itself, an antiquated DC-6 which had such terrible oil leaks that

I figured they had to fly with two men on the wings pouring in oil—but it did get the job done.

In New Orleans, I met and worked with Mario Callero, brother of Adolfo Callero, President of the FDN. Mario was the Supply and Procurement Officer for the Contra. He graduated from college in the US and spent a tour in the US Marine Corps. Like most of the Nicaraguans I met, Mario loves the United States and lives to see a democratic form of government like we have established in Nicaragua. Mario is dedicated to the cause, and a sixteen hour work day is the norm for this dynamic man.

In February 1986, Tom Posey, Jim Turney, David "Sparky" Sparks, Iowa State CMA Director, and I went to Washington to lobby on behalf of the Contra Aid Bill. We briefed the Inter-American Defense Council and several other Conservative groups. We met with representatives from other Freedom-Fighter Groups (Afghanistan, Angola, and Cambodia) and talked to as many Congressmen as we could. Posey appeared on several radio talk shows in the Washington area. We were pleased to find out how much the CMA was respected by the various conservative groups and feared by the liberal and left-wingers.

Brigadier General D.M. Schmuck, USMC Retired and a member of the CMA National Advisory Board, traveled to Honduras and visited the FDN. After returning to the US, General Schmuck submitted a report on the FDN to the Commandant of the Marine Corps. This thorough and objective report was circulated through Washington and became a major influence in finally getting the Contra Aid Bill passed. General Schmuck is a highly decorated veteran of World War II, the Korean War and Vietnam. His sage advice and assistance has been essential to CMA's success.

In May, CMA changed their name to Civilian Material Assistance, because it was felt this more described the idea of the organization.

In July, Jim Turney was invited to Guatemala and, as a result of his visit, CMA has joined the fight against the communist insurgents in that vital nation. So far, CMA has provided instructors to the National Police, special equipment to the Airborne School and Ranger School, and $150,000 worth of clothing, medical supplies and school equipment to refugee camps and orphanages. There are plans to establish and support a large refugee camp and four medical aid stations near the Mexican border. In conjunction with the Guatemalan Army, CMA is sponsoring a parachute training course and Central American Freedom Jump in Guatemala in July 1987.

1986 was a good year for CMA. Membership doubled and chapters are now in 44 states and 6 foreign countries. The State Director of Georgia is a women, and the oldest member is an 83 year-old-lady from Columbus, Ohio.

I cannot talk about CMA without pointing out the contributions and support of Herbert Humphreys, Jr., a well-known fourth generation Memphis, TN, businessman. "Herbo," as his friends call him, is Chairman of the National Advisory Board and Chairman of the Board of Directors of CMA. He is a dedicated American patriot who believes that the Communist advance must be stopped in Central America. A world traveler and adventurer, Humphreys has been to the Soviet Union, Cuba and has visited 161 other countries including 18 in which hostilities were or are going on—such as Angola, Rhodesia, South Africa, El Salvador, Guatemala and Nicaragua. A frequent visitor to Honduras, he has supported the Anti-Communist Freedom-Fighters (Contra) since their inception. He is a personal friend and confidant of Adolfo Callero, leader of the FDN, and Enrique Bermudez, the FDN field commander. Humphreys has provided thousands of dollars of humanitarian aid to the Contra, such as medical supplies, food and clothing. At his own expense, he has taken US Congressmen and members of the media to Central America to visit the FDN and see firsthand what is really going on there. And he has spent weeks in Washington talking to legislators and lobbying on behalf of the Nicaraguan Freedom-Fighters. The FDN respects Humphreys so much that they have made him an Honorary General in their Army.

"Herbo" has been principal backer of the CMA, donating thousands of dollars to the organization. The recent shipment of clothing sent to the refugees in Guatemala was collected by the CMA membership; however, Humphreys paid for the cost of shipping the two Conex containers.

An active Conservative, Mr. Humphreys is a member of the National Defense Council, Inter-American Defense Council, Republican National Committee and the President's Civilian Advisory Council.

Humphreys is an international businessman with interests throughout Central America, the Caribbean and the United States. He owns or is the major stockholder in investment companies, real estate, travel agencies, a charter airline and a large resort hotel in the British West Indies. He is President of Humphreys Shipping Company and Marine Archeological Research Ltd, a salvage and treasure hunting company owning and operating two Marine Research Vessels. He currently has a contract with the Bahamian Government to salvage the artifacts and treasure that were aboard the Spanish ship La Nuestra Senora de Maravilla which sank along the Bahama Banks in 1656 with a full cargo of Central American treasure. According to the manifest, the treasure aboard would be worth over $1.6 billion at today's prices. In 1986, Humphreys and his crew recovered riches estimated by the Bahamian Government to be some $1 million, including a giant emerald of 50 carats (give or take a few carats). Mr. Humphreys has commissioned me to write a book about him, his amazing crew and their hunt for the mother lode of the Maravilla, so this year I will be accompanying them on their ship, the BEACON. Some writers have all the luck! It is an adventure that I am looking forward to, especially since I consider Herbert Humphreys the most interesting man I have ever met.

The Memphis Businessman-Adventurer-Soldier of Fortune, is a commissioned Licensed Marine Master Mariner, a Captain in the Merchant Marine and Inactive Navy Reserve, a SCUBA diving master, a licensed pilot and qualified parachutist. He has also been trained in martial arts, small arms and demolitions. He is a man living life to its fullest and has crammed an awful lot in his 39 years.

There is no doubt that CMA has contributed to the efforts of the Anti-Communist Freedom-Fighters in Nicaragua. It is a viable "grass roots" organization that not only talks about stopping communism—it does something about it. As long as CMA limits itself to working within its own limited resources, it will continue to grow and assist in stopping the communist advance in Central America. There are many concerned Americans who want to get involved, and there are thousands of Vietnam Veterans who believe they still have a war to win against the communists—CMA may just be the organization for them. PERHAPS CMA IS AN IDEA WHOSE TIME HAS COME!!

G. Lee Tippin

FOR FURTHER INFORMATION ABOUT CMA WRITE:
CIVILIAN MATERIEL ASSISTANCE
P.O. Box 3012
Decatur, Alabama 35602

Publisher's Note

Colonel Tippin recently gave up his position with the CMA. He returned to Central America for a short period of time and then assumed duties as a crew member on Herbert Humphreys' salvage ship searching for treasures from the La Senora Nuestra de Maravilla. He is writing a book about the operation which will include numerous color photographs of the treasures and other findings.

Colonel Tippin was replaced by Jim Kent, a retired U.S. Marine Corps First Sergeant. Jim is an experienced warrior and he is doing an outstanding job for the CMA and the FDN. He has visited the Contra camps at least twice since assuming his duties.

During 1987, Jim Turney resigned as the Deputy Director of CMA in order to better support his family. He is still heavily involved in doing all he can to assist in the defeat of the communist threat around the world.

Appendix B

RELIGIOUS PERSECUTION IN NICARAGUA

"Three hundred and thirty priests and pastors have been accused by the Sandinistas of caring only for the rich and of being counter-revolutionaries. Cuban-style block committees report their every move. State Security agents record their services and threaten parishioners with losing jobs or ration coupons if they attend Mass or services.

"Nearly seven years after the revolution that toppled dictator Anastasio Somoza, the Sandinistas are waging war on religion. They have closed Protestant churches and expelled their pastors, accusing them of being CIA agents. They have deported missionaries and confiscated Managua's lone synagogue; and the city's Jews have fled.

"Now the communists have taken on the Catholic Church, to which most Nicaraguans belong. The Sandinista government banishes priests on trumped-up charges, taxes Church property and refuses to permit new construction on Church land. It promotes atheism in schools and tries to block the celebration of such holidays as Christmas (now officially called the 'Day of the Family') and Easter. And it promotes the growth of a so-called Popular Church, whose priests espouse armed violence and see 'no contradiction' between Marxism and Christianity.

"In 1980, the Sandinistas brought in thousands of Cuban teachers, purportedly to stamp out illiteracy. Instead, they promoted atheism. Entering classrooms, the Cubans barked, 'Children, close your eyes. Ask God if he will send you caramels.' Then they drove their point home: 'Look children, God doesn't give you candy. Now yell, 'FSLN (Sandinista Liberation Front), we want caramels.' And the Cubans gave them caramels.

"Traditionally, the church had been responsible for education. Now the Sandinistas began forcing children to sing their hymn, "We fight against the Yankee, enemy of humanity . . . "

The Reader's Digest
"The Lonely Struggle of a Nicaraguan Priest"
by Trevol Armbrister
April 1986

233

* * *

"There has been an international cover-up of the anti-Semitism of the Sandinista regime. Egged on by the Palestine Liberation Organization, for which the Sandinistas have often proclaimed undying love and identity of interest, the regime mounted a campaign of persecution of Nicaragua's small Jewish community. In fine Nazi style, old Jews were forced to scrub streets. Other Jews were beaten, their homes and property seized. Eventually, the entire Jewish community was forced to leave the country—and many among them believe that this was the only way to escape a miniature holocaust.

"The facts of this persecution have been fully and repeatedly documented by the Anti-Defamation League of B'nai B'rith. For years the ADL has been sending long reports to individual members of Congress and to the media on the Sandinista-PLO connection and on the brutal treatment of Jews in Nicaragua. (All of this has been confirmed by our own intelligence services.)"

The New American
"Soft on Anti-Semitism"
by Ralph de Toledano
June 1986

* * *

"The Catholic Church in Nicaragua has been the object of continual harassment. The Pope's visit in March 1982, was disrupted by Sandinista mobs, controlled by State Security, when the Pope tried to address a large crowd in Managua. Many Catholics who wanted to attend the Pope's address were forcibly prevented from attending, and Sandinista mobs were placed in the square to shout him down on loudspeakers provided by the government.

"The Sandinistas claim that they respect religious freedom and have created a "People's Church" which supports the government and preaches Marxist philosophy."

Defense Science
"The Nicaraguan Crisis"
by Rep. Jim Courter (R-NJ)
Oct/Nov 1985

* * *

"There should be no doubt: Nicaraguan Christians are confronting a Marxist-Leninist regime which, in spite of its promises regarding religious and other basic human rights, is bent on securing totalitarian rule. What seems unique in the Nicaraguan process—the participation of priests in the government and the support of some Christian groups—does not change the fundamental commitments and policies of a government determined to impose a Cuban-style Communist system on Nicaragua. This system will mean the progressive loss of human rights and the increasing persecution of Christians.

"Perhaps the greatest single success that the Sandinistas and their allies in the Christian churches have accomplished is to obscure from the view of Christians abroad the fact that there is religious persecution in Nicaragua.

"Western Christians concerned for the problems of the Third World must outgrow their tendency to naively welcome revolutions which use high-sounding rhetoric to disguise totalitarian convictions. Christianity can be manipulated in behalf of non-Christian causes. A romanticized view of Third-World revolutionaries fighting shocking injustices avoids confronting the fact that, regardless of their apparent, or even true, idealism, Marxist revolutions harbor the seeds of even more cruel oppressions than the ones they are striving to dethrone. Such forces are unyieldingly hostile to Christianity.

"Christians should also learn that there may be "liberation theologies" which are not liberating at all. The case of Nicaragua shows that what has been advanced as a form of liberation theology has been nothing else than a justification for Marxism-Leninism clothed in a religious garment—a revolution that is not for Christ, nor even for the poor, but for communism . . . in the name of Christ.

"Western Christians naivete about Third-World Marxist revolutions and about some forms of liberation theology has been conspiring against Nicaraguan Christians by depriving them of sorely needed support in an hour of trial. Countless individual Christians visiting Nicaragua (often invited by CEPAD and other pro-Sandinista organizations) have utterly failed to discover the communist nature of the Nicaragua regime. They have bypassed grave violations of human rights, and they have not discerned the presence of any anti-religious strategy. They have often exhibited an

unashamed use of double standards regarding elections, press freedom, and the vilification of religious figures. Even worse, their pleas for support have not been for the Nicaraguan Christians victimized by the Sandinistas but for their Sandinista oppressors."
Nicaraguan Christians Under Fire
by Humberto Belli
A former Marxist and collaborator
with the Sandinistas who became a
convert to Christianity in 1977.

* * *

"The headquarters for Liberation Theology in the US, and perhaps in the entire world, are located near the Hudson River at Maryknoll, New York, international center of America's most socialistic and active missionary order, The Maryknoll Fathers and Sisters. The current Foreign Minister of Nicaragua, 'Father' Miguel D'Escoto, a committed communist, was the Director of Communications at Maryknoll, using his priestly demeanor and his position as a cover for organizing communist propaganda activities on behalf of the Sandinistas within the US and abroad."
Commentary Magazine
"Liberation Theology and the Pope"
by Michael Nowak
June 1979

* * *

"Since May 1982, all churches in the Atlantic Coast region of Nicaragua have been required to submit all sermons to State Security for prior approval, while more that 50 Moravian Christian churches in that area have been burned to the ground by Sandinista forces. Protestant Minister Prudencio Baltodano, also from the Atlantic Coast, was abducted by Sandinista troops, tied to a tree, and had his ears cut off with a bayonet. The soldiers then slashed his throat and left him tied to a tree to die. Miraculously, he survived."
Permanent Commission of Human Rights of Nicaragua
May 1986

* * *

"Nicaragua can now be added to the ugly list of nations that have driven Jews from their midst. And, as usual, their exodus was violent. The lone Synagogue in Managua was partially burned and later desecrated. One Jewish cemetery was dug up, and the exhumed bodies were moved to another location. The 60 Jewish families who once prospered in Nicaragua have fled. Although the Somozas were repressive dictators, Jews were welcomed into the country and were not mistreated. Most were refugees from the Holocaust. Their small world came crashing down after the Sandinistas came to power. Many of the guerrilla leaders have been trained by the Palestine Liberation Organization, whose enemy is Israel.

"Caught up in the mob frenzy, a few of the rebels tossed Molotov cocktails at the Synagogue, and the front entrance burst into flames. The Jews rushed to the exit, but they found the entrance blocked with automobiles. 'Death to the Jews,' shouted the Sandinistas. 'What Hitler started we will finish.'

"Their synagogue was converted into a center for Sandinista youth and plastered with PLO posters and smeared with anti-Semitic graffiti. Jewish homes and factories have been confiscated by the government. The house of one prominent Jewish family is now the embassy of Bulgaria.

"There is no Israeli embassy. The Palestine Liberation Organization, however, enjoys full diplomatic privileges, with its own embassy."

Jack Anderson and Dale Van Atta
Washington Post
August 18, 1985

Appendix C

SELECTED QUOTES ON NICARAGUA

"If you fail in Nicaragua, we must ask, where will you fail next? If freedom and democracy are not worth defending in your own hemisphere, where are they worth defending? The free world awaits your answer. Its enemies are waiting too."

Winston Churchill II
Member of British Parliament

* * *

"Libyan fighters, arms and backing to the Nicaraguan people have reached them because they fight with us. They fight America on its own ground."

Moammar al Khadafy
October 1984

* * *

"Communism stops only when it encounters a wall, even if it is only a wall of resolve. The West cannot now avoid erecting such a wall in what is already its hour of extemity."

Alexander Solzhenitsyn
Author, Gulag Archipelgo

* * *

"The Sandinistas want to finish the church They think it is a wall that stops their advance."

Father Bismarck Corballo
Managua, August 1986

* * *

"First, we will consolidate the revolution in Nicaragua, then move it to neighboring countries, and finally to our ultimate target—the United States."

Tomas Borge
Nicaraguan Minister of Interior

* * *

"The national security of all the Americas is at stake in Central America. If we cannot defend ourselves there, we cannot expect to prevail elsewhere. Our credibility will collapse, our alliances will crumble, and the safety of our homeland will be in jeopardy."

President Ronald Reagan

* * *

"Here in Nicaragua, you must pay a price for believing in Christ. You must run many risks."

Father Oswaldo Mondragon
Parish Priest, El Calvario
Church, Managua May 1986

* * *

"The triumph of the Nicaraguans is the PLO's triumph."

Yasser Arafat July 23, 1980

* * *

"The price of containing Soviet adventurism in the Americas will never be as cheap as it is today. If we spend our dollars now, we will not have to spend American blood later."

John Sibler
President of Boston College

* * *

"Do we help the Nicaraguan people reclaim their revolution or begin readying our own troops to defend the Mexican border?"
Major General John Singlaub
Chairman of the US Council
of World Freedom

* * *

"Yes, in Nicaragua today one is free—free to be a communist."
Francis Campbell

* * *

"We say to our brother Arafat that Nicaragua is his land and the PLO cause is the cause of the Sandinistas."
Tomas Borge
July 22, 1980

* * *

"First will come thousands of refugees fleeing from Central American and Mexico, and intermingled with these refugees will come trained terrorists and guerrillas. Their mission will be to prepare and soften the United States for the onslaught that will surely follow."
Mario Calero
Nicaraguan Democratic Forces

* * *

"We must force America to fight on a hundred fronts all over the earth. We must force it to fight in Lebanon, to fight in Chad, to fight in Sudan, and to fight in Central America."
Moammar al Khadafy

* * *

"The American media is easily open to suggestion and false information given by communist states."

Truong Nhu Tang
Former Communist Official
in North Vietnam

* * *

"There are serious questions about the willingness of the Sandinistas to tolerate a truly independent religious community in Nicaragua."

Senator Edward Kennedy

* * *

"I was taken by force to the Evangelical Chapel and raped. Later that night, the Sandinista Army commander beat me, my house was burned, and my husband shot to death."

Candida Fernandez, 22
Batitan, Nicaragua

* * *

"The army was moving fast, treating everyone with extreme cruelty. They wanted to make us leave town as soon as possible. Gabino Flores approached me from behind and said, 'They killed Christina Mercado while she was giving birth to her twins . . . she could not finish quick enough to leave town with the others.'"

Miskito Indian Woman, 22

* * *

"We were 35 prisoners. That night the Sandinista soldiers took four of us out. When they gave us shovels, I knew that we were going to dig our own graves. The night before, they had beaten me until I could no longer see with my right eye. But I was lucky . . . they kicked the others until they vomited blood; and, then, while the drunken soldiers were shooting my friends and throwing them, still alive, into the graves, I managed to run away."

Vidal Poveda, peasant, 35
Leymus, Nicaragua

* * *

"The Sandinista troops went into the homes of the people and took the sleeping people out of bed and arrested the people and led them on to the street and said to them, 'You black people, you are monkeys, and you are used to dancing.' And they shoot bullets between the feet of the people to make them dance. There was one black lady that they took a newspaper and put it down her throat."

Theofilo Archibald
Black Nicaraguan (Creo) leader

* * *

"The people of Nicaragua have risen up against the Sandinista government as they did against Somoza. The current battle within Nicaragua is between the forces of progress and a repressive status quo; except five years later, the Sandinistas represent repression and oppression, while the Freedom-Fighters, the so-called 'Contras,' represent democratic pluralism, respect for human rights and economic progress. For the United States to fail to support this struggle is to deny our heritage and traditional support for freedom. It is simply an issue of whether we will support the establishment of freedom and tyranny in our own front yard."

Hon. Bob Livingston
Task Force Chairman
Task Force on Central America
US House of Representatives

* * *

"The stakes are very high in Nicaragua. Were it not for the Contras, who are putting the Sandinistas on the defensive, there would be a major Marxist Sandinista-backed guerrilla campaign in Honduras; those in El Salvador and Guatemala would be vastly expanded; and one in Costa Rica (a democracy without an army at all) would be seriously under way. I spoke with many people in Honduras who all noted that communist guerrilla activity, which had been increasing, suddenly evaporated in their country as soon as the Contras began operating."

Dr. Jack Wheeler
Director, Freedom Research Foundation

* * *

"If the Miskito Indians in Nicaragua survive as a culture and as a nation, it will be because of the Contras that are helping them. I would hope that we, as a nation that speaks for freedom and human rights, would do as much as we can to help these people."
> Othniel Seiden
> A doctor who lives or lived with the
> Miskito Indians, testifying before the
> House Task Force on Central America

* * *

"US church money, given to Nicaragua, paid for a massive ideological brainwashing of the peasants."
> Miguel Bolanos Hunter
> Former Sandinista Field Commander

* * *

"The free world should not turn its back on the terrible situation under which the people of Nicaragua are living. If we cannot obtain the support of the West for the people who are struggling on all fronts to prevent the perpetuation of communism, then it is quite easy to foresee that Soviet adventurism will attain a new triumph in its imperialist course."
> Dr. Jose Antonio Tijerino
> Former Professor of International
> Law at the University of Central
> America, Managua, Nicaragua.

* * *

"You boys have to understand that God does not exist, that Jesus Christ does not exist either, that God is revolution, and that Jesus Christ is you, is all the Sandinistas."
> Father Ernesto Cardenal
> Roman Catholic Priest, now
> Minister of Culture, Nicaragua
> Speaking to Sandinista troops
> on December 24, 1978

* * *

"The Sandinista dictatorship of Nicaragua, with full Cuban-Soviet bloc support, not only persecutes its people and the church and denies free press, but also supplies arms and provides bases for communist terrorists attacking neighboring states. Support for Freedom-Fighters is self-defense and totally consistent with the OAS and UN Charters."

President Ronald Reagan
State of the Union Message
February 6, 1985

* * *

"The Sandinista strategy is to prop up their communist regime in Nicaragua by sacrificing the freedom of the Nicaraguan people while they inspire, aid and arm, from Nicaragua, insurgencies throughout Latin America, 'movements of national liberation' that will convert the entire continent into an immense base of insurrection."

Edgar Chamorro
Washington Post
April 3, 1986

* * *

"What I have said, from the Salvadoran standpoint, is that we have a problem of aggression by a nation called Nicaragua against El Salvador, that these gentlemen are sending in weapons, training people, transporting bullets and what not, and bringing all of that to El Salvador. I said that at this very minute they are using fishing boats as a disguise and are introducing weapons into El Salvador at night.

"In view of this situation, El Salvador must stop this somehow. The Contras are creating sort of a barrier that prevents the Nicaraguans from continuing to send arms to El Salvador by land."

President Durarte
El Salvador
July 27, 1984